Character
as a Subversive Force
in Shakespeare

Character
as a Subversive Force
in Shakespeare

The History and Roman Plays

Bernard J. Paris

Rutherford • Madison • Teaneck
Fairleigh Dickinson University Press
London and Toronto: Associated University Presses

Associated University Presses
440 Forsgate Drive
Cranbury, NJ 08512

Associated University Presses
25 Sicilian Avenue
London WC1A 2QH, England

Associated University Presses
P.O. Box 39, Clarkson Pstl. Stn.
Mississauga, Ontario,
L5J 3X9 Canada

The paper used in this publication meets the requirements of the American National Standard for Permanence of Paper for Printed Library Materials Z39.48-1984.

Library of Congress Cataloging-in-Publication Data

Paris, Bernard J.
  Character as a subversive force in Shakespeare : the history and Roman plays / Bernard J. Paris.
      p.   cm.
  Includes bibliographical references (p.   ) and index.
  ISBN 0-8386-3429-X
  1. Shakespeare, William, 1564–1616—Histories. 2. Shakespeare, William, 1564–1616—Characters. 3. Shakespeare, William, 1564–1616—Knowledge—Rome. 4. Shakespeare, William, 1564–1616—Knowledge—Psychology. 5. Historical drama, English—History and criticism. 6. Characters and characteristics in literature. 7. Motivation (Psychology) in literature. 8. Rome in literature. I. Title.
  PR2982.P37   1991
  822.3'3—dc20
                                                                    90-55839
                                                                    CIP

PRINTED IN THE UNITED STATES OF AMERICA

For Dr. Albert Rhoton
and His Neurosurgical Team
without Whom This Book
Could Not Have Been Completed

Contents

Acknowledgments

The University of Florida has been generous in providing research leaves, clerical help, and travel support for this project, and I am grateful to the Division of Sponsored Research for grants that have funded research assistance. Catherine R. Lewis was my assistant for three years, and in addition to doing bibliographic research she transcribed tapes of my lectures, identified passages in critical studies that she knew I should see, and helped me in innumerable other ways that depended upon her ability to read my mind. Without her, this would have been a much greater effort and a lesser book.

I am indebted also to colleagues at the University of Florida and elsewhere who have read portions of this work. These include Maurice Charney, Alistair Duckworth, Barbara Freedman, Andrew Gordon, Norman Holland, Sidney Homan, H. S. Kakar, Randal Robinson, Robert Thomson, and Bertram Wyatt-Brown. Earlier versions of chapters of this book have been presented at meetings of the Shakespeare Association of America, at UCLA, and at the Group for the Application of Psychology (University of Florida). I have benefited greatly from the astute comments of the colleagues mentioned above and from the feedback I received on these public occasions. I wish especially to thank Harry Keyishian for his helpful critiques of a number of chapters and his sustained (and sustaining) interest in this project at every stage.

My chapters on Richard III, Prince Hal, and *Julius Caesar* have appeared in print in somewhat different forms (see Works Cited), and I am grateful to the Fairleigh Dickinson University Press and the *Aligarh Journal of English Studies* for permission to use here what they published originally. I have occasionally drawn material from *Bargains with Fate: Psychological Crises and Conflicts in Shakespeare and His Plays*, and I am indebted to Insight Books for permission to repeat some of my wording.

Although the focus of this book is somewhat different from that of *Bargains with Fate*, the two books are complementary and, taken together, constitute my reading of almost the entire Shakespearean corpus. There are numerous instances of bargains with fate in this book and of character as a subversive force in *Bargains*. My justification of character analysis is more fully elaborated here, while my rationale for an interdisciplinary approach to Shakespeare is more fully developed there.

I am deeply grateful, as always, to my wife, Shirley, for her unfaltering faith, encouragement, and support. It is she more than anyone who has given me patience, who has reminded me, in the midst of frustrations, that if I kept putting one word after another, I would finish the book. She was right.

Finally, a word about the dedication. In 1985, I was operated on for a brain tumor that was diagnosed as malignant but that turned out to be benign. Since this very large tumor was located on the language center of my brain, there was a significant risk of damage during surgery that would impair my ability to speak, read, and write. That I emerged without any deficit was owing to the skill and dedication of Dr. Albert Rhoton and his neurosurgical team. Without them I would not have been able to finish this book—or to lead a normal life. No words can adequately express my gratitude.

Character
as a Subversive Force
in Shakespeare

1
"Creations inside a Creation"

I

Shakespeare was gifted with remarkable powers of psychological intuition, and one of his greatest achievements was the creation of highly individualized characters who seem to have a life of their own and to invite the same kind of motivational analysis that we employ with real human beings. In the eighteenth, nineteenth, and early twentieth centuries, these characters received much praise and attention, but since the 1930s most critics have turned away from them as objects of study and have regarded those who talk about them in motivational terms as guilty of a profound misunderstanding of the nature of literature. Audiences have continued to be fascinated by Shakespeare's great characters, but critics have been busy denying the mimetic component of his art.

Under the influence of movements that emphasize internal linguistic and literary relationships and that dismiss the referential capacity of language most recent criticism has been hostile to motivational analysis. Archetypal critics, Formalists, Structuralists, and Deconstructionists tend either to see character in purely functional terms or to subject the whole concept of character, or of a self that can be represented, to attack.

In his essay on Bentham, John Stuart Mill speaks of "the essential law of poor human intellect, by which it can only see one thing at a time well" (1961, 51). This law manifests itself in literary criticism, of course, and results in the kind of partial truths and oscillation in intellectual fashions that Mill described in the history of culture. "Every reaction in opinion," says Mill in his companion essay on Coleridge, "brings into view that portion of the truth which was overlooked before" (1961, 83); but it tends also to obscure that portion of the truth represented by the position against which it is reacting. This is what has happened in the reaction against the study of character in Shakespearean criticism. Since the 1930s, the focus on character that had been dominant since the last quarter of the eighteenth century has been replaced by a series of other perspectives, most of which have not incorporated but have rather rejected the kind of character analysis that preceded them.

This has been, in many ways, a salutary development, since the new perspectives have called our attention to aspects of Shakespeare that had not been adequately appreciated before. But in the process something has been lost. Fortunately, there are signs of a change, of a reaction against the reaction against character study. Such critics as V. Y. Kantak (1977), Seymour Chatman (1978), George Levine (1981), Hugh Bredin (1982), Martin Price (1983), Thomas Docherty (1984), Baruch Hochman (1985), Elio Frattaroli (1987), and Robert Alter (1989) have defended a realistic approach to character; and in *A New Mimesis* (1983), A. D. Nuttall has confronted the antireferential bias of formalist, structuralist, and poststructuralist criticism.[1]

Shakespeare's greatest characters occur in the histories, the tragedies, and the Roman plays. I have tried to show elsewhere that the major tragedies are about individuals who are in a state of psychological crisis as a result of the breakdown of their bargains with fate (Paris 1991). Although the history and Roman plays are usually discussed in terms of their political themes, they too contain characters who must be understood motivationally if we are to recover Shakespeare's psychological intuitions and appreciate his mimetic achievement. When we understand these characters with the help of modern psychology, we find that they tend to escape the formal and thematic patterns of which they are a part and to subvert the authorial rhetoric. The greater the character creation, the more disruptive it tends to be of the larger structure within which it exists.

In the creation of a literary character, the author is often doing a number of things at once as he responds to a variety of artistic demands, but critics tend to focus only upon the aspect of characterization privileged by their particular approach. Northrop Frye, for example, in an admitted oversimplification, divides critics into *Odyssey* critics, who like comedy and romance, and *Iliad* critics, who like tragedy and realism; and he ascribes to each kind a different method of interpreting character. For *Odyssey* critics each work is "a self-contained unit. The author starts with a certain kind of story: this develops certain kinds of characters, occupying the strategic positions of that story, and each character owes his characteristic features . . . to his place and function in the story" (1965, 39–40). *Iliad* critics "think of literature as a criticism of life";

they see the character "as owing [his features] rather to his place as a symbol of the truths about life that the play illustrates" (1965, 40). Since the author is usually creating characters as part of both a formal and thematic structure, each of these perspectives is necessary to account for some aspects of their behavior, and in some cases they account for the same things in different but equally legitimate ways. Each kind of critic, however, tends to regard all characters in the same way, regardless of their multiple functions or the different types of works in which they appear.

In the case of realistically drawn characters, there will be many aspects of their behavior that cannot be explained from either of the above perspectives and that may go unnoticed if we confine ourselves to them. In the creation of these characters, many details have been called forth not only by the work's formal and thematic requirements, but also by the mimetic impulse of the author. As W. J. Harvey observes, the mark of mimetic characterization is "a surplus margin of gratuitous life, a sheer excess of material, a fecundity of detail and invention" that "often overflows the strict necessities of form" (1965, 188). Harvey is talking about novels, but Douglas Peterson makes a similar point when he speaks of "the particularizing detail, historical and psychological, of which [Shakespeare's] memorable characters . . . are created." The "substantiality" of such characters is due in part "to the rich texture . . . of their speeches, . . . which, though always consistent with their characters, is not always explicitly relevant to dramatic action" (1973, 216).

Shakespeare's mimetic characters have been rendered in such rich particularizing detail that they must be understood as though they were actual persons. They are not real people, of course, but are "imagined human beings" whose behavior makes sense in motivational terms.[2] In the realistic plays, as Bradley observes, "the calamities and catastrophes follow inevitably from the deeds of men, and . . . the main source of these deeds is character" (1964, 13). The outcome of the action is affected by the source and genre of the play, but Shakespeare's practice is to make the fates of the characters appear to be the inevitable result of personality interacting with circumstance. In some cases, he even suggests ways in which their personalities have been formed by prior experience.

One reason for the resistance to seeing characters as imagined human beings who can be understood in motivational terms is a failure to distinguish between different kinds of characterization and hence between the different kinds of interpretation they require. In the case of Shakespeare, it is important to distinguish between characterization in the histories and tragedies and characterization in the comedies and romances, though there *are* some psychologically intelligible characters in the latter group.[3] According to Northrop Frye, "Shakespeare's technique is the opposite of . . . Chekhov's, where the characters seem to be prior to the plot, in the sense that the action of the play is presented as the logical behavior of the characters in it. Shakespeare tells a story that stylizes his characters and may force them to do quite unreasonable things. This is more obvious in his comedies than in his tragedies . . . but it is true in general of Shakespeare" (1965, 39–40). Frye is basically right about the comedies, but the histories and tragedies are well described, I think, by his account of Chekhov. The action of *Othello* "is presented as the logical behavior of the characters in it." Frye's remarks on character apply to Leontes or Posthumus, but not to Othello; to Don John or Iachimo, but not to Iago; to Hermione or Imogen, but not to Desdemona (see Paris, 1991). A more appropriate position is taken, I think, by Douglas Peterson, who in defining "the mimetic mode" of Shakespeare'e romances contrasts it with the mode of the tragedies: "Given the protagonist as the dramatist has conceived him, the situation in which he finds himself, and the choices open to him, we must be convinced that the choices he makes are inevitable and their consequences inevitable" (1973, 216). The same is true of the histories. The kind of arbitrary behavior that is perfectly acceptable in the comedies and romances would be disturbing in the realistic plays, where, by convention, characters are supposed to think, feel, and act in accordance with their natures.

One of the most frequent objections to character analysis is that it tries to understand characters in their own right, rather than in relation to the play as a whole. The controversy over this procedure is well summarized in Marvin Mudrick's account of the "realist" and "purist" positions:

> One of the recurring anxieties of literary critics concerns the way in which a character . . . may be said to exist. The 'purist' argument—in the ascendancy nowadays . . .—points out that characters do not exist at all except insofar as they are a part of the images and events which bear and move them, that any effort to extract them from their context and to discuss them as if they are real human beings is a sentimental misunderstanding of the nature of literature. The 'realist' argument—on the defensive nowadays—insists that characters acquire, in the course of an action, a kind of independence from the events in which

they live, and that they can be usefully discussed at some distance from their context. The purists have trouble with Chaucer, Shakespeare, and the great novelists, many of whose characters manifest an individual vitality which . . . seems so extravagantly in excess of any specifiable dramatic or fictional function as to invite further inquiry. The realists have trouble with almost all dramatists except Shakespeare, and with writers of allegory, whose characters manifest only as much individual vitality as is necessary to . . . discharge their function in the events that beget and contain them. (1960, 211)

The purist and realist positions can be reconciled by the taxonomy of characterization set forth by Robert Scholes and Robert Kellogg in *The Nature of Narrative*.

Scholes and Kellogg distinguish between aesthetic, illustrative, and mimetic characterization. Aesthetic characters predominate in highly formulaic works that are close to the mythic center of literature and in which there is little emphasis upon verisimilitude. They are stock types who must be understood primarily in terms of their technical functions and their formal and dramatic effects. They figure as minor characters in works of every kind, and all characters have some aesthetic functions. Illustrative characters are most important in works with a strong allegorical or thematic interest. Illustration "does not seek to reproduce actuality but to present selected aspects of the actual, essences referable for their meaning not to historical, psychological, or sociological truth but to ethical and metaphysical truth" (1966, 88). Illustrative characters are "concepts in anthropoid shape or fragments of the human psyche parading as whole human beings." We try to understand "the principle they illustrate through their actions in a narrative framework" (1966, 88). Behind realistic literature there is a strong "psychological impulse" that "tends toward the presentation of highly individualized figures who resist abstraction and generalization, and whose motivation is not susceptible to rigid ethical interpretation" (1966, 101). When we encounter a fully drawn mimetic character, "we are justified in asking questions about his motivation based on our knowledge of the ways in which real people are motivated" (1966, 87). Mimetic characters usually have aesthetic and illustrative functions, but they are so highly individualized that they may also be understood in psychological terms.

The Scholes and Kellogg taxonomy suggests that what the purists say is true for aesthetic and illustrative characters, but that we must employ the realists' approach if we are to appreciate mimetic characterization. Strictly functional analysis of such characters is highly reductive, since it neglects a vast amount of detail that is there primarily for the sake of the mimetic portrait.[4]

It is Bradley, of course, who epitomizes the realist approach to Shakespeare and who has borne the brunt of our century's attack upon character analysis. Bradley has often been accused of misreading Shakespeare's plays by treating them like nineteenth century novels whose protagonists can be discussed as though they were actual human beings. There are many affinities, however, between Shakespeare's mimetic characters and those we encounter in realistic fiction. As John Galsworthy observed, "If Shakespeare had not chanced to be an actor, or at least intimately connected with dramatic enterprise, he might well have innovated the character novel in this country, and taken precedence of Cervantes as the first great realistic novelist" (1931, 14).

The most pervasive objection to Bradley is that he misunderstood the nature of Shakespearean tragedy, that he interpreted it in terms of the wrong set of conventions. We are frequently reminded that "Shakespeare wrote a *poetic* drama and not an Ibsenian one" (Kirschbaum 1962, 1), and this, of course, is true in the sense that the conventions of Shakespeare's realism were in some respects different from those of Ibsen's. He gave less attention to verisimilitude in his handling of time and place, ghosts, entrances and exits, coincidental encounters, and so on; and his characters speak poetry rather than an approximation of ordinary speech. But this does not mean he was less concerned about the plausibility of their behavior. Mimetic characterization almost always exists alongside of other less realistic conventions and inside of more or less manipulated plots. Two of Shakespeare's unrealistic conventions, soliloquies and poetic speech, contributed greatly, in fact, to his mimetic portraiture, for they enabled him to render inner conflict and to provide a great deal of psychological detail in very few words. Think of Browning's dramatic monologues, which give us a sense of a character's motivations and personality that it would take a novelist many chapters to convey. Despite the differences in convention, Shakespeare's realism is like Ibsen's in its treatment of character. Peterson's description of the mimetic mode of the tragedies could easily be a description of Ibsen's mature plays.

Shakespeare's histories, tragedies, and Roman plays far surpass all previous literature in their detailed portrayal of character and motive. Since his achievement was so new in its time, it cannot be properly understood by those who insist upon seeing his works solely from the perspective of preceding and contemporary theory and practice. Aristotle's theory of characterization was dominant through the Renaissance, and for Aristotle character is "that which reveals moral purpose, showing what kinds of things a man chooses or avoids" (1952, 23). Speeches "in which the speaker does not choose or avoid anything . . . are not expressive of character" (1952, 23). Sidney's view of character is equally illustrative:

> If the poet do his part aright, he will show you in Tantalus, Atreus, and such like, nothing that is not to be shunned: in Cyrus, Aeneas, Ulysses, each thing to be followed; where the historian, bound to tell things as things were, cannot be liberal (without he will be poetical) of a perfect pattern, but, as in Alexander or Scipio himself, show doings, some to be liked, some to be misliked. And then how will you discern what to follow but by your own discretion, which you had without reading Quintus Curtius? (1952, 90)

In Sidney's terms, Shakespeare's practice in his mimetic characterization is closer to that of the historian than to that of the poet. In the illustrative view of character that is espoused by Aristotle and Sidney, there is no room for psychological portraiture, and to see Shakespeare's characters exclusively from this perspective is to ignore one of the chief sources of their interest.[5]

Since criticism tends to lag behind practice and realistic characterization did not become a dominant feature of literature until the rise of the novel, it is not surprising that an appropriate response to Shakespeare's mimetic characterization did not begin to develop until the late eighteenth century.[6] In 1777, Maurice Morgann articulated the position I am defending here when he observed that in the characters of Shakespeare "there is a certain roundness and integrity . . . which give them an independence as well as a relation, insomuch that we often meet with passages which . . . cannot be sufficiently explained in words, without unfolding the whole character of the speaker" (qtd. by Knights 1933, 20). L. C. Knights marvels at "how narrowly Morgann misses the mark." He recognized "the full-bodied quality" of the plays, but instead of realizing that it sprang from Shakespeare's "use of words, . . . he referred it to the characters' 'independence' of the work in which they appeared" (1933, 21). What impresses me about Morgann is how precisely he has *hit* the mark.[7]

II

There are many ways of conceiving Shakespeare's history and Roman plays and of making sense of their characters. If we regard the characters only in terms of their functions, we can explain their behavior without having recourse to motivational analysis. Once we see the most fully developed characters as imagined human beings, however, we shall not feel that we have understood them completely until we have grasped "the inner movements which produced these words and no other, these deeds and no other, at each particular moment" (Bradley 1964, 2).

Some critics argue that if we are to analyze these characters motivationally, it should be from the perspective of Renaissance psychology, as Shakespeare would have understood them. Shakespeare had to make sense of human behavior for himself, as we all do; and he undoubtedly drew upon the conceptual systems that were available in his culture. To see his characters in the light of Renaissance psychology, therefore, is to recover what may have been Shakespeare's conscious understanding of them, the way in which he and some members of his audience may have explained their behavior to themselves. This is historically interesting, and it helps to satisfy our need to understand what the plays meant in their own time. It also constitutes one of the most common ways of interpreting characters, which is to imagine how the author must have understood them and to submit oneself to his presumed intentions.[8]

Such a procedure does not help us, however, to recover Shakespeare's psychological intuitions and to appreciate his genius in mimetic characterization. We cannot identify Shakespeare's conceptions of his characters with the characters he has actually created, even if we could be certain of what his conceptions were. The great artist sees and portrays far more than he can comprehend. To analyze Shakespeare's characters primarily in terms of Renaissance psychology is to deny the vitality that is the source of their greatness. Renaissance psychology has long been outmoded, but we still respond to Shakespeare's characters as imagined human beings who are very much like ourselves.

Literature as a form of knowledge is usually far in advance of the conceptual systems that are contemporaneous with it, and it is highly reductive to understand it primarily in terms of those systems. As Murray Krieger observes, the "history that enters literature as its raw material is the living, felt, pulsing history of breathing men and not the static formulae of ideology. . . . it is history as institutionalized in ideology that comes after, thanks in part to what literature shows us" (1964, 59). Literature embodies perceptions that are "*under* or before language," that are "not yet analyzed, realized in institutions, or perhaps even understood"

(1964, 59). Shakespeare's mimetic characters embody perceptions about human behavior that had not been adequately conceptualized in his own day. Our understanding of such characters is bound to change, moreover, along with our changing conceptions of human nature. Each age must interpret them for itself, using its own modes of explanation. The characters will, of course, outlive every interpretation.[9]

In the past fifty years, the most commonly used tool for character study has been Freudian psychoanalysis. The chief weakness of this approach has been its use of a diachronic mode of analysis that explains the present in terms of the past. Because of its reliance upon infantile experience to account for the behavior of the adult, it must often posit events in a character's early life that are not depicted in the text. This results in the generation of crucial explanatory material out of the premises of the theory, with no corroborating literary evidence except the supposed results of the invented experiences, which were inferred from these results to begin with. This procedure has inspired a justifiable distrust of the psychological study of character.[10] Because of its emphasis upon infantile origins, psychoanalysis has, ironically, made literary characters seem less accessible to motivational analysis than they did before its development.

Meredith Skura has argued, indeed, that "we have no basis for psychoanalyzing" Shakespeare's characters (1983, 38). The poet and the analyst both ask about "a character's unacknowledged motives," but "unlike the poet, [the analyst] traces these back to other thoughts, other experiences, other contexts, which give rise to the motives and give them their only meaning" (1983, 39). Since these other thoughts, experiences, and contexts are not present in the literary work, they cannot be evoked to explain current behavior. The "reality" of a literary character "does not include the kind of unconscious experience on which an analysis is based" (1983, 38). If we presuppose or invent unconscious or prior experience in order to make analysis possible, we are no longer constrained by the text: "If purely unconscious motives *are* there, they are hard to locate: Is Brutus unconsciously killing his father when he kills Caesar? there is no room for these motives in the fully explained world of the play; or, rather, there is room for too many of them" (1983, 40). (In my chapter on *Julius Caesar* below, I shall argue that Brutus does have unconscious motives for killing Caesar and that they can be precisely identified through an analysis of the text.) When we psychoanalyze a real person, we have ways of determining which of a whole range of possible causes are actually responsible for his behavior, but there is no way of doing this with a literary character. "It is only in the psychoanalytic process," says Skura, "that characters, and people, can be psychoanalyzed" (1983, 38); and since characters cannot enter into that process, they cannot be analyzed.

Skura has made a powerful case against the use of the Freudian paradigm for analyzing literary characters, but I cannot conclude with her that characters cannot, therefore, be understood in motivational terms. She is driven to this conclusion because her "conventions for analyzing behavior in life" (1983, 41) are not applicable to literary characters, but hers are not the only conventions. There are contemporary theories that focus upon the character structure and defensive strategies of the adult, rather than upon infantile origins. These are synchronic theories that enable us to understand the present structure of the psyche as an inwardly intelligible system and to explain behavior in terms of its functions within that system.[11] Skura's conventions for analyzing behavior involve tracing motives "back to other thoughts, other experiences, other contexts, which give rise to the motives and give them their *only* meaning" (1983, 39; my italics). This diachronic approach supplies one kind of meaning, but by no means the only kind. An individual's motives are meaningful also when we understand them synchronically, in terms of their function within the present constellation of defenses. Such an approach is highly suitable for the analysis of literary characters, since we are often supplied with ample information about their adult personalities. It permits us to account for the character's thoughts, feelings, and actions on the basis of what has actually been given in the text.

III

The interpretations I shall offer in this study have been inspired in large part by Third Force psychology, especially the theories of Karen Horney. For Horney, as for Freud, the current character structure has its origins in early childhood, but she does not see the adult as simply repeating earlier patterns. The personality of the adult is the product of a complicated evolutionary history that can be reconstructed if we have enough information, but it can also be understood in terms of its present structure. Though Horney's theory has a diachronic component, it is predominantly synchronic in nature. If childhood material is available, it can be utilized; but if it is absent, it need not be invented.

Third Force psychology offers a view of human nature that is distinct from Freudian and behaviorist theories. Human beings are not simply tension-reducing or conditioned animals, but there is inherent in them a third force, an "evolutionary constructive force," that urges them "to realize [their] given potentialities" (Horney 1950, 15). Individuals have an intrinsic nature, a "real self," that it is their object in life to fulfill; and they develop in either a self-actualizing or a self-alienated way, or in some combination of both, depending upon the degree to which their psychological needs are gratified. According to Abraham Maslow, in addition to our physiological needs, we also have basic needs for safety, love and belonging, esteem, beauty, and knowledge and understanding. If these needs are reasonably well gratified, we remain in touch with our real thoughts, feelings, and interests and are able to actualize ourselves (Maslow 1970). If they are frustrated, we develop defensive strategies designed to compensate for our deprivations, and we are motivated by them rather than by our genuine desires.

While Maslow offers the most comprehensive account of healthy development, it is Karen Horney who best describes the strategies we employ to cope with frustration and anxiety.[12] According to Horney, we defend ourselves against a threatening environment by moving toward, against, or away from other people, by becoming compliant, aggressive, or detached. Each of these strategies entails a constellation of behavior patterns and personality traits, a conception of justice, and a set of beliefs about human nature, human values, and the human condition. Each involves also a bargain with fate in which obedience to the dictates of that solution is supposed to be rewarded. In the course of their development individuals tend to make all of these moves, and since the moves involve incompatible character structures and beliefs, they will be torn by inner conflicts. In order to gain some sense of wholeness, they will emphasize one solution more than the others, but the subordinate trends will continue to operate. If they should rise to the surface, they will produce inner turmoil and perhaps paralysis. When the predominant solution fails, individuals may embrace a previously repressed set of attitudes.

People in whom compliant trends are dominant try to gain love, self-esteem, and protection by being good, affectionate, and

weak. They need to feel part of something larger and more powerful than themselves, a need that often manifests itself as religious
devotion, identification with a group or cause, or morbid dependency in a love relationship. They value sympathy, love, humility,
and unselfishness and have powerful taboos against pride, ambition, and vindictiveness. They do not hold these values as genuine ideals, but because they are necessary to their solution. They
must believe in turning the other cheek, and they must see the
world as displaying a providential order in which virtue is rewarded. Their bargain is that, if they are giving, submissive people who shun pride and do not seek their own gain or glory, they
will be well treated by fate and other people. If their bargain is not
honored, they may despair of divine justice, they may conclude
that they are the guilty parties, or they may have recourse to belief
in a justice that transcends human understanding. They need to
believe not only in the fairness of the world order, but also in the
goodness of human nature, and here, too, they are vulnerable to
disappointment.

Compliant people are full of resentment, but this threatens
their self-image, their philosophy of life, and their bargain with
fate; and they must repress, disguise, or justify their anger in
order to avoid arousing self-hate and the hostility of others. They
may satisfy their repressed needs vicariously by attaching themselves to an aggressive person in a relationship of morbid dependency.

There are many predominantly compliant (or self-effacing)
characters in Shakespeare, the most striking of whom are Henry
VI, Helena (A Midsummer Night's Dream), Antonio (The Merchant of
Venice), Silvius (As You Like It), Viola, Hamlet, Desdemona, Duke
Vincentio, Antony, Timon of Athens, Prospero, and the poet of
the Sonnets.[13] There are other characters in whom self-effacing
trends are subordinate, and in the characters I have mentioned
there are usually inner conflicts.

Though I have given this list of examples, let me caution immediately that psychological categories should be used not to label
characters, but to help us appreciate their uniqueness and complexity. Defensive strategies manifest themselves differently in
different people, are combined with different qualities and tal-
ents, and generate different kinds of personality structures and
relationships.

People in whom aggressive tendencies are predominant have
goals, traits, and values opposite to those of self-effacing people.
Since they need to achieve power and prestige, what appeals to

them most is not love but mastery. There are three aggressive (or expansive) solutions: the narcissistic, the perfectionistic, and the arrogant-vindictive.[14]

Narcissists were often spoiled children who grew up seeing the world as a fostering parent and themselves as favorites of fortune. The ordinary rules of life do not apply to them. They are full of self-admiration, have an unquestioned belief in their greatness, and often display unusual charm and buoyancy. They run into difficulties as adults because they overrate their capacities, expect everything to be easy, and are not prepared for the vicissitudes of human existence. Since their exalted sense of themselves is in excess of their actual accomplishments, they have an underlying insecurity that manifests itself in boasting and in an insatiable need for admiration. Their magic bargain is that if they hold onto their dreams and their exaggerated claims for themselves, life is bound to give them what they want. If it does not, they may experience a psychological collapse, since they are ill-equipped to cope with reality. The most fully developed narcissists in Shakespeare are King Lear and Richard II.

Perfectionists take great pride in their rectitude and strive for excellence in everything they do. The imposition of their standards on others leads to admiration for a select few and a critical or condescending attitude toward the majority of mankind. They believe that there is a just order in the universe and that success is a proof of virtue. They have a legalistic bargain in which correctness of conduct insures fair treatment by fate and their fellows. Through the height of their standards they control reality. Ill fortune or errors of their own making threaten their bargain and may overwhelm them with feelings of helplessness or self-hate. The predominantly perfectionist characters in Shakespeare include Talbot (1 Henry VI), Humphrey of Gloucester (2 Henry VI), Titus Andronicus, Henry V, Brutus, Angelo (Measure for Measure), Othello, Cordelia, Kent, Macbeth (before the murder), and Coriolanus. Again, despite their similar defenses these characters are quite different from each other in their human qualities and inner conflicts.

Whereas narcissists received early admiration and perfectionists were subjected to rigid standards, arrogant-vindictive people were often harshly treated in childhood. They have a need to retaliate for injuries and to achieve invulnerability through their superior manipulative abilities. In their relations with others, they are competitive, ruthless, and cynical. They trust no one and are out to get others before they get them. They avoid emotional dependency and use friendship and marriage as means by which they can possess the desirable qualities of others and enhance their own position. They believe that might makes right and that the world is a jungle in which the strong annihilate the weak. They want to be hard and tough and regard those who value love, compassion, and loyalty as fools who are asking to be exploited. They fear the emergence of their compliant trends because this would make them vulnerable in a dangerous world, would confront them with self-hate, and would threaten their bargain, which is essentially with themselves. They do not count on the world to give them anything but are convinced they can reach their ambitious goals if they remain true to their vision of life as a jungle and do not allow themselves to be influenced by their softer feelings or the traditional morality. If their expansive solution collapses, self-effacing trends may emerge quite powerfully. There are many arrogant-vindictive characters in Shakespeare. The most notable include Richard III, Shylock, Cassius, Iago, Edmund, Goneril, Regan, Lady Macbeth, and Macbeth after the murder.

Basically detached people worship freedom, peace, and self-sufficiency. In order to avoid being dependent on the environment, they try to subdue their inner cravings and to be content with little. Their resignation from active living gives them an "onlooker" attitude that frequently permits them to be good observers of their own inner processes. They pride themselves on their ability to see through both their own folly and that of others. They often have a pessimistic outlook and feel, in the words of Ecclesiastes, that all is vanity and a striving after wind. They do not usually rail against life, however, but resign themselves to things as they are and accept their fate with ironic humor or stoical dignity. They try to escape suffering by being independent of external forces, by feeling that nothing matters, and by concerning themselves only with things within their power. Their bargain is that if they ask nothing of others, they will not be bothered; that if they try for nothing, they will not fail; and that if they expect little of life, they will not be disappointed. There are only a few predominantly detached characters in Shakespeare (Jaques, Horatio, Thersites, Apemantus), but detachment is often an important defense when other solutions collapse, as it is for Richard II and Antony and Cleopatra.

Individuals develop not only interpersonal, but also intrapsychic strategies of defense. To compensate for feelings of inadequacy, they create an "idealized image" and embark upon a search for glory in which they try to actualize their grandiose conception of themselves. The idealized image is designed to enhance their feeling of worth, but it leads to increased self-contempt. Since they can feel worthwhile only if they *are* their idealized image, everything that falls short is deemed worthless, and there develops a "despised image" that is just as unrealistic as its idealized counterpart. There are now four selves competing for allegiance: the real (or possible) self; the idealized (or impossible) self; the despised self; and the actual self, which is what a person realistically is at the moment.

The creation of the idealized image produces not only the search for glory but a whole structure of intrapsychic strategies that Horney calls "the pride system." Individuals take an intense pride in the attributes of their idealized image and on the basis of this pride make "neurotic claims" upon others. These claims are based on an assumption of specialness or superiority, they deny the world of cause and effect, and they are "pervaded by expectations of magic" (Horney 1950, 62). People do not see their claims as unrealistic, of course, but only as what they have a right to expect given their magnificent qualities, and they will feel that life is unjust if their expectations are frustrated. The creation of the idealized image also leads to the imposition of stringent demands and taboos upon oneself, which Horney calls "the tyranny of the should." The shoulds are also pervaded by expectations of magic, since people believe they can control external reality by obeying their inner dictates. Their bargain is that if they live up to their shoulds, their claims are bound to be honored. Since the idealized image is for the most part a glorification of the self-effacing, expansive, and detached solutions, people's shoulds are determined largely by the character traits and values associated with their predominant defense. Their subordinate trends are also represented in the idealized image, however; and, as a result, they are often caught in a "crossfire of conflicting shoulds" as they try to obey contradictory inner dictates. Because the shoulds are contradictory and unrealistic, they are impossible to live up to and expose individuals to increased self-hate and anxiety. They cannot keep their bargain with themselves, and it will not, of course, be honored by the world.

IV

I have argued so far that the leading characters in Shakespeare's realistic plays are imagined human beings who can be understood in motivational terms and that the theories of Karen Horney are particularly useful in helping us to recover Shakespeare's psychological intuitions and to appreciate his mimetic achievement. As I shall show when I look at individual plays, there is often a remarkable congruence between Horney's analysis of human behavior and Shakespeare's dramatic portrayal of characters and relationships.

I have also argued that when we understand mimetic characters in motivational terms, we find that while they are part of the fictional world in which they exist, they are also autonomous beings with an inner logic of their own. In Maurice Morgann's words, they have "a certain roundness and integrity . . . which give them an independence as well as a relation" (qtd. by Knights 1933, 20). They are the product of a character-creating impulse that tends to go its own way as the author becomes absorbed in making his characters lifelike, complex, and inwardly intelligible. They say, do, think, and feel things that belong to the portrayal of their psyche but that may have no other function in the work. This gives rise to what Norman Holland describes as "the paradox of literary realism": "that highly realistic events can exist in the highly formal, unreal atmosphere of a work of art: an imaginary garden with real toads in it, as though an early creative movement toward shaping and order were canceled by a subsequent impulse toward verisimilitude" (1970, 50). E. M. Forster is making a similar point when he describes "round" characters as "creations inside a creation" who are "full of the spirit of mutiny": they "try to live their own lives and are consequently often engaged in treason against the main scheme of the book" (1949, 64).

We normally operate upon the assumption that the meaning of parts can be understood only in relation to a conception of the whole. With round or mimetic characters, however, we must understand the part as a whole before we can understand its relation to the whole of which it is a part. Arthur Sewall argues that "when character is understood separately from moral vision it is not in fact understood at all" (1951, 59). I contend that we cannot grasp the moral vision of a play until we have first understood its characters and that understanding the characters often makes the moral vision difficult if not impossible to grasp.

The subordination of character to the critic's conception of the play as a whole often results in too easy a sense of the work's artistic coherence, since mimetic characters tend, in Forster's words, to " 'run away,' " to " 'get out of hand,' " to be "inharmonious toward" the whole of which they are a part (1949, 64). As Galsworthy says, the "enduring characters in literature . . . have kicked free of . . . their creators" (1931, 27). If round characters "are given complete freedom," says Forster, "they kick the book to pieces," but if "they are kept too sternly in check, they revenge themselves by dying, and destroy it by intestinal decay" (1949, 64). This is the dilemma of the realistic writer. In the histories, the tragedies, and the Roman plays, Shakespeare did not keep his great characters "too sternly in check" but allowed them to come alive in such a way that they have seemed like fellow humans to a wide variety of subsequent audiences. Their vitality, however, has often generated unresolvable tensions within the plays and controversies among the critics, as they have undermined the very structures they were presumably designed to serve.

As Wayne Booth (1961) has pointed out, authors employ a variety of rhetorical devices in an effort to influence our moral, intellectual, and emotional responses to their characters. In Shakespeare's history and Roman plays, this rhetoric is sometimes in conflict with itself and sometimes in conflict with the mimetic portrayal of character. Both *Richard II* and *Antony and Cleopatra* begin by criticizing the protagonist for his flaws of character but end by glorifying him and romanticizing his fate. The rhetorical treatment of Cassius and Brutus is also inconsistent. Cassius is initially presented as a villain but becomes a sympathetic figure, and Brutus is presented as self-deceived until his exalted version of himself is confirmed by Antony's final speech. In the two parts of *Henry IV* and in *Henry V*, there is conflict between rhetoric and mimesis. The rhetorical treatment of Hal as a self-possessed young man whose virtue is vindicated is subverted by the mimetic portrait of him as a wayward adolescent who must be forced to grow up. The celebration of Henry V as an exemplary monarch is undermined by the concrete depiction of the darker sides of his character. In *Richard III*, the subversion of rhetoric by characterization takes a somewhat different form. Though Richard is judged in a way that is consistent with his Machiavellian behavior, his sheer vigor and magnetism and the inside view of his psyche give him an appeal that conflicts with our response to his villainy.

Sometimes the rhetoric is in conflict with both the mimesis and itself. In *Richard II* and *Antony and Cleopatra*, for instance, the rhetoric at the end conflicts with both the rhetoric at the beginning and the characterization throughout, though the rhetoric at the beginning is in harmony with the mimetic portrait. Both plays begin as tragedies of character in which the protagonist is responsible for his downfall, but both exchange blindness for insight in the last two acts. Only in *Coriolanus* is the rhetoric consistent with both itself and the mimesis; hence Coriolanus is the only character who does not subvert the structure of the play as a whole.

The conflicts of rhetoric with itself and with the mimesis generate disagreement among interpreters, since some critics respond to one set of signals, some to another, and some to several or all of a play's contradictory messages. A Horneyan approach enables us to recognize inconsistencies and to make sense of them without resorting to the sort of rationalization that is common in literary criticism. In *Shakespeare and the Common Understanding* (1967), Norman Rabkin deals with contradictions by invoking the principle of complementarity. In *Shakespeare and the Problem of Meaning*, he maintains his sense of the Shakespeare play as "an autonomous, coherent, and meaningful whole" (1981, 22) in the face of seemingly insoluble difficulties by citing the disparity between our experience of a work and our schematic interpretations. While such a disparity no doubt exists and is sometimes responsible for contradictory readings, it is often the case that Shakespeare's "confusion accounts for tension in the work and its audience" (1981, 7) and that a play's inconsistencies can be explained as manifestations of the author's psychological conflicts (see Paris, 1991).

Rabkin rejects the possibility that Shakespeare could be confused and argues instead, in the words of Stanley Cavell, that "the artist is responsible for everything that happens in his work—and not just in the sense that it is done, but in the sense that it is *meant*" (1981, 23). We have a tendency to attribute to the author a higher degree of conscious intention and psychic integration than he actually possesses; we want him to have a greater self-awareness and a more coherent set of values than most human beings have been able to attain. Whatever his gifts, however, the artist is subject to the same inconsistencies that plague the rest of us, the same waverings, uncertainties, and blind spots. This is true even for Shakespeare. The approach I employ at once sharpens our awareness of these inconsistencies and helps us to understand them as part of an intelligible structure of psychological conflicts.

2
Richard III

Shakespeare's genius in mimetic characterization first manifests itself in the history plays, which contain three great psychological portraits—Richard III, Richard II, and Hal, both as prince and as king. Richard III is Shakespeare's first great mimetic portrait and his most fully developed arrogant-vindictive character before Iago; Richard II is a younger version of the narcissistic Lear; and Prince Hal is an extraordinary study of a man who is afraid of becoming king and who has, therefore, a powerful resistance to growing up.

The three *Henry VI* plays were the workshop in which Shakespeare learned the art of mimetic characterization. They contain a multitude of psychological types: Talbot, Bedford, and Humphrey of Gloucester are perfectionistic; Winchester, Suffolk, Somerset, Margaret, Eleanor, York, Beaufort, and Clifford are arrogant-vindictive; and Henry is self-effacing. They contain also a number of psychologically interesting relationships that foreshadow similar relationships in later plays. Margaret and Suffolk are aggressive partners who share similar goals and a similar contempt for the submissive Henry, while Margaret and Eleanor and Margaret and York are aggressive rivals each of whom needs to triumph over the other. Margaret and Eleanor are ruthless women who, like Lady Macbeth, try to shame their less aggressive husbands with charges of unmanliness. A major contrast in the last two plays is between Henry, who finds the kingship a burden, and York, who is driven by an unquenchable ambition for the throne. The most fully developed of all these characters is Henry, who is an interesting study of the inability of a self-effacing man to exercise power and to cope with a world full of aggressive people. He is in some ways a prefiguration of Hamlet.

However vivid some of these characters may be, they are rendered from the outside only and are psychologically uncomplicated when compared with Richard of Gloucester. York has several soliloquies in *2 Henry VI,* but these give us insight into his political rather than his psychological motivations. It is with Richard's soliloquies in *3 Henry VI* that Shakespeare suddenly emerges as a psychological dramatist, taking us deep inside the psyche of his character and enabling us to understand the formation of his personality and the sources of his behavior. Richard is usually seen as a melodramatic villain, a Senecan tyrant, a Vice, or a Machiavel. He is all of these things, but he is also perhaps the most fully drawn mimetic character in Western literature up to the point at which he appears. Like Michael Neill, I am interested in "the surprising psychological insight which Shakespeare manages to produce from the manipulation of such thoroughly traditional material" (1975, 103).

There are many critics, of course, who focus on Richard's relationship to the traditional material or on his thematic function and who fail to see him as a mimetic character. William B. Toole argues, for instance, that we should not "seek a modern psychological explanation for Richard's behavior" on the basis of his opening soliloquy in *Richard III* because "the delineation of Richard's character is ultimately conditioned more by his structural role in the overall design of the play than by psychological reality" (1974, 25). Richard Wheeler is close to my own position when he points to the way in which Shakespeare's realistic presentation of political and psychological processes disrupts the play's "stated meaning" (1971–72, 305).[1]

Richard is less complex than Iago, who is Shakespeare's supreme portrait of an arrogant-vindictive person (see Paris, 1991), but in some respects he is more fully drawn since we are given enough information about his childhood to understand the genesis of his character structure, whereas we can only guess at the origin of Iago's. Like Shylock, and like Edmund in *Lear,* Richard has been treated unfairly because of an accident of birth, and he is burning with a bitter resentment. His needs for love and belonging and for esteem have been severely frustrated, and this has led him to develop the compensatory strategies that he talks about in his soliloquies and that he acts out in the course of the plays. These strategies are designed to restore his pride, to help him forget his loveless state, and to give some sense of purpose to his life. They work fairly well until he becomes king, but the internal and external consequences of his ruthless behavior finally catch up with him, and his defenses break down, momentarily at least, the night before the battle of Bosworth. The emergence of his feelings of guilt and self-hate reawakens the sympathy for him that had been generated by his soliloquies. One of the functions of Richard's soliloquies is to create dramatic irony by informing us of his true motives while his victims are deceived by his role playing. At the same time that they unmask his villainy, however, they also give us insight into his pain. Richard is not a motiveless villain, like Aaron the Moor; he is a suffering human being, like Shylock, whose behavior is monstrous but understandable.

In his two soliloquies in 3 *Henry VI* and in the opening soliloquy of *Richard III*, Richard is obsessed with his physical deformity, which fills him with self-loathing, makes him feel unlovable, and gives him a sense of being excluded from the human community. Richard's self-loathing is in large part an internalization of the loathing with which he has been regarded by others, a loathing that can now be justified by his moral character but that was originally a response to his physical deformity. One of the chief sources of his negative feelings about himself is his mother. It is understandable that the Duchess of York should be horrified that Richard is her son, given his terrible crimes, but it seems evident that her horror was there from the beginning. She describes Richard as "the wretched'st thing when he was young" (2.4) and tells him that she has never had a "comfortable hour" in his company (4.4). Richard has always been "disgracious" in his mother's "eye" (4.4), a source of shame and disappointment. Since Richard could not possibly accept himself in the face of his mother's rejection, it is no wonder that his infancy was "tetchy and wayward" and his "schooldays frightful, desp'rate, wild, and furious" (4.4). When Richard has his drummers drown out his mother's speeches, he is acting out a desire that must have been with him all his life to get away from her criticism. Though he displays positive feelings toward his father, he is constantly hostile toward his mother. He even has Buckingham spread the story that she conceived his brother Edward while his father was abroad.[2]

Richard has been subjected not only to his mother's rejection, but also to a widespread, culturally inspired abhorrence of his deformity. Over and over again he has been given the message that he is an anomaly, a monstrosity from whom normal people shrink with horror. Even the meek and mild Henry assaults Richard by repeating the stories about how the "owl shriek'd," the "crow cried," and "Dogs howl'd" at his birth:

Thy mother felt more than a mother's pain,
And yet brought forth less than a mother's hope,

To wit, an indigested and deformed lump,
Not like the fruit of such a goodly tree.

(*3 Henry VI*, 5.6)[3]

Richard had come to the Tower to commit a political murder, but he kills Henry in a fit of passion, as an act of revenge, striking back through Henry at all who have regarded him as a monster. He stabs Henry initially in order to shut him up, much as he later drowns out his mother; and then he stabs him again after he is dead as a way of releasing his still unsatisfied anger: "Down, down to hell, and say I sent thee thither!" (5.6). Henry's words trigger Richard's rage because they remind him of his mother's disappointment and reflect back to him his despised image of himself, which is the product of just such words in the mouths of those by whom he has been surrounded since infancy.

Richard grows up, then, in the midst of a mythology about himself in which he is a demonic figure. Not only does this mythology generate self-hate and a corresponding rage at those who make him feel so terrible about himself, but it also releases Richard to act out his rage, to seek revenge. He stabs Henry as Henry begins to recite the terrible things that Richard has come into the world to do: "Die, prophet, in thy speech. / For this (amongst the rest) was I ordain'd" (*3 Henry VI*, 5.6). The prophecies about Richard are self-fulfilling; he embraces the scenario that society has laid out for him. He does this not only because it satisfies his need to act out his rage and to pursue vindictive triumphs, but also because it seems futile to do otherwise. Since people regard him as a monster and expect him to be evil, he has little hope of gaining approval and sees no point in trying. He might as well accept his fate:

The midwife wonder'd, and the women cried
"O, Jesus bless us! He is born with teeth!"
And so I was; which plainly signified
That I should snarl and bite and play the dog.
Then, since the heavens have shap'd my body so,
Let hell make crook'd my mind to answer it.

(*3 Henry VI*, 5.7)

Richard tries to acquire self-esteem by making evil his good and excelling as a Machiavel. He is proud of his ability to manipulate, deceive, and destroy his enemies. The measures he takes to get rid of his self-hate tend to increase it, however. He sees his mind as crooked, shaped by the agents of hell. His moral self-condemnation is largely unconscious, but it emerges fully, for a moment at least, before the battle of Bosworth.

One of Richard's greatest sources of pain is his feeling that his physical deformity has made him unlovable. In his first soliloquy in 3 *Henry VI*, he considers giving up his pursuit of the crown because there are too many others whose claim is prior to his:

> Well, say there is no kingdom then for Richard:
> What other pleasure can the world afford?
> I'll make my heaven in a lady's lap
> And deck my body in gay ornaments
> And witch sweet ladies with my words and looks.
> O miserable thought! and more unlikely
> Than to accomplish twenty golden crowns!
> Why, love forswore me in my mother's womb;
> And, for I should not deal in her soft laws,
> She did corrupt frail nature with some bribe
> To shrink mine arm up like a wither'd shrub;
> To make an envious mountain on my back,
> Where sits deformity to mock my body;
> To shape my legs of unequal size;
> To disproportion me in every part,
> Like to a chaos, or an unlick'd bear-whelp,
> That carries no impression like the dam.
> Am I then a man to be belov'd?
> O monstrous fault to harbor such a thought!
>
> (3.3)

This speech and the repetition of similar sentiments at the beginning of *Richard III* reveal, among other things, the intensity of Richard's desire for love. Despite his sense of its impossibility, he has a recurring fantasy of being loved by a woman, of making his "heaven in a lady's lap." Since the fantasy arouses his self-hate by making him conscious of his repulsiveness, he is angry with himself for allowing himself to entertain it. His hopelessness about winning love is partly the result of his deformity, but it is also the result of his mother's rejection. In order to feel lovable, we must have received love in childhood, but Richard has never been loved by anyone. He feels, therefore, that "love foreswore [him] in [his] mother's womb," that it is part of his fate to be unlovable, just as it is part of his fate to be evil. His feeling of unlovableness makes it easier for him to be evil. Since love is unavailable, he is not afraid of losing it by moving against others.

Richard feels not only cut off from love but hostile to it and to all who are able to enjoy it. Since he "cannot prove a lover," he is "determined to prove a villain / And hate the idle pleasures of these days" (1.1). He hates the sight of romantic dalliance because it reminds him of his undesirability and makes him feel rejected, excluded, inferior. He is bitterly envious of those who are attractive to their fellows, and he needs to assuage his own misery by spoiling their pleasure. As long as his family was fighting for the throne, Richard could occupy himself with political scheming and warfare and gain some measure of approval for his aggressive activities. Now that peace has come, men are turning their attention to activities from which he feels excluded and in which he cannot compete. By being a villain he will not only poison their delight; he will make the world a jungle once more, a place where he is at home and in control while others are at a disadvantage.

Because of his loveless state, Richard feels excluded from the human community. Men love one another because they are like each other, because they share a common nature. Richard has been made to feel like a creature of another species, one who is repulsively different from the mass of mankind. He has no sense of kinship even with his brothers and is prepared, in the pursuit of his own interests, to commit fratricide:

> I have no brother, I am like no brother;
> And this word "love," which greybeards call divine,
> Be resident in men like one another,
> And not in me! I am myself alone.
> Clarence, beware.
>
> (3 *Henry VI*, 5.7)

Because he is so different from others and is therefore excluded from love, Richard feels that he is a law unto himself and is free to follow his own desires. His loveless state at once generates enormous rage and provides him with a rationale for acting it out. If no one loves him, why should he care about anyone else? Let those who have love be loving. Since he is not part of the human community, he is not subject to its laws.

Because of the accident of his birth, then, Richard is deprived of love, of esteem, of fellowship, of all the normal pleasures of life. Like the bastard Edmund, he feels victimized and is in rebellion against his fate. Edmund feels that it is "the plague of custom" and the "curiosity of nations" (*Lear*, 1.2) that have deprived him of his rights, and he turns to "Nature" as his goddess. Richard has nowhere to turn; he feels persecuted by all of the supposedly good forces in the universe. In the soliloquies that I have been examining, he blames "love" (*3 Henry VI*, 3.2), "the heavens" (*3 Henry VI*, 5.7), and "dissembling Nature" (I, i) for his deformity. Like Edmund, he feels terribly "cheated" (1.1); but there are no gods who will stand up for Richard. He has a profound distrust of life and no one to turn to for comfort and understanding. He is a lonely man at war with the whole universe, trying to get justice in the only way that seems possible to him, through vindictive triumphs. Because he has been so badly cheated he feels that he has a right to some kind of compensation, but he does not expect that compensation to be provided by fate, or nature, or anyone else. He relies entirely on himself, on his ability to be ruthlessly aggressive. He is so uninhibited in his aggressiveness in part because he has no respect at all (consciously, at least) for traditional values. Why should he defer to the so-called divine order when it has dealt so unfairly with him? He is in rebellion not just against society, like Edmund or Iago, but against the whole system of the universe.[4]

II

The arrogant-vindictive person pursues vindictive triumphs as a way of retaliating for humiliations suffered in childhood. In the case of Richard, the humiliations have been almost unimaginably severe, and, as a result, his need for vindictive triumphs is overwhelmingly intense. When we add to this the fact that Richard is free of most of the usual restraints and that he has no choice but to think of himself as evil, we can begin to understand why his behavior is so extreme. Vindictive triumphs have two major functions: to provide a feeling of potency by hurting our enemies even more than they have hurt us, and to restore self-esteem by raising us above those to whom we have felt inferior. They involve, that is, both vindictiveness and self-vindication. Richard's pursuit of vindictive triumphs becomes the meaning and purpose of his life.

We can see the way in which Richard consciously turns to vindictive triumphs as a compensatory strategy in his first soliloquy in *3 Henry VI*. After he concludes that he cannot make his heaven in a lady's lap, he reverts to his determination to pursue the crown:

Then, since this earth affords no joy to me
But to command, to check, to o'erbear such
As are of better person than myself,

I'll make my heaven to dream upon the crown
And, whiles I live, t'account this world but hell
Until my misshap'd trunk that bears this head
Be round impaled with a glorious crown.

(3.2)

Richard feels it is hopeless to try to move toward people, and he is too full of outrage to resign himself to his fate. His search for glory can only take the form of achieving mastery, and what form of mastery can surpass that of becoming king? Life is hell for Richard because of his negative feelings about himself, but he hopes to escape his anguish by becoming the most powerful and glamorous figure of all, the great object of deference and respect. He sees the crown as an antidote to his self-contempt; possession of it will make up for his "misshap'd trunk." Richard either must be all or he is nothing. If he cannot actualize his idealized image of himself, he will be left with his feelings of worthlessness: "Counting myself but bad till I be best" (*3 Henry VI*, 5.7). His drive for the crown is fueled by his enormous self-hate.

Richard's self-vindication takes the form that it does because of the influence of his father and the position of his family in the state. Like his son, York harbors a deep sense of injustice at the way in which he has been treated; and he engages, as a result, in an obsessive pursuit of the throne. He is a dissembler, a schemer, a ruthless seeker of power. Richard is rejected by his mother, but he receives approval from his father for his aggressive behavior. He feels that he "carries no impression like the dam," but he identifies with his father, who is the same psychological type. He feels himself to be more his father's son than are his other brothers, and hence his rightful heir. He instructs Buckingham to tell the commons that Edward was not his father's issue, "Which well appeared in his lineaments, / Being nothing like the noble Duke my father" (3.5). When he speaks to the people, Buckingham develops Richard's fantasy: "Withal I did infer your lineaments, / Being the right idea of your father / Both in your form and nobleness of mind" (3.7). Richard fights against the injustice of his fate at first by identifying with the family cause. He saves his father several times in battle and is outraged by the murder of Rutland. He accounts for the fact that he "came into the world with [his] legs forward" by attributing it to his eagerness "to make haste / And seek their ruin that usurp'd our right" (*3 Henry VI*, 5.6). Once his father is dead, however, and Edward is on the throne, Richard's family loyalty disappears. He is obsessed by his

personal wrongs and is ready to sacrifice everyone, his brother
Clarence included, to pursue his dream of the crown.

At the beginning of his first soliloquy in *3 Henry VI*, Richard is
discouraged by the many obstacles between himself and the
throne; but, when he reflects that the world affords him no "other
pleasure," he decides to pursue the crown. He realizes that the
difficulties are immense, but he is also aware that he has an
advantage over his adversaries because of his utter ruthlessness
and ability to dissemble:

> Why, I can smile, and murder whiles I smile,
> And cry "Content!" to that which grieves my heart,
> And wet my cheeks with artificial tears,
> And frame my face to all occasions.
> I'll drown more sailors than the mermaid shall;
> I'll slay more gazers than the basilisk;
> I'll play the orator as well as Nestor,
> Deceive more slily than Ulysses could,
> And, like a Sinon, take another Troy.
> I can add colours to the chameleon,
> Change shapes with Proteus for advantages,
> And set the murderous Machiavel to school.
> Can I do this, and cannot get a crown?
> Tut, were it farther off, I'll pluck it down.
>
> (3.2)

Richard's search for glory involves not only gaining the throne,
but also actualizing his arrogant-vindictive idealized image of
himself. In this passage he sees himself outdoing those who are
famous for violence, seductiveness, and deceit. He will be slyer
than Ulysses and more murderous than the Machiavel. He aspires
to become a legendary villain.

The obstacles Richard faces have a positive value for him, since
they give him an opportunity to prove his mettle. When he
succeeds in deceiving or disposing of his adversaries, he exults
not only because he has moved a step closer to the throne, but
also because he has lived up to his shoulds. We can see this most
vividly, perhaps, in his euphoria after his wooing of Lady Anne:

> What? I that kill'd her husband and his father
> To take her in her heart's extremest hate . . .
> Having God, her conscience, and these bars against me,
> And I no friends to back my suit withal
> But the plain devil and dissembling looks?

And yet to win her—all the world to nothing?
Ha!

(1.2)

Richard has an idealized image of himself as a man who can overcome all obstacles by the sheer force of his cleverness and ability to dissemble. His victory over Lady Anne feeds his pride and assuages, to some extent at least, the self-hate he displayed in his opening soliloquy. He still does not find himself to be "a marv'llous proper man," but he has "crept in favor with himself" by virtue of his vindictive triumph. Critics frequently account for Richard's conscious delight in his villainy by placing him in the tradition of the Vice. His behavior fits that pattern, but, as we have seen, it also has psychological motivations.

Critics have been puzzled as to why Richard woos Lady Anne in the first place. He does not love her, he does not plan to "keep her long," and the marriage seems to offer no particular advantage. He speaks of having a "secret close intent / By marrying her" (1.1); but we never learn what it is—or perhaps we do. Richard has decided that since the earth affords no joy to him "But to command, to check, to o'erbear such / As are of better person than" himself, he'll make his "heaven to dream upon the crown" (3 Henry VI, 3.2). He has a bitter envy of those with normal bodies, and his primary form of vindictive triumph will be to have them all in his power by becoming king. There are other forms of triumph, however. His wooing of Anne is aimed not so much at Anne herself as at Edward, a man with whom he has a particularly strong sense of rivalry:

Hath she forgot already that brave prince,
Edward, her lord, whom I, some three months since,
Stabb'd in my angry mood at Tewkesbury?
A sweeter and a lovelier gentleman—
Fram'd in the prodigality of nature,
Young, valiant, wise, and (no doubt) right royal—
The spacious world cannot again afford;
And will she yet abase her eyes on me,
That cropp'd the golden prime of this sweet prince
And made her widow to a woeful bed?
On me, whose all not equals Edward's moiety?

(1.2)

Richard sees Edward as his opposite: Edward was "fram'd in the prodigality of nature," whereas he was "Cheated of feature by dissembling Nature" (1.1). Edward is just the sort of man to exacerbate Richard's feelings of inferiority. He gets even with Edward, and with "Nature," and assuages these feelings first by killing Edward and then, more satisfying still, by winning his wife. He makes her humiliate her husband by forgetting him so soon and by doing it for his murderer, a man vastly inferior to himself. She does it, moreover, for a man who does not love her, does not value her, and does not plan to keep her long. Richard has made a fool of Anne and has greatly diminished the stature of Edward. It is no wonder that he is exultant.

Critics have been puzzled not only by Richard's wooing of Lady Anne, but also by Anne's capitulation, which seems to many to be psychologically unrealistic.[5] Because we know so little about Anne, Richard's seduction of her lacks the richness and intelligibility of Iago's seduction of Othello. We can appreciate not only the ingenuity of Iago's techniques, but also their impact upon Othello. What we know about Anne we must infer from the success of Richard's approach. We do not have a prior knowledge of her character, but Richard does, and he chooses his method of attack accordingly. He flatters her, professes his love, and claims that he killed her husband and father-in-law only because of his passion for her. His primary method of manipulating Anne is to appear self-effacing himself and to appeal to her self-effacing value system.

At the beginning of the scene, Anne is full of rage toward Richard, and he tries to disarm her by appealing to her to behave in a more Christian manner: "Lady, you know no rules of charity, / Which renders good for bad, blessings for curses" (1.2). He is trying to make her feel guilty about her vindictiveness. He behaves himself according to the model he holds up to her. No matter how angry and scornful she is (and she says some terrible things to him), he unfailingly renders good for bad, blessings for curses. He presents himself as a proud, hard man who has been transformed by his love for her. He has never before shed "an humble" or a "remorseful tear," but his longing for her has made him "blind with weeping" (1.2). He has never asked anyone for anything; but now his "proud heart sues, and prompts [his] tongue to speak" (1.2). This feeds Anne's pride in a number of ways. It is a testimony to her desirability, and it gives her a sense of having great power over a very powerful man. It appeals to a fantasy that is frequent in the self-effacing woman—that through his love for her, she will be able to soften and redeem a wildly aggressive man.

When none of his techniques seem to be working, Richard hits upon his master stroke:

If thy revengeful heart cannot forgive
Lo, here I lend thee this sharp-pointed sword,
Which if thou please to hide in this true breast
And let the soul forth that adoreth thee,
I lay it naked to the deadly stroke
And humbly beg the death upon my knee.

(1.2)

Anne is so angry with Richard that she wishes to kill him, but having the opportunity to do so throws her into inner conflict. She does not want to think of herself as vengeful and unforgiving. Richard has made her confront her vindictive impulses and recoil from them. If she should actually kill him, she would surely hate herself. She "offers at" his breast with his sword but cannot stab him. Richard urges her to proceed, reminding her that he killed Henry and Edward, but protesting again that he did it for love of her. When she drops the sword, saying that, though she wishes his death, she will not be his executioner, he offers to kill himself at her bidding. He is saying to her, in effect, if you cannot forgive me, kill me; if you cannot kill me, forgive me. He knows, of course, that she cannot kill him, but she does not know that he knows this. He is trying above all to convince her of his sincerity by offering her his life.

Anne is not convinced, but she is no longer certain that he is lying: "I would I knew thy heart" (1.2). His earlier tactics could not succeed as long as she felt he was dissembling. Now that she thinks he may be sincere, they have considerable effect. Perhaps he does think her a saint, perhaps he did kill Edward and Henry for her sake, perhaps he is a changed man because of his love for her. When Richard proposes solemnly to inter "this noble king / And wet his grave with my repentant tears," Anne is completely taken in: "much it joys me, too / To see you are become so penitent" (1.2). Once Anne believes that Richard has been converted to Christian values, she is compelled to give him a chance. I am not sure that this explains, however, her willingness to marry him.

Richard has won Anne in the face of tremendous obstacles and with nothing on his side "but the plain devil and dissembling looks" (1.2). He employs the techniques he uses on Anne again and again in the course of the play. His primary method of

manipulating others is to dissemble, and the chief object of his
dissimulation is to appear self-effacing himself and to play upon
the self-effacing tendencies of others. Like Iago, Richard despises
self-effacing values as they are embodied in the traditional morality, and he loves to exploit other people's virtue and their naive
belief in his appearance of goodness. By assuming a self-effacing
posture, he manages to overcome the mythology that has surrounded him since birth and the animosity aroused by his evil
actions as an adult. It is no wonder that this gives him a tremendous sense of triumph. It is a testimony to his skill and the folly of
others.

Richard begins the next scene, with the Queen, Rivers, and
Grey, by protesting that he has been unfairly accused of not loving
them and attributing this to his lack of hypocrisy:

> Because I cannot flatter and look fair,
> Smile in men's faces, smooth, deceive, and cog,
> Duck with French nods and apish courtesy,
> I must be held a rancorous enemy.
> Cannot a plain man live and think no harm
> But thus his simple truth must be abus'd
> With silken, sly, insinuating Jacks?
>
> (1.3)

As in his dealings with Anne, it is essential that Richard overcome
the distrust of his adversaries if his dissembling is to have any
effect. He tries to do it here by accusing others of his own prac-
tices, by pretending to abhor hypocrisy, and by professing, like
Iago, to be "a plain man." He has so much trouble in this world
because to be direct and honest is not safe. He deflects suspicion
from himself for Clarence's imprisonment by accusing the
Queen's party of being responsible and expressing great sorrow
for his brother: "I would to God my heart were flint like Edward's,
/ Or Edward's soft and pitiful like mine. / I am too childish-foolish
for this world" (1.3). (This is, of course, the way in which Richard
sees self-effacing people.) When he asks God to "pardon them
that are the cause" of Clarence's imprisonment, Rivers is taken in:
"A virtuous and a Christianlike conclusion—/ To pray for them
that have done scathe to us" (1.3).

Richard deceives not only his enemies, but also his allies,
whom he regards as "simple gulls." He gets them to whet him

> To be reveng'd on Rivers, Dorset, Grey.
> But then I sigh, and with a piece of Scripture,

Tell them that God bids us do good for evil;
And thus I clothe my naked villainy
With odd old ends stol'n forth of holy writ,
And seem a saint when most I play the devil.

(1.3)

This reminds us of Iago's exultation at the end of act 2 of *Othello:*
"Divinity of hell! / When devils will the blackest sins put on, /
They do suggest at first with heavenly shows, / As I do now."
Richard and Iago both understand thoroughly the psychology of
self-effacing people and are experts at imitating and exploiting it.
Richard concludes this scene by putting on one of the blackest of
sins, as he orders the murder of his brother.

There are several other instances of Richard's playing at being
self-effacing. He tells Rivers that he "had rather be a pedlar" than
be king (1.3), and he welcomes Edward's efforts to make peace:
" 'Tis death to me to be at enmity: / I hate it, and desire all good
men's love" (2.1). He claims to be totally free of hostility:

I do not know that Englishman alive
With whom my soul is any jot at odds
More than the infant that is born to-night.
I thank my God for my humility.

(2.1)

After the death of Edward, while he is plotting against the
princes, he pretends piety and humility again in his behavior
toward his mother: "Humbly on my knee / I crave your blessing"
(2.2). Shakespeare rather heavy-handedly has him mock his
mother's blessing in an aside. His constant exposure of Richard's
hypocrisy may reflect a fear that the audience will be taken in.

Richard's most elaborate display of self-effacing behavior occurs
in 3.7, the scene in which he pretends reluctance to accept the
throne. This scene is carefully orchestrated by Richard and Buckingham, who work the crowd like a pair of con men. When
Buckingham arrives with the Lord Mayor and the citizens,
Richard is "within, with two right reverend fathers / Divinely bent
to meditation." He appears reluctantly—"So sweet is zealous
meditation"—between two bishops, and refuses Buckingham's
offer of the crown. Playing the role of the humble man who shuns
"greatness" and "glory," he cites his "desert / Unmeritable," his
"poverty of spirit," and his "many . . . defects": "Alas, why would
you heap this care on me? / I am unfit for state and majesty."

Buckingham understands his reluctance to depose his "brother's son; / As well we know your tenderness of heart / And gentle, kind, effeminate remorse." But he insists that, whether Richard accepts or not, Edward's son shall never be king, and Richard regretfully accepts the "burden." As the scene ends, he is off to his "holy work" again with the bishops. Throughout this scene, Richard and Buckingham play upon the Christian morality, with its taboos against pride, ambition, and the desire for glory. They present Richard as a model of self-effacement. He is self-deprecating, unambitious, and reluctant to seek his gain at the expense of others. He is a humble, unassuming, religious man who would rather pray than exercise power. There is no soliloquy at the end of this scene, but we can imagine Richard's exultation at the success of his pretense and his scorn for the gullibility of the people, who are deceived by their belief in the value system that he and Buckingham are mocking.

Richard, of course, is the opposite of the self-effacing image he presents to the world. He seems to be a man without scruples, without remorse, without inner conflicts. He has an advantage over everyone else because he acts out his aggressive impulses, whereas they are subject to inner restraints. Even Buckingham, whom he describes as his "other self" (2.2), is hesitant about murdering the young princes. Richard feels that men have been brainwashed by their culture into believing that the voice of conscience is the voice of God and that they cannot violate the moral law without guilt and retribution. From Richard's point of view, "Conscience is but a word that cowards use, / Devis'd at first to keep the strong in awe" (5.3). He believes that might makes right and that society keeps down the strong by making them afraid to use their strength. Anyone who sees through this deception is able to throw off all moral restraint and to take advantage of other people's belief in the traditional pieties.

III

The traditional pieties have more power over Richard than he cares to admit. He needs to exploit self-effacing people in part because he is trying to prove to himself that he is right to suppress the self-effacing side of his own personality. He cannot entirely suppress it, however. He believes, like Lady Macbeth, that he can murder without guilt and remorse; but he finds, also like Lady

Macbeth, that conscience is a reality he cannot escape, that it
pursues him in his sleep no matter what he believes while he is
awake. Margaret's curse on Richard is that

> The worm of conscience still begnaw thy soul! . . .
> No sleep close up that deadly eye of thine,
> Unless it be while some tormenting dream
> Affrights thee with a hell of ugly devils!

$$(1.3)$$

This, like all of Margaret's curses, comes to pass. Lady Anne later
reports that "never yet one hour in his bed / Did I enjoy the golden
dew of sleep, / But with his timorous dreams was still awak'd"
(4.1). Richard's most terrifying attack of conscience occurs the
night before the battle of Bosworth. It is the climax of Shakespeare's treatment of conscience in the play as a whole, which is
designed to refute Richard's position.

Richard III is commonly seen as a justification of the Tudor
dynasty. It is that, of course; but it is also, and perhaps more
importantly, a justification of the traditional model of man and the
traditional morality, both of which are challenged by Richard's
arrogant-vindictive belief system. Shakespeare is out to show,
through action and through characterization, that crime does not
pay and that conscience is inescapable. Like *Macbeth, Richard III*
asks whether a human being can, indeed, sin with impunity, and
in both plays the answer is a resounding NO. The arrogant-vindictive solution does not work; its view of human nature and of the
world order is false. Crime or the intention to commit crime
activates the conscience, even in hardened men. The murderers of
Clarence are troubled by conscience before the deed, and one of
them repents after. The dialogue between them (2.4) is similar to
conversations between Macbeth and his Lady. Despite the fact
that they are "flesh'd villains," the murderers of the princes are
stricken "with conscience and remorse" (4.3); and Tyrrel, who
commissioned them, is deeply shaken. Sometimes it is misfortune or the threat of retribution that activates the conscience.
Clarence's accusing dream occurs while he is in prison and fills
him with remorse. Buckingham, who is as proud of his villainy as
Richard, recognizes the justice of his fate as he is about to be
beheaded: "Wrong hath but wrong, and blame the due of blame"
(5.1). Both Richard and Buckingham swear great but insincere
oaths in order to get people to believe them. They do this with
ease because they do not believe in the religious doctrines that

make an oath a sacred thing. In the case of Buckingham, the very fate he has called upon his head if he should be lying comes to pass, and he undergoes a religious conversion:

That high All-seer which I dallied with
Hath turn'd my feigned prayer on my head
And given in earnest what I begg'd in jest.
Thus doth he force the swords of wicked men
To turn their own points in their masters' bosoms.

(5.1)

The emergence of conscience in Richard parallels the process that Shakespeare has depicted in other aggressive characters in the play. It is not prepared for by a detailed portrayal of his psychological development, but it is compatible with his character structure. Gerald Zuk argues that "Richard's downfall would seem to have been precipitated by his ascent to the crown," that he is one of those people in whom "latent forces within the superego" are liberated by "a powerful wish-fulfillment" (1957, 38–39). Richard's ascent to the throne does seem to have something to do with the emergence of his inner conflicts, the prior presence of which is indicated by his "timorous dreams." The arrogant-vindictive person lives for the day of reckoning, the moment of vindictive triumph when his superiority is established and his revenge upon his detractors is complete. Richard anticipates having such a triumph when he ascends the throne. He has made his "heaven to dream upon the crown" and has invested the kingship with wonderful properties. In 3 *Henry VI*, he urges his father to "but think / How sweet a thing it is to wear a crown, / Within whose circuit is Elysium / And all that poets feign of bliss and joy" (1.2). Though Shakespeare does not portray the process very fully or explicitly, Richard seems, like the Macbeths, to find the possession of the throne a disappointing experience; and this may increase his uneasiness about the crimes he has committed to achieve it.

We do not see Richard experiencing any bliss or joy when he becomes king. Instead, he is immediately anxious about holding onto the throne ("But shall we wear these glories for a day?") and stopping "all hopes whose growth may damage" him (4.2). In the first scene in which he appears as king, he arranges the deaths of the princes (over which he breaks with Buckingham), he decides to kill Anne, he plans to marry his niece, and he worries about Henry VI's prophecy that Richmond will become king. He does

not contemplate the pursuit of Elizabeth with the same zest and
self-satisfaction that we saw earlier in his wooing of Anne:

> I must be married to my brother's daughter,
> Or else my kingdom stands on brittle glass.
> Murder her brothers, and then marry her—
> Uncertain way of gain! But I am in
> So far in blood that sin will pluck on sin.
> Tear-falling pity dwells not in this eye.
>
> (4.2)

It had filled Richard with delight that he was able to win Anne
despite his murder of her husband and father-in-law. He has a
sense now of the monstrousness of what he is contemplating in
relation to Elizabeth, and he must overcome his reluctance by
reminding himself of its necessity and his taboo against feeling
pity. He seems in this passage to believe in the reality of sin,
whereas he had formerly regarded it as just a scare word. He sees
both his past bloody acts and his intended ones as sinful, and he
is uncertain as to what they will gain. As soon as he ascends the
throne, he seems to expect to lose it, perhaps because at some
level he believes in the traditional values and in the retribution
that is supposed to follow their violation.

The emergence of Richard's inner conflicts may be related also
to the fact that as soon as he becomes king things start going
badly for him and he is subjected to severe moral condemnation.
In 4.3, we learn that Richmond aims at Elizabeth ("And by that
knot looks proudly on the crown"), that Morton has fled to Richmond, and that Buckingham is in the field with an army of
Welshmen. In 4.4, we see Richard rattled for the first time, as he
sends Catesby off to the Duke of Norfolk but forgets to give him a
message and as he strikes the messenger who brings him news of
Buckingham: "Out on ye, owls! Nothing but songs of death?"
Richard is inundated with news of desertions and the growing
strength of his enemies, and he does not entirely trust his remaining friends. In addition, he is subjected in this scene to his
mother's curse and to a scathing attack by Queen Elizabeth as he
tries to gain her assistance in wooing her daughter. All of these
things may give him the feeling that another day of reckoning is
approaching at which he will have to pay for his sins. He fears
failure at Bosworth in part because his sense of sinfulness has
been activated, and his fear of failure exacerbates his sense of
sinfulness, for self-effacing trends rise to the surface in an expansive person when his quest for mastery is threatened. It is not

surprising that, despite his superiority in numbers, Richard has "not that alacrity of spirit / Nor cheer of mind that [he was] wont to have" (5.3). He is no longer convinced of his ability to master his fate through the sheer force of his aggressiveness but is burdened by guilt and fear and is full of inner conflicts.

Shakespeare's mimetic portrait of Richard is not as consistently rich and interesting as are some of his later characterizations. We can understand the genesis of Richard's defense system with exceptional clarity, but Richard is for the most part a rather static character who repeats his strategies rather than one who undergoes a complex development in the course of the play. There are some signs, as we have seen, of the weakening of his defense system; but it is not until the night before the battle of Bosworth that he experiences a psychological crisis. In his dream he is visited by those he has murdered, each of whom tells him to despair and die. Richard has believed that might makes right and that he can violate the moral law with impunity. The traditional belief is that right makes might, that the good will triumph and the evil will be undermined by their sins. The play is set up to vindicate the traditional morality. The battle of Bosworth is presented as a trial by combat in which the righteousness of Richmond's cause assures him victory despite his inferiority in numbers and experience. Oxford proclaims that "Every man's conscience is a thousand men, / To fight against this guilty homicide" (5.2). While Richmond's righteousness gives him additional strength, Richard's guilt has the opposite effect. Because of its unrealistic mode of presentation, we cannot treat Richard's dream as a purely psychological phenomenon, but it does seem to be linked to his other "timorous dreams" and to mark the point at which his unconscious guilt emerges so powerfully that it breaks down his defenses.

If Richard's dream is not presented realistically, his reaction to it is. The soliloquy that follows his awakening is the high point of Shakespeare's mimetic portrait. Richard awakes in a panic, calling for a horse and treatment of his wounds. He has evidently been dreaming of battle and has been experiencing the misfortune predicted for him by the ghosts of those he has murdered. In the midst of his fright, he calls upon Jesus for mercy. This is a self-effacing response to the collapse of his feelings of mastery and an indication that at some level he still holds traditional beliefs. When he realizes that he was only dreaming, he is filled with self-hate. His guilt-ridden dream and his plea for mercy undermine his idealized image and make him feel like his despised self. In

order to restore his pride, he heaps scorn on his conscientious
side ("O coward conscience") and tries to master his fear:

> What do I fear? Myself? There's none else by.
> Richard loves Richard: that is, I am I.
> Is there a murderer here? No. Yes, I am.
> Then fly. What, from myself? Great reason why—
> Lest I revenge myself upon myself?
> Alack, I love myself. Wherefore? For any good
> That I myself have done unto myself?
> O no! Alas, I rather hate myself
> For hateful deeds committed by myself.
> I am a villain. Yet I lie, I am not.
> Fool, of thyself speak well. Fool, do not flatter.

(5.3)

This is Shakespeare's first detailed presentation of a character in
the grip of inner conflict. Richard is schizoid in this soliloquy: his
self-effacing side has emerged and he is caught in a cross-fire of
conflicting shoulds. He realizes that what he is afraid of is the
conscientious side of himself, and he tries to cope with his fear by
holding onto his code of egoism. If everyone is out for himself,
then Richard must love Richard, and he has no reason to be afraid
of himself. The problem is that he hates himself because of his
violations of traditional values and he is afraid that he will punish
himself in order to reduce his self-hate. He has an impulse to seek
revenge on himself for having been so self-destructive. For a
moment the forces in conflict seem evenly balanced. His self-
effacing side tells him that he is a villain, but his arrogant-vindictive side tells him that he is not. One set of shoulds tells him that
he is a fool for thinking ill of himself, while the other set tells him
that he is a fool for engaging in self-deception. Then his defenses
collapse, and he is overwhelmed with guilt and self hate:

> My conscience hath a thousand several tongues,
> And every tongue brings in a several tale,
> And every tale condemns me for a villain.
> Perjury, perjury, in the high'st degree,
> Murder, stern murder, in the dir'st degree,
> All several sins, all us'd in each degree,
> Throng to the bar, crying all "Guilty! guilty!"
> I shall despair. There is no creature loves me;
> And if I die, no soul will pity me.

Nay, wherefore should they, since that I myself
Find in myself no pity to myself?

(5.3)

Richard is in despair because there is no way in which he can
either cope with his guilt or satisfy his yearning for love. He feels
that he has gone too far ever to put himself in harmony with his
conscience. He has tried to deny its existence, but now he knows
that it is indisputably there, and he fears that he can never escape
his self-hate. He is experiencing not only his guilt, but also,
perhaps for the first time, the full force of his need for love. He
has tried to deny this also, but with his self-effacing side now
dominant, he experiences the pain of his alienation from the
human community. No one loves him and if he dies no one will
pity him. He understands that his isolation is something he has
deserved. He cannot expect compassion from others when he is
so full of rage with himself. His despair awakens our compassion,
of course, as had the evidences of suffering in his earlier soliloquies. Because of such deep inside views, he is much more real to
us than his merely illustrative adversaries.

Richard seems to be heading for a psychological collapse; but,
when we next see him, he has pulled himself together and has
rebuilt his defenses.

Let not our babbling dreams afright our souls;
Conscience is but a word that cowards use,
Devis'd at first to keep the strong in awe.
Our strong arms be our conscience, swords our law!
March on, join bravely, let us to't pell-mell,
If not to heaven, then hand in hand to hell.

(5.3)

This speech is addressed to himself, of course, more than to those
who are with him. Richard deals with his guilt and anxiety by
once more dismissing conscience as a ruse and a sign of cowardice. He reaffirms his belief that might makes right and confronts
his fate defiantly. Even if he is wrong and is headed for hell, his
spirit is unbroken. He fights valiantly and dies with his harness
on his back. His ability to fend off despair and to behave in a way
that conforms to his own system of values wins a certain respect,
much as similar behavior does for Macbeth.

I have presented Richard's inner conflict as being between the
self-effacing and arrogant-vindictive components of his person-

ality. It can be seen in other ways, of course. Many critics see it as being between the traditional values that Shakespeare's culture inherited from the Middle Ages and the new ideas that were springing up in the Renaissance. This is certainly a valid perspective. Richard is the first of the "new men," the individualists, whom Shakespeare depicted and destroyed again and again in his plays. We can reconcile the ideological and the psychological interpretations of Richard's inner conflict by recognizing that belief systems often reflect our defensive strategies and appeal to us because they reinforce our dominant solution. Characters like Richard III, Iago, Edmund, and Lady Macbeth can be seen as embodying certain radical ideas, the challenge of which Shakespeare rose to resist; but their belief systems are presented by Shakespeare himself as integral to their personalities and not as merely the product of cultural influences. The plays invite a psychological reading. Whatever his thematic intentions, Shakespeare seems intuitively to have understood the relationship between character structure and belief.

Shakespeare may have been trying to work out in *Richard III* a conflict between arrogant-vindictive and self-effacing components of his own personality. Part of him seems to be drawn to Richard. He imagines him with such force that Richard is not simply a villain but is also a vividly drawn figure whose behavior seems understandable and even, at times, delightful and whose magnetism threatens to subvert the effects of the rhetoric. Shakespeare needs to repudiate the aggressive part of himself, however, even more than he needs to give it expression, and so the play is heavily weighted on the side of conventional values. Shakespeare seems to be showing himself that though the intellect may see through and dissolve the traditional beliefs, they still have psychological force, that even in the most ruthlessly ambitious person there is a suppressed self-effacing side which makes it impossible for him to commit crimes without incurring self-hate.

3
Richard II

I

Is *Richard II* primarily a political play or a tragedy of character? Many critics agree with Hazlitt that "the part of Richard himself gives the chief interest to the play" (1964, 276), while others feel that the play is "too often read as the tragedy of a private individual" and that its "political implications . . . are correspondingly neglected" (Palmer 1948, 118). Those who focus upon the part of Richard disagree about the coherence of his characterization, the reasons for his psychological collapse, and the degree to which he grows as a result of his suffering, while those who focus on the play's political implications see it as dramatizing the consequences of violating Tudor notions of divine right, or the preferability of "a strong and efficient king with illegal title [to] such a man" as Richard (Ribner 1971, 33), or the ultimate insolubility of the problems with which it is grappling. Some critics find the play confusing. A. L. French complains that it starts out as a story of abdication and turns into a story of deposition, "giving us one truth in one place and another in another, with apparently equal weight and conviction" (1967, 431). For Travis Bogard it begins as the story of a king whose deposition results in civil strife and turns into the story of a complex and fascinating individual. Shakespeare stumbled into the creation of his greatest character so far through his growing interest in Richard, but the play's "preliminary assurance" is "destroyed midway" by this unexpected development (Bogard 1955, 193).

I, too, find the play confusing, for several reasons. Shakespeare presents the problem of what to do about a capricious, ill-ruling king without providing a solution.[1] Richard seems to deserve his fate: it is he, after all, who first brings disorder into the realm. He is responsible for Gloucester's death and in his treatment of Bolingbroke he himself violates the principle of succession by which he holds the throne. Gaunt says that "God's is the quarrel"

(1.2) and that He will "rain hot vengeance on offender's heads" (1.2); but how is God to rain vengeance upon Richard except through his subjects, who thereby incur divine wrath? Richard's subjects are confronted by a choice of evils: either submit to injustice or seek out right with wrong and bring about the dreadful consequences of rebellion. York's confusion within the play indicates the inability of the traditional value system to deal with such choices. The rhetoric of the play seems to affirm that rebellion is the greater evil, but this does not feel like a satisfactory response to the situations confronted by Bolingbroke, the Duchess of Gloucester, and the many other victims of Richard's injustice. As Wilbur Sanders has said, the play leaves us with a sense of "the moral impenetrability of the political order" (1968, 160), but I am not sure, as Sanders seems to be, that its "riddling complexity" (1968, 158) "has been deliberately cultivated" (1968, 164).

Perhaps the greatest source of confusion about the play is "the imaginative blur" (French 1967, 413) connected with Richard's deposition. It is clear that Bolingbroke was grievously wronged by Richard; it is less clear what Bolingbroke should have done about this (hence York's bewilderment in 2.2 and 2.3); and it is not clear at all that he returned to England with the intention of deposing Richard. Many critics think that he did, but many others feel that his motives cannot be ascertained and/or that Richard was more responsible for his loss of the throne than was Bolingbroke.[2] While Bolingbroke keeps insisting that he will lay down his "arms and power" provided that his banishment is repealed and his lands are restored (3.3), Richard introduces the topic of deposition and prompts Bolingbroke to take the throne through his readiness to relinquish it. If Richard abdicates or invites his deposition, then the play becomes even more difficult to interpret thematically, though it is all the richer as a study of character.

Irving Ribner tries to put character and theme together by arguing that Shakespeare makes Richard "the author of his own downfall" in order to justify Bolingbroke's succession "without seeming an advocate of rebellion" (1971, 35), but this conflicts with the fact that our sympathies shift from Bolingbroke to Richard as the play progresses. They do so partly because Bolingbroke and Richard exchange roles of victim and victimizer, with Bolingbroke's crime against Richard being by far the more serious, but also because Richard becomes more and more highly individualized while Bolingbroke remains an illustrative character. Though Richard begins as an illustrative character, he emerges in 3.3 as a complex and vulnerable human being; and, since a mimetic character always engages us more deeply than an illustrative one (witness Satan and God in *Paradise Lost*), the terribly flawed but humanly real Richard is far more sympathetic than the sketchily drawn, problematic Bolingbroke. Our sympathy for Richard overcomes the antipathy that has been generated by his bad behavior and the negative rhetoric of the first two acts. The play begins as the story of a man who brings destruction upon himself and his country by abusing his royal powers, and it becomes, like *King Lear,* the story of a humiliated monarch who is more sinned against than sinning. Richard's sufferings, like Lear's, are so vividly portrayed that they tend to obscure his faults and the thematic issues associated with them.

Richard II is confusing, then, because it does not provide a satisfying answer to the question of what should have been done about Richard, because Bolingbroke is treated as a usurper even though his motives are unclear and Richard seems intent upon undoing himself, and because it begins as a critique of Richard but then makes him predominantly a victim by presenting the story from his point of view and surrounding him with sympathetic rhetoric. It begins as a political play full of illustrative characters (hence the relative thinness of the first two acts); but with the emergence of Richard as a mimetic character, it becomes primarily a psychological drama. Since the already impenetrable political issues become even more blurred as Richard escapes his illustrative role, the play is bound to be endlessly perplexing when we try to make sense of it thematically. Richard is one of those "creations inside a creation," of whom E. M. Forster speaks, who kick the book to pieces. He is the chief source of the play's difficulties and also of its greatness.

II

As I have indicated, some critics feel not only that the play as a whole lacks coherence, but also that there is an "incoordination of the elements of Richard's portrait" (Bogard 1955, 205). Bogard finds "three, possibly four Richards in the play, no one of them brought fully into conformity with any other" (1955, 199), and Rossiter complains of "a lack of continuity between the Richard of Acts I and II and the melancholy introvert re-imported from Ireland" (1961, 24). I think that the characterization of Richard is consistent and that the appearance of incoordination derives from the shift to a more detailed psychological portraiture that occurs in act 3 and from the "rapid transition[s] from one feeling to its opposite" (Coleridge 1960, 140) that have often been noted in Richard. Richard is a difficult character to comprehend.[3] Why does he oscillate between "ungrounded hope" and "unmanly despair" (Coleridge, 1960, 140)? Why does he give "up his . . . crown with such alacrity" (Wangh 1968, 215)? Why does he switch so rapidly from the arrogant king of the first two acts and the beginning of the third to the self-abasing, self-martyring man of the rest of the play?

Richard's behavior makes sense, I believe, if we see him as one of the many characters in Shakespeare who undergo a psychological crisis as a result of the breakdown of their bargain with fate (see Paris 1991). Indeed, he is the first character whose crisis is presented in the kind of rich psychological detail that we find in the major tragedies. Richard resembles King Lear, of whom he is, in many ways, a younger version. He has a grandiose image of himself that is the result of his having been indulged as a king, he has enormous claims based on that image, and he has very little sense of the duties that accompany his position. He responds with rage to hearing the truth about himself (compare his reaction to Gaunt with Lear's reaction to Kent), and he courts flattery through his "liberal largesse" (1.4) in order to have his idealized image confirmed. His narcissism leads him, like Lear, to make disastrous political decisions. The first two acts of the play show Richard preparing his own destruction while the last three portray his psychological collapse and his effort to develop new defenses.

Because he regards the realm as his property rather than as his trust, Richard indulges himself and his favorites on a lavish scale without counting the cost to his people or being concerned about loss of support. His wastefulness leaves him short of money for his Irish wars, and he is forced to "farm" the realm and issue "blank charters" (1.4), thereby increasing his unpopularity. His need for money leads him also to "seize into [his] hands" the plate, goods, money, and lands of his uncle Gaunt, an act of usurpation that the mild-mannered York sternly warns against: "Take Hereford's rights away, and . . . / Be not thyself—for how art thou a king / But by fair sequence and succession?" (2.1). Richard dismisses this because he sees himself as being above both the legal code and the law of cause and effect, but his violation of an order larger than himself leads to the loss of his kingdom. Like Lear's, his delusion that he is "everything" is shattered when he confronts a reality that refuses to honor his claims.

We get our most vivid sense of Richard's self-idealization from the speeches that he utters when he lands on the coast of Wales (3.2). He reverses the normal relationship between earth and human by seeing himself as the mother and the earth as his child. He is not dependent upon the earth for his sustenance but rather does the earth "favours with [his] royal hands." He is sovereign not only of the people of England but also of the animal, vegetable, and mineral kingdoms, which he calls upon to fight against his enemies. His followers urge him to embrace "the means that heaven yields," but Richard's bargain is based on maintaining his grandiose claims, and he therefore mocks Aumerle's admonitions ("Discomfortable cousin!") and reaffirms his magical powers. As anointed king, his exceptional status has been conferred upon him once and for all, and he need not fear deposition by "the breath of worldy men."

As king, Richard does have an exceptional status, of course, and legitimate claims to obedience. The reactions of his supporters make clear, however, that even for those who believe in his divine right, he seems out of touch with reality. His allies are threatened by his fantasies of omnipotence, which make him all the more vulnerable, while he is threatened by their scepticism, which undermines his idealized image. Richard cannot cope with adversity in part because it is one of his claims that he should not have to do so, and he is afraid to give up his claims lest his entire solution collapse. He feels that as the Lord's anointed he is above the moral, legal, and physical constraints that govern ordinary men. His bargain is that if he holds onto these claims, they are bound to be honored by God. Anything that threatens his faith in his claims activates his defenses. He reacts to Gaunt's denunciation with rage and an invocation of his "seat's right royal majesty" (2.1), and when York compares him unfavorably to his father, "whose hands were guilty of no kindred blood," Richard seems uncomprehending: "Why, uncle, what's the matter?" (2.1). He ignores York's warning against seizing Gaunt's possessions, persists in believing that his uncle "always loved [him] well" (2.1), and appoints him Governor of England in his absence. York's words are so threatening to Richard that he simply refuses to give them conscious recognition.

The most serious threat to Richard's claims is, of course, Bolingbroke's rebellion. He dismisses it, as we have seen, by invoking his status as the Lord's anointed, but he is overwhelmed by anxiety when Salisbury reports that his Welsh allies, hearing he was dead, "Are gone to Bolingbroke, dispers'd, and fled" (3.2). This is the first of Richard's rapid transitions from one feeling to its opposite. Having just claimed that an army of angels will fight on his side, he now feels that "time hath set a blot upon [his] pride" and warns "all souls that will be safe" to "fly" from him (3.2). We can understand this rapid transition if we recognize the fact that while Richard's idealized image is extraordinarily lofty, it is also very fragile—he must surround himself with flatterers in order to protect it. It is so fragile in part because it is so lofty and in part because Richard has done nothing to earn self-esteem, the respect of others, or a feeling of being able to cope with reality. There is in Richard a good deal of insecurity that he deals with by clinging all the more fiercely to his exalted conception of himself. He is unscrupulous in his exercise of power and seems impervious to criticism, but he registers the indictments of Gaunt and York and is haunted by them later. Beneath his claims of potency and righteousness lurk hidden feelings of weakness, inadequacy, and guilt. These feelings emerge when he hears about the Welshmen because this stroke of ill fortune calls into question his conviction that he is the favorite of God. If God does not honor his claims, then he has been guilty of a pride for which he is now being punished. He oscillates between identifying with his idealized self, which is not subject to necessity, and with his despised self, which is totally vulnerable.

When Aumerle, now alarmed by Richard's excessive pessimism, tries to rally his spirits by telling him to "remember who" he is, Richard swings back to the opposite extreme. He attacks himself for having given up his claims and reaffirms his supernatural power: "Is not the King's name twenty thousand names? / Arm, arm, my name! A puny subject strikes at thy great glory" (3.2). Aumerle's feeding of his pride assuages Richard's guilt and anxiety and allows him to reestablish his sense of the vast disparity between himself and his subjects. Richard does not rely entirely on the magic of kingship, however, as he had done at the beginning of the scene, but comforts himself with the thought that York will have a sufficient power to oppose his enemies. He is no longer indifferent to "the means that heaven yields" "of succor and redress" (3.2).

Richard's confidence quickly collapses when Scroop's demeanor indicates that there is more bad news to come, and although it rebounds again, from this point on Richard is in a state of psychological crisis. As Michael Manheim observes, in "all the . . . memorable scenes that follow" he is searching for ways to make his "intolerable situation somehow tolerable" (1973, 63). His initial response is to turn to resignation. Since his kingdom was his care, it is no great loss; and since "death will have his day" (3.2), why bother to evade it? By immediately embracing the worst, Richard is seeking to attain emotional invulnerability. To resist or to hope is to expose himself to further disappointment. He defends himself also by adopting a self-effacing posture. The worst that he faces is "worldly loss," but from a religious point of view this is unimportant. Bolingbroke cannot become greater than he because he will not be able to serve God any better. Indeed, since his revolting subjects are breaking "their faith to God as well" as to him, Richard, though defeated, is morally superior to them.

After he hears Scroop's tale of woe and learns of the deaths of Wiltshire, Bushy, and Green, Richard rejects all talk of comfort and assumes that his fate will be deposition and death. He does not stop to consider either his remaining resources or Bolingbroke's objectives, which are not necessarily so radical. Scroop's account of how "Both young and old rebel, / And all goes worse than I have power to tell" (3.2) delivers a series of blows to Richard's pride; and, with no reality-based sense of worth or strength to fall back upon, Richard swings from self-glorification to self-minimization. He is either everything or nothing, either Fortune's favorite or her victim, either the owner of England or a man who can call nothing his "own but death / And that small model of the barren earth / Which serves as paste and cover to our bones" (3.2). Bolingbroke is now the favorite of fortune and the possessor of everything. Richard does not make a fight for his throne and his life in part because he feels so impotent and in part because without the aura of glory by which they have been surrounded, they are worth nothing to him.

In his great speech upon "the death of kings," Richard's inner conflicts are reflected in his shifting conceptions of kingship. Instead of seeing kings as superior to moral and physical law, he now sees them as subject to guilt and doomed to be victims of murder. He may, as some critics have suggested, expect and even want to die because he is haunted by the ghost of Gloucester.[4] The collapse of his claims leaves him vulnerable to the reproaches of Gaunt and York and to York's dire warning that "by bad courses may be understood / That their events can never fall out good" (2.1). He mocks himself for having been infused with such "self and vain conceit" that he thought his "flesh" was "brass impregnable," and he imagines that Death all the while was "grinning at his pomp" (3.2). As many critics have observed, Richard comes here to recognize his bond with the rest of humanity, but he still lacks a balanced conception of what it means to be a king. He recognizes the absurdity of his former claims, but he seems to be saying that because kings die, they have no right to "respect" or "duty." In the remainder of the speech, however, he reverts to his former conception of kingship. Since he is "subjected" to "want," "grief," and the need of "friends," how can anyone say to him that he is a king? Kings are presumably above such subjection, but since Richard is not, he does not feel like a king. He is once again glorifying kingship, but because his claims are not being honored, he feels unworthy of the title.

Richard's oscillations are not over, of course. When Carlisle chides him for his fear and Aumerle reminds him of York's power, Richard swings from his despised to his idealized image and proclaims that it is an "easy task . . . to win our own" (3.2). This is a characteristic claim of a narcissistic person, for whom nothing should be difficult.[5] It is also an affirmation of the doctrine that right makes might; since the throne is legitimately his, he should have no trouble defending it. When he learns that York has defected, Richard once again embraces despair. Without allowing anyone to advise him, he dismisses his troops and sets out for Flint Castle to "pine away." As in the "death of kings" speech, he glamorizes his suffering by presenting himself as an exceptionally pathetic figure: "A king, woe's slave, shall kingly woe obey" (3.2).

III

Despite his self-defeating behavior, Richard's fate does not yet seem to be sealed. In 3.3, Bolingbroke assures York that he will not take "further that [he] should"; and in his dealings with Northumberland, Richard behaves with regal dignity. He asserts his right to the "awful duty" of his subjects and warns that "God omnipotent" is mustering "Armies of pestilence" on his behalf. He has considerably reduced his claims, however, since his threats are of future rather than of immediate retaliation. According to Northumberland, Bolingbroke swears by their "royal grandsire's" tomb, by "the royalties of both [their] bloods," by "the buried hand of warlike Gaunt," and by "the worth and honour of himself" that he has come but for "his lineal royalties" and "Enfranchisement" (3.3). Once these are granted, he will commend his arms "to rust," his steeds "to stables, and his heart / To faithful service of your Majesty." This is a powerful oath, and we have no reason to think that Bolingbroke does not intend to honor it. Richard grants all of Bolingbroke's "fair demands" and then, as many critics have pointed out, invites his deposition when it seems as though he could have retained the throne by taking Bolingbroke at his word:

> What must the King do now? Must he submit?
> The King shall do it. Must he be depos'd?
> The King shall be contented. Must he lose
> The name of king? A God's name, let it go!

> (3.3)

This is not a response that Bolingbroke had expected. Northumberland reports that "Sorrow and grief of heart / Makes him speak fondly, like a frantic man." How can we explain this most puzzling of Richard's rapid transitions?

As we have seen, Richard has been oscillating between his idealized and his despised self-images. His idealized image is that of a king, and in order to feel like a king he must be above the human condition and must partake of God's omnipotence. Anything that frustrates his claims throws him into a state of despair. Despair is hopelessness about actualizing—or, in the case of the narcissist, maintaining—one's idealized image. Richard's fragility and his resilience are both characteristic of narcissism, in which the idealized image is in large part an introjection of a grandiose conception of self provided by others. Because the narcissist has not *done* anything to warrant his self-exaltation, his feelings of grandiosity are quite vulnerable; but because he has always been made to feel special, his illusions about himself are persistent. Richard alternately sinks into despair and reaffirms his claims as he is assaulted by piece after piece of bad news. The final blow to his idealized image is his accession to Bolingbroke's demands. This marks a new stage in his psychological crisis and leads to his self-deposition.

Granting Bolingbroke's demands is such a devastating blow to Richard because it is an irrevocable relinquishment of his claims. When he felt in "the death of kings" speech that his claims were not being honored, he at first identified all kings with himself and felt that if kings are subject to necessity, like ordinary men, they have no right to ceremonious duty and respect. He returned at the end of the speech, however, to his exalted conception of kingship, and he maintains this conception to the end of his life. It is this conception of kingship that results in Richard's collapse after he has granted Bolingbroke's demands, for he cannot be less than absolute and continue to feel like a king. If he had had a less lofty notion of kingship, he might have been able to live with his concessions to Bolingbroke and thus to have remained on the throne.

Bolingbroke has a legitimate grievance and his "demands," so far, are "fair," but it is intolerable to Richard to have to recognize other people's rights and to feel himself in their power. When he violates his bargain by relinquishing his claims, he is flooded with self-hate and despair. He has debased himself irrevocably and he begins to mourn for his lost idealized image:

> O that I were as great
> As is my grief, or lesser than my name!
> Or that I could forget what I have been!
> Or not remember what I must be now!

(3.3)

He is crushed by the disparity between his former grandeur and the present reality, and he wishes that he could escape his consciousness of this disparity by repressing awareness of either his former or his present state. His suffering would also be lessened if he were "lesser than [his] name," that is, if he were not a king, for then his expectations would be more in accord with his lot. This, then, is one of his reasons for embracing deposition. He wishes to rid himself of the contradiction between his actual limitations and the status to which he feels entitled.[6]

Richard would rather be a martyr than a king with limited powers. He turns to a self-effacing solution in which suffering and victimization, lowliness and humility, raise one to the heights. He will give his "jewels for a set of beads," his "gay apparel for an almsman's gown," his "sceptre for a palmer's walking staff," and his "subjects for a pair of carved saints" (3.3). In this speech, Richard at once exalts his new religiosity and evokes pathos by contrasting his former opulence with the austerity of his future life. At the thought of exchanging his "large kingdom for a little grave," he is overwhelmed by his sense of betrayal:

> A little grave, an obscure grave;
> Or I'll be buried in the king's highway,
> Some way of common trade, where subject's feet

May hourly trample on their sovereign's head;
For on my heart they tread now whilst I live,
And buried once, why not upon my head?

(3.3)

Richard derives a distinct pleasure from the thought of his subjects trampling on his head. He envisions himself as a legendary
figure because of the distance of his fall and the magnitude of his
griefs, and in order to actualize this new idealized image, he must
nurse his sense of injustice and bring about his own deposition
and death. The worse he is treated, the greater his glory.

When Richard comes face to face with Bolingbroke, his fate is
still undecided. Bolingbroke tells all to "show fair duty to his
Majesty," he kneels before Richard, and he affirms once again that
he has "come but for [his] own" (3.3). Even when Richard replies
"Your own is yours, and I am yours, and all," Bolingbroke answers like a dutiful subject: "So far be mine, my most redoubted
lord, / As my true service shall deserve your love" (3.3). If Richard
had been able to feel and act like a king despite having had to
make concessions, Bolingbroke would not, I think, have tried to
take the throne from him. As it is, Richard refuses to accept a
conditional submission and instead keeps thrusting the crown
upon Bolingbroke.

The confusion about abdication versus deposition is of both
Richard's and Bolingbroke's making. In 4.1, Bolingbroke tries to
justify his ascension to the throne by showing that Richard has
yielded his sceptre willingly *and* that he deserves deposition,
while Richard tries to thwart Bolingbroke's efforts to do this.
Though Richard *is* ready to "resign the crown," for the reasons
discussed above, he wants to nourish his sense of betrayal and to
make others feel guilty by presenting himself as unjustly deposed. He needs both to abdicate the throne and to feel that he is
still rightfully king. He tries to force Bolingbroke to "seize the
crown," and he gives it up in such a way as to reaffirm his claim to
it:

With mine own tears I wash away my balm,
With mine own hands I give away my crown,
With mine own tongue deny my sacred state,
With mine own breath release all duteous oaths.

(4.1)

The implication is that he cannot himself "undo" his "sacred
state," and if he cannot, neither can anyone else. Having forsworn

his "pomp and majesty," he finds himself "a traitor with the rest; / For I have given here my soul's consent / To undeck the pompous body of a king" (4.1). Richard is at once expressing self-hate for having "Made glory base and sovereignty a slave" and condemning those who have "usurp'd" his title.

Richard thwarts not only Bolingbroke's attempt to legitimize himself as a willingly adopted "heir," but also Northumberland's effort to get him to recite his "crimes" so that men "may deem" him "worthily deposed" (4.1). Instead of allowing himself to be put on the defensive, he accuses his former subjects of being Judases and Pilates, and he reminds Northumberland that among his own crimes there is

> one heinous article,
> Containing the deposing of a king
> And cracking the strong warrant of an oath,
> Mark'd with a blot, damn'd in the book of heaven.
>
> (4.1)

He does not deny that he has been guilty of follies, but he deflects every attempt to get him to acknowledge specific offenses and succeeds in presenting himself as a man more sinned against than sinning.

Richard presents himself above all as the king of grief. This is partly an effort to induce guilt by showing others what they have done to him and partly a means of thwarting their objectives by controlling the emotional situation. Both of these motives are operative in the mirror episode. How can Northumberland insist that Richard read the accusations against him when he is already so devastated? Richard says that he will read his sins in his face, but he dwells instead upon his sorrows, which others have inflicted upon him, and upon the contrast between his former glory and his present humiliation. He is disappointed that his face looks much the same, since he wants to be a pitiful spectacle, and he dashes the glass to the floor as a symbolic expression of "the unseen grief / That swells with silence in the tortured soul" (4.1). It is extremely important for everyone to know how much he is suffering.

Being the king of grief enables Richard to turn his downfall into a new source of glory. He not only accuses his former subjects of having delivered him to his "sour cross," but he sees himself as being even more of a martyr than Jesus, since "he, in twelve, / Found truth in all but one; I, in twelve thousand, none" (4.1).

Because the lower he falls the greater his sense of injustice, Richard keeps focusing upon his state of nothingness. His lack of even a title or a name makes him all the more pitiable. He longs for death partly as an escape from his pain and partly because this will complete his victimization: "Long mayst thou live in Richard's seat to sit, / And soon lie Richard in an earthy pit" (4.1). He feeds his self-pity by contrasting Bolingbroke's rise with his decline and invites his own murder, as he had invited his own deposition. When he requests "leave to go" at the end of the scene, Bolingbroke asks, "Whither?" This gives Richard an opportunity to propose a mode of life for himself. Instead he replies, "Whither you will, so I were from your sights" (4.1); and Bolingbroke sends him to the Tower. Bolingbroke could have acted differently, of course, but Richard keeps insisting that he is rightful king, even though he has abdicated; and he makes no effort to propose how they might coexist, for that would be inconsistent with his self-destructive scenario.

As he bids farewell to his queen, Richard urges her to think of him as dead, and, when "good old folks" tell tales "Of woeful ages long ago betid," to requite them with his story (5.1). As in "the death of kings" speech, he takes comfort in the thought that others have experienced similar woes, and he imagines that his story, like theirs, will go down in history. Indeed, his "lamentable tale" will be sadder than any of the others. Not only will it "send the hearers weeping to their beds," it will move "the senseless brands" to "weep the fire out" (5.1). Richard's suffering has become the basis of a new set of magical claims and a new dream of glory.

IV

At the beginning of the play, Richard has a conception of himself as king that is loftier than the already grandiose conception of kingship that is sanctioned by his culture. Because he sees himself as exempt from human and natural law, he expects to be able to violate the rights of his subjects with impunity. The discovery that he cannot do this precipitates a psychological crisis with which he copes in the manner that we have examined. There is considerable disagreement as to whether Richard undergoes not only an emotional breakdown but also a process of growth as a result of his misfortunes. Perhaps the most positive view of his development has been taken by Norman Rabkin, who sees him at the end as "a fully sentient human being" (1967, 92). He has been "instructed by his suffering," and by the beginning of act 5 "he is a new man, strong and able to bear his adversity" (1967, 91). He "reaches by the point of his death a full acceptance of his responsibility for his demise" (1967, 91). In striking contrast to this is the position of Wilbur Sanders, who argues that his "despairing cadences" in prison show Richard to be in a state of "desolation" (1968, 181). He has occasional "searing insights," but he "retreats" from them into a kind of "nihilism" (1968, 182). According to James McPeek, Richard's "consideration of the lives he might have led is a characteristic evasion of the facts about the life he has led" (1958, 380). What light does our psychological perspective shed on the issue of Richard's maturation? Are his insights fleeting, like Lear's, or does his suffering enable him to achieve "self-knowledge . . . and a new awareness of the common lot of mankind" (Humphreys 1967, 59)?

Richard learns that he has been living in "a happy dream" (5.1), that he had been beguiled by his "followers in prosperity" (4.1). The "truth of what we are" shows that he has no supernatural powers, that "glory" is "brittle" (4.1), and that he is "sworn brother . . . / To grim Necessity" (5.1). He "live[s] with bread," like ordinary men; his "flesh" is not "brass impregnable" (3.3). Richard's insights are genuine, but his reactions to them are extreme. If his wishes aren't magic, there is no use trying to cope with reality; if he cannot be absolute monarch, he does not want to be king; and if he must die, there is no point in living. The discovery of his mortality results in an obsession with death. Richard cannot accept his human limitations and strive for the possible but is driven to embrace destruction. He has not really given up his claims, since it seems profoundly unfair that *he* must be human. If his claims are not being honored, life seems absurd, and he strives to give it meaning by developing a new idealized image.

This new idealized image contains self-effacing elements that give an impression of spiritual growth. Richard's initial defense is to profess service to God and indifference to "worldly loss" (3.2); and after his deposition, he tells his wife to enter a religious house: "Our holy lives must win a new world's crown, / Which our profane hours here have thrown down" (5.1). He imagines himself as an "almsman" and a "palmer" (3.3); and in the deposition scene, he (half-ironically) asks God to forgive those who have broken their oaths to him, he turns the other cheek, and he blesses Bolingbroke. His new idealized image contains inner conflicts, however. He is both a man whose wrongs will become legendary and a humble, pious man who has submitted to necessity and acknowledged his sinfulness; but if he accepts "responsibility for his demise," he cannot also attain glory through his undeserved suffering. As a result, his acknowledgements of folly or guilt tend to be fleeting, and they are usually accompanied by displays of anguish and attacks on his enemies that restore his position as a man more sinned against than sinning. The mournful tale he would have his wife tell is not of a man who has thrown himself down through his "profane hours," but of "the deposing of a rightful king" (5.1). When Northumberland announces that he must go to Pomfret, Richard attacks him savagely, speaking of "foul sin," "wicked men," "unrightful kings," and his "usurped throne" (5.1). He keeps reminding others of their heinous offenses while evading their efforts to get him to acknowledge his own.

In the prison scene, which many critics point to as evidence of Richard's growth, there is only one brief passage that shows genuine awareness of the connection between his sins and his suffering. As he listens to someone playing music, he realizes that though he has "the daintiness of ear / To check time broke in a disordered string," he "Had not an ear to hear" the discordance he created as king (5.5). He quickly shifts, however, from acknowledging that he "wasted time" to seeing himself as a victim, first of time, which is now wasting him, and then of Bolingbroke, whose "Jack o' th' clock" he is. His train of thought leads him not to self-knowledge and an acceptance of responsibility, but to bitter reflections on the contrast between Bolingbroke's "proud joy" and his own "sighs and tears and groans" (5.5). Instead of soothing his spirit, the "music mads" him, and he wishes it to sound no more.

William Toole points to the earlier part of Richard's soliloquy, in which he compares his prison to the world, as a place where "he is in the process of acquiring self-knowledge. The emotional purgatory to which he has been subjected has given way, for a time, to an attitude of quiet contemplation. . . . his psychological perspective has broadened as he sees what he has in common with all men" (1978, 178). These are the lines in which Wilbur Sanders finds "desolation," "nihilism," and despair (1968, 181). There *is* a kind of contemplativeness here, but it derives, I think, from a detached perspective that is, indeed, nihilistic. Richard compares his three kinds of thoughts—religious, ambitious, and stoic— with three kinds of people, and he finds that neither the thoughts nor the people are "contented." As we have seen, Richard has been oscillating among three defensive strategies—self-effacing, expansive, and resigned. In this soliloquy, he consoles himself by seeing through all of these strategies and finding his own lack of contentment to be the common lot. This is, in part, as McPeek points out, an evasion of responsibility for the mess he has made of his life: "No matter what sort of life I might have led, he rationalizes, I should have still been discontent" (1958, 380). It is also a preparation for death, which Richard sees as welcome. There is self-knowledge in his realization of the inadequacy of his defenses, but there is nihilism in his conclusion that because these strategies do not work, man "With nothing shall be pleas'd till he be eas'd / With being nothing" (5.5).

Some critics feel that Richard redeems himself by dying in a heroic manner, and the rhetoric of the play seems to support this point of view. "The king of tears who has been reduced to nothing . . . [rises] in rage," says Toole, and dies "like a lion" (1974, 182). What produces this last of Richard's rapid transformations? In his comparison of the prison to the world, Richard had reached the conclusion that it does not matter whether he is a king or a beggar, for nothing brings ease but death. This detached perspective gives way to a more self-effacing frame of mind when the music leads him to reflect on his earlier lack of attention to "the concord of [his] state and time" (5.5). Self-blame is soon replaced by self-pity, however, and Richard is maddened by the contrast between Bolingbroke's triumph and his own humiliation. Richard's self-pity, here and elsewhere, is one of the means by which he expresses his impotent rage. His rage is reinforced by the sympathy of the groom and by the groom's account of Bolingbroke's ride on roan Barbary. Richard turns his anger on the horse, which should have broken "the neck / Of that proud man that did usurp his back" (5.5); but then he forgives Barbary, which "Wast born to bear," and turns upon himself instead: "I was not made a horse; / And yet I bear a burden like an ass, / Spurr'd, gall'd and tir'd by jauncing Bolingbroke" (5.5). There is some self-pity here and a great deal of anger toward Bolingbroke, but the dominant emotion is disgust with himself for having accepted such treatment so passively. When the keeper says that Sir Pierce of Exton, who has come from the King, has commanded him not to taste Richard's food, Richard finally explodes with rage: "The devil take Henry of Lancaster, and thee! / Patience is stale, and I am weary of it. [*Beats the Keeper.*]" (5.5). He fights his assassins with the energy of his liberated aggression.

Richard has been a disappointment to his friends because of his lack of aggressiveness. His behavior has not conformed to the code of martial and manly honor that is widely accepted in his culture and that is spelled out by Carlisle in response to "the death of kings" speech: "Fear, and be slain—no worse can come to fight; / And fight and die is death destroying death, / Where fearing dying pays death servile breath" (3.2). Richard responds to this not with a display of courage but with a reaffirmation of his narcissistic claims—"An easy task it is to win our own"—which immediately gives way to despair. The only time that he shows a fighting spirit is after he grants Bolingbroke's demands: "Shall we call back Northumberland and send / Defiance to the traitor, and so die?" (3.3). He is dissuaded from this by Aumerle, who wants to placate Bolingbroke "Till time lend friends, and friends their helpful swords"; but Richard is incapable of being pragmatic and capitulates entirely instead. When his narcissism is crushed, he tries to restore his pride not by fighting but by resignation and self-effacement. It is his queen who comments on this most directly:

> The lion dying thrusteth forth his paw
> And wounds the earth, if nothing else, with rage
> To be o'erpow'r'd; and wilt thou pupil-like
> Take thy correction, mildly kiss the rod,
> And fawn on rage with base humility,
> Which art a lion and the king of beasts?
>
> (5.1)

These lines, and Carlisle's, provide the scenario for Richard's death.

The play ends well for Richard. He redeems himself in terms of the martial code by showing that he is "full of valour" (5.5), he escapes his suffering in the only way possible, and he achieves once and for all the status of a man more sinned against than sinning. He dies affirming his royal title and his heavenly destination. Above all, he turns the tables on Bolingbroke, the man by whom he has been so badly beaten. He has felt threatened by Bolingbroke from the beginning, and it may well be that he banishes him and wrongs him in order to assure himself of his mastery. Once he feels that Bolingbroke has replaced him as the favorite of fortune, he falls under his spell and is unable to resist him. The queen asks if he has been "both in shape and mind / Transform'd and weak'ned? Hath Bolingbroke depos'd / Thine intellect? Hath he been in thy heart?" (5.1). When he rebels against the Keeper, Richard is also rebelling against Bolingbroke; and when he dies at Bolingbroke's hands—in fulfillment of his own quest for martyrdom—he revenges himself on his enemy in the most effective possible manner. It is now Richard who invades Bolingbroke's psyche, transforming and weakening his intellect. Instead of rewarding Exton, Bolingbroke tells him to take "guilt of conscience" for his labor and "With Cain" to "wander through the shades of night" (5.6). Bolingbroke is expressing his own Cain-like feelings, of course, and he resolves to "make a voyage to the Holy Land / To wash this blood off [his] guilty hand" (5.6). He never makes the voyage, and he is haunted by Richard's murder for the rest of his life. I do not think that Richard matures very much, but by dying in a way that establishes his valor, confirms his victimization, and burdens his nemesis with guilt, he makes his solutions work and achieves victory in his defeat.

4

Prince Hal

I

Shakespeare's presentation of Prince Hal in the two parts of *Henry IV* has been the subject of considerable critical controversy. There is widespread agreement (though not universal) that the plays develop "in such a way as to exhibit in the prince an inclusive, sovereign nature fitted for kingship" (Barber 1959, 195); but there is disagreement about whether Hal is "from the very first a commanding character, deliberate in act and in judgment" (Tillyard 1944, 277) or an immature young man who must undergo growth or reformation. Those who feel that Hal is virtuous from the start point to his opening soliloquy in which he announces his intention of throwing off his "loose behaviour" at the appropriate *a* moment (*1 Henry IV*, 1.2); but this soliloquy is itself a subject of *Machiavell* controversy, since it makes Hal appear a calculating schemer who *Schemist* heartlessly uses (and later rejects) Falstaff for his own political purposes. So the evidence for Hal's being a model prince from the start presents him in a rather unflattering light. This view of Hal does not take into account, moreover, his feelings of guilt, his tormenting behavior toward his father in part 1, and his reversion to such behavior in part 2 after the reconciliation at Shrewsbury.

Hal's backsliding in part 2 creates problems for the reformation theory as well. Indeed, much of the debate over the relationship of parts 1 and 2 is fueled by the fact that in the second part Hal seems to repeat his earlier behavior, despite his apparent movement in part 1 away from the irresponsibility of his connection with Falstaff and toward a reconciliation with his father. "It is not tolerable," argues Harold Jenkins, "that the victor of Shrewsbury should do as critics sometimes say he does, relapse into his former wildness and then reform again. The Prince cannot come into Part Two unreclaimed without destroying the dramatic effect of Part One. Yet if Part Two is not to forgo its own dramatic effect, and especially its splendid last-act peripeteia, it requires a prince who is unreclaimed" (1965, 232). Jenkins solves this problem by his elaborate theory of the relation between the two parts in which "though Part Two frequently recalls and sometimes depends upon what has happened in Part One, it also denies that Part One exists" (1965, 232).

Another source of controversy about Hal is his rejection of Falstaff. Both the virtuous-from-the-start and the reformation schools see Hal as the perfect prince, either all along or by the end; and both tend to see his rejection of Falstaff as justified and appropriate. There are members of both schools, however, who feel that his rejection of Falstaff is a perhaps necessary but nonetheless regrettable narrowing of his personality. C. L. Barber observes, for example, that "Hal's lines, redefining his holiday with Falstaff as a dream, and then despising the dream, seek to invalidate the holiday pole of life, instead of including it, as his lines on his old acquaintance did at the end of *Part One*" (1959, 219). Bradley, however, finds in Hal a "readiness to use other people as means to his own ends which is a conspicuous feature in his father" and suggests that his "conduct in his rejection of Falstaff is in perfect keeping with his character on its unpleasant side as well as on its finer" (1963, 257, 258). In his famous essay on "Prince Hal's Conflict," Ernst Kris argues that Hal shuns the court for the tavern as a way of expressing "his hostility to his father" and escaping "the temptation to parricide" (1953, 282). When his father dies, his hostility rises to the surface and "he turns against the father substitute; hence the pointed cruelty of Falstaff's rejection" (1953, 282). Modifying Kris's interpretation, M. D. Faber sees Hal as wishing for Falstaff's death all along because he feels guilty about having substituted Falstaff for his father. Hal's treatment of Falstaff in the rejection scene is not "dispassionate, just, 'moderate,' and 'necessary,'" but is unjustifiably cruel because "Hal's murderousness is much closer to the surface, much more bound up with fury and profound, irrational resentment than it has ever been, a turn which may be traced, of course, to the guilt arousing aspects of the actual father's recent death" (1970, 221–22).

Shakespeare's presentation of Prince Hal in the *Henry IV* plays has generated, then, the following critical questions: Is Hal virtuous from the start or does he undergo a process of growth or reformation? Is his character in part 2 continuous with his character in part 1, or does Shakespeare have him behave in ways that are incompatible with his earlier development? Is his rejection of Falstaff necessary and just, or is it excessively harsh, a manifestation of irrational forces in Hal's personality? Is Hal a model prince, a man in control of his acts, or is he a struggling, suffering human being who is full of inner conflicts? I shall offer my answers to these questions through an analysis both of Shakespeare's rhetoric and of Hal's character, which, I shall try to show, is mimetically sound and consistent from part to part.

II

We can resolve the issue of whether Hal is virtuous from the start or undergoes a process of reformation, I believe, by distinguishing between Shakespeare's rhetoric and his mimetic portrayal of character. Rhetorically, Hal's is a story of vindication; it is not he who must be educated but others who must learn his worth. Those who feel that Hal is a model prince from the first are responding correctly to Shakespeare's interpretation of him. As a mimetic character, however, Hal escapes his author's rhetoric and takes on a life of his own. When we see him as an imagined human being, a "creation inside a creation," we recognize that he is not as flexible and self-possessed as the rhetoric would have us believe. He pains his father greatly, and suffers guilt as a result, because his behavior is not entirely under his conscious control. Despite his denials, he is powerfully drawn to Falstaff and what he represents, and he is repelled by the court and the responsibilities he is destined to assume. Those who see Hal's as a story of reformation are responding to Shakespeare's mimetic portrait, which shows him as a troubled young man who first struggles against and then accedes to the demands of his adult role. The disagreement between the reformation and the vindication schools is partly a result of each group's looking at a different aspect of the play, but it is also sponsored by the play itself, by the disparity between Shakespeare's interpretation of Hal and his representation of his character.

A vindication pattern is one in which a truly noble protagonist, often a child or a young person, is rejected or held in low esteem by parental figures and/or the surrounding community, is given an opportunity or a series of opportunities to prove his or her worth, and is the recipient, by the end, of much praise and recognition and often of an appropriate position in society. This is a variation of the Cinderella archetype and is a common pattern in fiction, where it has a comic and a tragic form. In the comic form the vindication occurs in time for the protagonist to be appropriately rewarded, while in the tragic form it comes too late, but the protagonist receives posthumous recognition. Both forms occur in *King Lear*, the comic in Edgar's story and the tragic in Cordelia's. The reader or audience always knows the true worth of the protagonist from the start because of the author's rhetoric, which often includes the use of direct praise, inside views, or appreciative observers. This pattern gives rise, therefore, to many ironic effects. The detractors are either defeated or converted, and by the end almost everyone is praising the protagonist.

In *1 Henry IV*, Hal's detractors are King Henry and Hotspur. In the opening scene Henry envies Northumberland for having "A son who is the theme of honour's tongue," while "riot and dishonour stain the brow / Of my young Harry"; and he wishes that Hotspur were his son instead of Henry. When Hal returns to court, the King attacks him for his "inordinate and low desires," accuses him of "vassal fear" and "Base inclination," and compares him unfavorably to Hotspur, who "hath more worthy interest to the state / Than thou, the shadow of succession" (3.2). Hotspur refers to him contemptuously as the "madcap Prince of Wales" (4.1) whom he "would have poisoned with a pot of ale" were it not for the fact that "his father loves him not / And would be glad he met with some mischance" (1.3). The play as a whole moves toward the battle of Shrewsbury where Hal proves both his loyalty and prowess, defeats one of his detractors, converts the other, and demonstrates his worthiness of the throne.

From the beginning, however, Shakespeare is at pains to let us know that Henry is wrong in his judgment of Hal's character and of his worth in relation to Hotspur. Immediately after the King's complaints about Hal, we see Hal with Falstaff, who is proposing that thievery be countenanced and gallows removed when Hal becomes king. The issue, says Barber, is whether "the interregnum of a Lord of Misrule, delightful in its moment, might develop into the anarchic reign of a favorite dominating a dissolute king" (1959, 196). When Hal responds to Falstaff's "Do not thou, when thou art king, hang a thief" by saying that Falstaff shall "have the hanging of thieves" (1.2), he is making it clear that he will not be a dissolute king. Unlike the Prince in *The Famous Victories of Henry the Fifth*, Hal is not himself a criminal. He refuses to participate in the Gadshill affair ("Who, I rob? I a thief? Not I, by my faith"), wavers a moment under pressure from Falstaff ("Well, then, once in my days I'll be a madcap"), then determines to "tarry at home" (1.2). He goes along only after Poins proposes that the two of them rob the thieves rather than the travelers, and he arranges to have the booty returned.

Shakespeare's presentation of Hal in the second scene of the play is a response to Henry's complaints in the first. He raises the question through Falstaff's speeches of whether Hal will be a lawless king and immediately provides us with evidence that he will not. In case we have missed the point, Hal's soliloquy should leave no doubt. What this speech tells us about Hal's character is a matter of considerable controversy, but it seems fairly clear that it is an important rhetorical device. It lets us know that Hal is aware of the deficiencies of his companions and means to remain with them for only a limited period of time, that he will "throw off" his "loose behaviour" when the right moment arrives, and that he will live up to the demands of his role and the values of his community. The soliloquy generates a great deal of dramatic irony, since it gives us more information about Hal than is possessed by the characters in the play and makes us aware of the inappropriateness of their expectations and anxieties. It creates expectations in the audience that are then fulfilled by the ensuing action, partially in part 1 and completely in part 2. The expectation is not for reformation, but for vindication. We know that Henry and Hotspur are wrong about Hal, and we await their acknowledgement of his worth. We know that his vindication will seem like a reformation to other people, but we also know that Hal will not change in any fundamental way. Rather, he will appear to be what he really is; he will display his virtues at last.

As the play progresses, Shakespeare employs other foreshadowing devices that contribute to the rhetoric of vindication. Hal assures Falstaff that he is not afraid of the approaching confrontation with Douglas and Percy (2.4); he lets Falstaff know, only half in jest, that he will banish him (2.4); he promises his father that he "shall hereafter . . . / Be more [him]self" (3.2); and he predicts his battlefield triumphs, which will win him all the glory Percy has accumulated and will wash away his shame. Since the action confirms all that Hal says, we are left with the impression that he can do whatever he wishes; he is not torn between virtue and vice, nobility and degeneracy, but is simply choosing when to display his true self. His vindication, both in this play and the next, is foreshadowed also by Vernon's praise, which, coming from an adversary, carries much weight: "England did never owe so sweet a hope, / So much misconstrued in his wantonness" (5.3). There is a similar speech by Warwick in part 2, in which he tells Henry that his son "but studies his companions," whom he will "cast off" in "the perfectness of time" (4.4). His "memory" of them will help to form his judgment, thus "turning past evils to advantages." Both of these speeches present Hal not as a dissolute young man who will reform, but as a noble young man who has been "misconstrued," and the audience knows that they are right before the action proves them to be so.

In *1 Henvy IV*, the primary contrast is between Prince Hal and Hotspur, to whom the King twice compares his son, to Hal's great disadvantage. Part of Shakespeare's rhetoric of vindication is to develop the comparison dramatically in such a way as to show Hal to be the better man, and this from the start. The King is mistaken not only about Hal, but also about Hotspur, who does embody certain martial virtues in which Hal is, for the moment, deficient, but who also embodies the defects of those virtues, and who behaves self-destructively as a result. Whereas Shakespeare consistently justifies Hal, he consistently satirizes Hotspur, who lacks all balance and self-control.

Hotspur is shown again and again to be "A hare-brain'd Hotspur, govern'd by a spleen" (5.2). In the first scene in which he appears he becomes so "drunk with choler" that he will not let others speak, and his father calls him "a wasp-stung and impatient fool" (1.3). After his baiting of Glendower, Mortimer and Worcester attack him for his willfulness (3.1). Whereas Hal is praised by his adversary, Hotspur is criticized by his friends; and, unlike the King's complaints against Hal, the charges against Hotspur are shown to be true. His pride and impatience lead him to give battle foolishly at Shrewsbury, thus precipitating his own destruction.

Hal seems by comparison to be rational, clear-headed, and flexible, capable of fierceness and determination when these qualities are called for, but not in a state of perpetual aggression. Hotspur is dominated by a single humor, an obsession, a ruling passion. He has no use for love, music, humor, poetry, or colorful characters like Glendower, but only for military glory. Shakespeare presents Hal as a many-sided man who can perform brilliantly in every sphere of life. This contrast is developed throughout the play, but most vividly, perhaps, in the juxtaposition of the third and fourth scenes of the second act, in which Hotspur is so obsessed with thoughts of war that he has stopped sleeping with his wife, while Hal is sporting with Francis and Falstaff in the tavern. Whereas Hotspur has only one humor and one conception of honor, to which he devotes his life, Hal has many humors and pursues honor in a variety of ways. He explicitly rejects Hotspur's obsessiveness: "I am not yet of Percy's mind, the Hotspur of the North; he that kills me some six or seven

dozen of Scots at breakfast, washes his hands, and says to his
wife, 'Fie upon this quiet life! I want work' " (2.4). Hal does with
ease, almost casually, that which is Hotspur's entire occupation;
and at the end he aquires all the marital honor Hotspur has won
so laboriously and adds it to the other forms of honor that he has
gathered along the way.

Whereas the King feels that "riot and dishonor stain the brow"
of young Harry (1.1), Shakespeare presents Hal's consorting with
the Boar's Head crowd as a source of honor, a mark of his ability to
sound "the very brass-string of humility" (2.4). Hal's low-life ad-
ventures are presented as being essential to his later success as
king, since they enable him to produce the sensation that gets his
reign off to such a fine start and give him a rapport with the men
he will lead into battle. Warwick spells out the pattern: "past evils"
are turned into "advantages." The Prince's descent into the tavern
is a kind of fortunate fall, except that it is not really a fall but only
appears to be one. The intention of Shakespeare's rhetoric has
been well expressed, I believe, by Maynard Mack: "[B]y the play's
end, Hal casts an inclusive shadow. He has met the claims of
Hotspur's world, of Falstaff's and of Henry's without narrowing
himself to any one. He has . . . brought into a practicable balance
court, field, and tavern." He combines "valor, courtliness, hard
sense, and humor in an ideal image of the potentialities of the
English character" and is "on the way to becoming the luminous
figure toward whom, in *Henry V*, Welshman, Irishman, Scot, and
Englishman will alike be drawn" (1965, xxxv).

As many critics have observed, in its treatment of Hal, part 2
repeats the pattern of part 1. The concern about Hal is expressed
near the beginning not by the King, but by the Lord Chief Justice,
who tells Falstaff that he has "misled the youthful prince" (1.2).
Before the climactic scene with his father, Hal's most serious
accuser is, strangely enough, Poins, who comments on his talking
so idly and asks "how many good young princes would do so,
their fathers being so sick as yours at this time is?" (2.2). Poins
clearly believes that because Hal has "been so lewd and so much
engraffed to Falstaff," he does not love his father and would
welcome his death. He is expressing, of course, a widespread
perception of Hal that will be changed by the end of the play. Lest
the audience share this perception, Shakespeare gives Hal a
speech that functions like his soliloquy in part 1: "By this hand,
thou thinkest me as far in the devil's book as thou and Falstaff for
obduracy and persistency. Let the end try the man. But I tell thee,
my heart bleeds inwardly that my father is so sick" (2.2). Once

again we have a rhetoric of vindication in which the Prince is misconstrued, both at court and in the tavern, while the audience knows in advance what will happen when the end tries the man. Shakespeare may be relying on our memory of Hal's soliloquy to provide even more reassurance, but the speech I have just quoted is a clear signal to a sensitive audience that, despite appearances to the contrary, Hal is a loving son.

As he did in part 1, Shakespeare tends to accompany every accusation against Hal or anxiety about his future behavior with a rhetoric of reassurance that lets us know Hal is being misconstrued and will be vindicated. Hearing that Hal is accompanied "with Poins and his other continual followers," the King fears for the future of England, envisioning "th' unguided days / And rotten times that [it] shall look upon / . . . when his headstrong riot hath no curb" (4.4). This is followed immediately by Warwick's speech, which presents the Prince as being misunderstood and predicts that he will turn "past evils to advantages." The most scathing denunciation of Hal comes after he has wandered off with the crown, when his father accuses him of wishing for his death and evokes a picture of what will happen when "the Fifth Harry from curb'd license plucks / The muzzle of restraint." England will become "a wilderness again, / Peopled with wolves, [its] old inhabitants" (4.5). This speech is highly ironic, and unjust, in light of the soliloquy some fifty lines earlier in which Hal remonstrates with the crown for burdening his father, expresses his "filial tendernees," and vows to preserve the "lineal honour" for his posterity. Hal once again explains himself to his father, predicts his "noble change," and effects a reconciliation.

Having vindicated himself in the eyes of his father, Hal must now do so in the eyes of the court and the people. Upon the death of King Henry, there is intense anxiety as to the future of England ("O God, I fear all will be overturn'd"—5.2), followed by the great scene in which Hal reassures the court by accepting the Lord Chief Justice's explanation of why he had imprisoned him ("You are right, Justice"), by making the Justice his chief adviser, and by proclaiming that his wildness has been buried with his father. This is the climax toward which we have been moving since Hal's soliloquy near the beginning of part 1; the vindication pattern is almost complete. Hal will "rase out / Rotten opinion" that has "writ [him] down / After [his] *seeming*" (5.2—my italics).

It has been even clearer in part 2 than in part 1 that in order to do this he must break with Falstaff. To prepare us for this painful event, Shakespeare has darkened the picture of Falstaff, making him one of those predatory moderns who invokes nature as his guide, thinks might makes right, and has no respect for law and order. He sees "no reason in the law of nature but [he] may snap at Shallow" (3.2); and when he hears that Hal is king, he says, "Let us take any man's horses; the laws of England are at my commandment" (5.3). Shakespeare makes Falstaff's crew seem unsavory, too, by having Doll and Pistol involved in a murder. The rejection of Falstaff is made to seem justified, and it vindicates Hal publicly, for all to see. Its harshness is softened by Shakespeare's final bit of rhetoric, a speech by Prince John near the end of the play:

> I like this fair proceeding of the King's.
> He hath intent his wonted followers
> Shall all be very well provided for;
> But all are banish'd till their conversations
> Appear more wise and modest to the world.
>
> (5.5)

Who could object to that?

III

I have tried through a rhetorical analysis to establish how Shakespeare meant us to respond to Prince Hal. Such an analysis supports the view of Tillyard and others that Hal is not a "dissolute lout awaiting a miraculous transformation" but "is from the very first a commanding character, deliberate in act and in judgment, versed in every phase of human nature" (1944, 277).[1] As I indicated at the outset, however, there are problems with this view of Hal that are generated, in large part, by the richness of Shakespeare's mimetic portrait. If we look at Hal's opening soliloquy not merely in terms of its rhetorical function but as an expression of his character, it makes him seem unattractively cold and calculating, hardly a "luminous figure." If we take Hal's explanation of his motives at face value, he proposes to achieve his grand effect not only by exploiting Falstaff and his crew, but also by tormenting his father, whose feelings are really quite bitter. This aspect of Hal's behavior is obscured by Shakespeare's rhetoric. We do not take Henry's anguish as seriously as we might because he is wrong about Hal and all is made right at the end, but when he is in his father's presence, Hal himself seems to realize how deeply he has grieved him. He expresses the hope that his exploits in the coming battle will "salve / The long-grown wounds of [his] intemperance" (3.2). Henry misconstrues Hal, to be sure; but given Hal's behavior, it is only natural that he should; and Hal seems, for the most part, indifferent to his father's suffering. If it costs his father so much, is Hal's plan really a good one? In staying away from the court, is Hal, as Kris suggests, expressing his hostility and escaping the temptation to parricide? Is Hal, that is, really as noble and as self-controlled as Shakespeare's rhetoric makes him out to be?

Such questions occur even more insistently in part 2, where Hal is once again playing the truant, to his father's even greater distress. The inappropriateness of his behavior while his father is seriously ill is evident even to Poins, and Hal himself seems uncomfortable with the way he is living: "Well, thus we play the fools with the time, and the spirits of the wise sit in the clouds and mock us" (2.2). He launches upon his prank with Falstaff nevertheless, while his father is beset by illness and news of rebellion. When, as the prank draws to a close, Peto brings word of the troubles at court, Hal reproaches himself: "By heavens, Poins, I feel me much to blame / So idly to profane the precious time, / When tempest of commotion . . . doth begin to melt / And drop upon our bare unarmed heads" (2.4). Hal's blaming himself tends to disarm our criticism of him, but we cannot help wondering if he has not good reason to feel guilt, especially when we see the ailing King surrounded by his other sons and anguishing over the future of his country.

Hal's "relapse," moreover, is difficult to reconcile with the vindication pattern that seems intended in both plays. It may be necessary if the pattern is to be repeated in part 2, but it seems incompatible with what has been accomplished in part 1. It is easier, in fact, to fit his relapse into a reformation pattern, for backsliding can easily be part of a process of moral education. But if Hal is a model prince from the first and is consorting with the Boar's Head crew only to increase his skill in dealing with all kinds of people and to prepare a grand effect, his objectives seem to have been achieved by the end of part 1. Does he really need to study his companions further? It could be argued that his plan is to emerge from the company of base contagious clouds only when he becomes king and that he returns to his "dissolute" ways in order to protect this scenario, but this is not a very attractive reason for his behavior, especially when we consider how deeply it is worrying his father.

As we have seen, critics have been troubled not only by Hal's relapse in part 2, but also by his rejection of Falstaff. Despite the care with which Shakespeare has prepared for it rhetorically, Hal's treatment of Falstaff has left many people feeling uncomfortable. As Edward Berry observes, "the political necessity of Falstaff's rejection . . . is today accepted without debate" (1977, 201). What critics object to is Hal's priggishness and hypocrisy, "the pious tone, the bluntness of the rejection, the simplification of the past" (Berry 1977, 207). I find it difficult not to be sympathetic with this. Does Hal need to express such contempt for Falstaff, to remind him of his age and the approach of death? We know from earlier scenes that Falstaff is full of anxiety about growing old, and Hal must know it too. Is it really fair, moreover, to characterize Falstaff as "the tutor and the feeder of [his] riots" (5.5), to blame Falstaff for leading him astray? This is not compatible with Hal's earlier image of himself as a man who knows what he is doing, who so offends as "to make offense a skill" (1 Henry IV, 1.2). However necessary it is for Hal to disengage himself from Falstaff, we cannot help asking if it had to be done with such cruelty. Hal's final act of self-vindication casts a shadow upon his character.

IV

So many problems arise in part 2 that we may, indeed, wonder if the two parts are meant to be integrated and if Hal's character is consistent from part to part. I believe that Hal's character is consistent and that it is his behavior in part 2 that enables us to understand his motivations. We must understand the Hal of part 1 retrospectively, as we do people in life whose earlier behavior makes sense as we come to know them better. The key to Hal's character is not his first soliloquy, but the scene in part 2 in which he offends and then is reconciled with his father. With the aid of this scene, it is possible to develop an interpretation of Hal's character that will account for his opening soliloquy, his involvement with the Boar's Head crew, his behavior toward his father, his reversion to his old ways in part 2, and the harshness of his rejection of Falstaff. This interpretation will not resolve the conflict between Shakespeare's rhetoric and his concrete portrayal of Hal—indeed, it will bring that conflict into sharper focus; but it will help us understand why so many critics have treated Hal's story as one of reformation. It will also help us to appreciate

Shakespeare's genius in mimetic characterization and to see how his portrayal of Hal binds the two parts of *Henry IV* together.

Many critics feel that Hal's mistaking his father for dead and wandering off with the crown are indications of his wish for his father's death and his eagerness to ascend the throne. That, indeed, is King Henry's interpretation:

> PRINCE. I never thought to hear you speak again.
> KING. Thy wish was father, Harry, to that thought.

(4.5)

The Prince gives, of course, a different explanation:

> Coming to look on you, thinking you dead—
> And dead almost, my liege, to think you were—
> I spake unto this crown as having sense,
> And thus upbraided it: "The care on thee depending
> Hath fed upon the body of my father.
> Therefore thou best of gold art worst of gold.
> Other, less fine in carat, is more precious,
> Preserving life in med'cine potable;
> But thou, most fine, most honour'd, most renown'd,
> Hast eat thy bearer up." Thus, my most royal liege,
> Accusing it, I put it on my head,
> To try with it (as with an enemy
> That had before my face murdered my father)
> The quarrel of a true inheritor.
> But if it did infect my blood with joy
> Or swell my thought to any strain of pride, . . .
> Let God for ever keep it from my head.

(4.5)

The King accepts Hal's explanation and so do I. Hal's feelings are, no doubt, ambivalent, but I think he has described his dominant emotions. He does dread the death of his father, he does regard the crown as an enemy, and he does not feel much joy at the thought of becoming king.

We know that Hal is not lying to his father because his explanation is corroborated by the soliloquy he utters when he first enters his father's chamber and thinks he is sleeping:

> Why doth the crown lie there upon his pillow,
> Being so troublesome a bedfellow?
> O polish'd perturbation! golden care!

That keep'st the ports of slumber open wide
To many a watchful night! Sleep with it now!
Yet not so sound and half so deeply sweet
As he whose brow, with homely biggen bound,
Snores out the watch of night. O majesty!
When thou dost pinch thy bearer, thou dost sit
Like a rich armour worn in heat of day,
That scald'st with safety.

(4.5)

When Hal concludes that his father is dead, he expresses great
sadness—"thy due from me / Is tears and heavy sorrows of the
blood, / Which nature, love, and filial tenderness / Shall, O dear
father, pay thee plenteously"; and he takes up the crown with a
sense of the responsibility that he has to defend the "lineal honour." Since Hal is alone, he is not trying to deceive anyone, unless
it be himself. His behavior toward his father throughout most of
parts 1 and 2 has been such as to cause us to distrust his present
expressions of "filial tenderness," but the true motives for that
behavior are compatible, I believe, with the attitudes toward both
the crown and his father that he is expressing in the present
scene. Indeed, we cannot understand those motives unless we
take quite seriously what Hal says here, both in his soliloquy and
to his father.

Hal has often been perceived as an adolescent who is in the
process of growing up. This is a more useful perspective for
understanding his character, I think, than is the view of him as a
model prince who is first misconstrued and then vindicated. "A
motivation for a 'last fling,'" observes Alexander Aarons, "is the
reluctance to relinquish a known pleasure for an unknown one"
(1970, 330; see also Lichtenberg 1969). What Hal is confronting is
the prospect of relinquishing the pleasures of youth for an adult
role that he perceives to be crushingly burdensome. It is his
destiny to follow his father as king; and when he looks at his
father, he sees a man who has been consumed by care, who
cannot sleep, and who is dying prematurely. The very first line of
part 1 strikes this note—"So shaken as we are, so wan with care";
and in the course of that play, the King's hair turns white. In part
2, Hal watches the crown murder his father. His address to the
crown dwells upon one of Henry's own obsessions, the inability
to sleep. It is almost as though he had heard the great soliloquy in
which his father envies "the vile" who sleep peacefully "in loath-
some beds" while he lies awake "under the canopies of costly

state": "Then, happy low, lie down! / Uneasy lies the head that wears a crown" (3.1).

Hal fears that for him, too, the crown will be "polish'd perturbation," "golden care," that he, too, will be pinched by majesty, consumed by worry and responsibility. When the King believes that Hal has taken the crown because he "hungers for his empty chair," he admonishes him severely: "O foolish youth! / Thou seek'st the greatness will overwhelm thee" (4.5). Henry is expressing here what must be one of Hal's deepest anxieties, that he will, indeed, be overwhelmed by the greatness he does not seek but that will one day be thrust upon him. After their reconciliation, Henry tries to be reassuring, telling Hal that the crown will descend to him "with better quiet, / Better opinion, better confirmation; / For all the soil of the achievement goes / With me into the earth" (4.5). Some of Henry's troubles and Hal's anxieties are derived, of course, from the "indirect crook'd ways" by which Henry attained the throne; but majesty is presented, both here and in *Henry V,* as a burden for all kings. We can credit, then, Hal's account of his feelings toward the crown.

We can credit also, I believe, his expressions of love toward his father. We cannot help wondering why, given his awareness of his father's suffering, he adds to it by staying away. The degree to which Hal's address to the crown echoes his father's soliloquy indicates that he has a strong identification with the King. He enters into his father's feelings, experiences his suffering as though it were his own, and fears that a similar fate is in store for him. He stays away from court less because he wants to torment his father than because he is tormented himself at the sight of his father's suffering. The worse his father gets, the more difficult it is for Hal to be in his presence, but this does not mean that he is uncaring. He tells Poins that his "heart bleeds inwardly that his father is so sick" and asks, "What wouldst thou think of me if I should weep?" (2.2). Poins, assuming that Hal wants his father's death, thinks that he would be "a most princely hypocrite"; but Hal talks idly and "profanes the precious time" in an effort to escape the anxiety and depression brought on by his father's illness.

Hal's method of defending himself against the anxieties associated with assuming his adult role is to move away from his father and toward Falstaff. In both his father's soliloquy on his sleeplessness and Hal's address to the crown, a contrast is developed between the watchfulness of those who rule and the blissful sleep of the poorest subjects. Falstaff is one of those "happy low" whom the King so envies. He falls "fast asleep behind the arras" (*1 Henry IV*, 2.4), even though the sheriff is in the house searching for him. Hal flees his careworn father in order to consort with a group of relatively carefree people to whom life is a game. Falstaff is a wonderful playmate, an antidote to the deadly seriousness of the court and a refuge from the burdens of state that Hal will eventually have to assume.

Hal's riotous living, then, is a form of escape from the demands of his role and the harsh realities of life. He revels in the perpetual adolescence that Falstaff represents. In his relation to age, death, time, law, and responsibility, Falstaff is the opposite of the King. Whereas Henry is prematurely old, Falstaff, though nearing sixty, thinks of himself as young and behaves like a youth. He still has adolescent attitudes toward sex. While Henry is growing feebler and approaching death, Falstaff has a seemingly endless supply of vitality. Henry is concerned about what Hal's way of spending his youth means for the future of England; Falstaff is oblivious of time and gives no thought to the morrow. Henry represents the rule of law; Falstaff is anarchistic. Henry carries the weight of the nation on his shoulders and calls men to their duty; Falstaff appeals to Hal so much because he is so much the opposite of his father, because he is on the side of light-heartedness and gaiety, and because he is himself engaged in a flight from reality. He throws off the very burdens that are threatening Hal and crushing the King and lives in a dream of eternal youthfulness and unrestrained desire.

Hal is not comfortable, of course, about his dissipation and irresponsibility. He knows that he is a "truant to chivalry" (*1 Henry IV*, 5.1) and that he is deeply wounding his father. He is disturbed that Hotspur is winning all the glory, and the King's approbation, while he is regarded as "degenerate" (his father's word, 3.2), a threat to the future well-being of the state. Hal is not prepared to give up his way of life, however, nor is he able to do so until it is absolutely necessary. He develops instead a way of interpreting his behavior that makes him more comfortable with it. He turns his offenses into virtues and his compulsions into evidence of his flexibility. He makes drinking in the tavern a source of honor, and feels himself superior to Hotspur because of the many-sidedness of his personality.

It is his opening soliloquy, of course, that presents the most favorable interpretation of his behavior. This soliloquy tells us a great deal about Hal if we analyze it in the light of our later knowledge of his character.

I know you all, and will awhile uphold
The unyok'd humour of your idleness.
Yet herein will I imitate the sun,
Who doth permit the base contagious clouds
To smother up his beauty from the world,
That, when he please again to be himself,
Being wanted, he may be more wond'red at
By breaking through the foul and ugly mists
Of vapours that did seem to strangle him.
If all the year were playing holidays,
To sport would be as tedious as to work;
But when they seldom come, they wish'd-for come,
And nothing pleaseth but rare accidents.
So when this loose behaviour I throw off
And pay the debt I never promised,
By how much better than my word I am,
By so much shall I falsify men's hopes;
And, like bright metal on a sullen ground,
My reformation, glitt'ring o'er my fault,
Shall show more goodly and attract more eyes
Than that which hath no foil to set it off.
I'll so offend to make offense a skill,
Redeeming time when men think least I will.

(1.2)

Hal is not, I think, a Machiavellian schemer who is cold-bloodedly using Falstaff for his own political purposes; he is a young man with inner conflicts who has found a way of doing what he wants, indeed needs, to do and feeling virtuous about it. His soliloquy is a series of rationalizations designed to justify, to glorify, and to reassure himself.[2]

The political cleverness of his plan is essential to its psychological value, for it makes Hal feel that he is modeling himself upon his father and that his father would approve if he knew about it. The King later reproaches Hal for making himself common, like Richard, whereas he had kept his "person fresh and new": "By being seldom seen, I could not stir / But like a comet, I was wond'red at" (3.2). It is precisely Hal's plan to be wondered at. He will achieve this effect by using his dissolute self as a foil to his reformed self in the same way that his father had used Richard. We are supposed to be struck, I think, by the irony of Henry's misunderstanding of his son, who is following exactly the course that he recommends. The similarities between Hal's soliloquy and Henry's speech in 3.2 are additional evidence of Hal's identification with his father. A major difference between the two, of course, is that Bolingbroke's plan was deliberate whereas Hal's is a rationalization, a way of satisfying his conscience while giving himself permission to continue his self-indulgence.

What Hal is telling himself in his soliloquy is that he is not really like his low companions, that he truly condemns their "idleness," and that he has retained his nobility despite the fact that it has been obscured for others by the bad company he keeps. He assures himself that he is in control of his behavior, that he has sound political reasons for what he is doing, and that his present dissipation will bring him more glory in the end. Hal needs to feel that his behavior is deliberate, and critics tend to believe that it is because everything works out exactly as Hal predicts. The reason it does, however, is that Hal's guilt and his need for vindication put him under tremendous pressure to reform when the situation demands it. The only way he can justify his dissolute behavior is to become a model prince in part 1 and a model king in part 2.

Hal is presented in part 1 as being a flexible, self-controlled man, in contrast to the rigid, compulsive Hotspur. In fact, however, he is caught between two compulsions, one to escape the crushing burdens of his role for as long as he can and the other to redeem himself by performing to perfection the demands of his role when he must.[3] This accounts for both his dissipation and his reformation. When reality breaks in upon him, as it does in the form of the Percy rebellion, Hal responds to the challenge. He cannot tear himself away from his escapist pursuits as long as he is not absolutely needed, but he could not live with himself if he seriously failed of his duty. He welcomes, moreover, the opportunity to vindicate himself in his father's eyes and to prove his superiority to Hotspur. When the crisis passes, however, he returns to his old haunts, which is where we find him early in part 2.

Hal seems considerably less light-hearted, however, than he was in the corresponding scenes of part 1. His father's illness weighs heavily upon him and may account for the fact that he is "exceeding weary" (2.2). He tries to escape the anxieties it arouses by playing the madcap prince, but his gaiety seems forced, and he feels uncomfortable about the inappropriateness of his behavior. In running away from the court once again, he activates his inner conflicts, which may also account for his weariness.

The imminent death of his father confronts Hal with his greatest crisis, for upon his father's demise, he will have no choice but to fulfill the duties of the kingship. When he enters his father's chamber and sees him sleeping with the crown by his side, his dread of what awaits him rises to consciousness. He does not experience it directly on his own behalf, however, but as a quarrel with the crown on behalf of his father. His behavior toward the crown is, among other things, a reflection of his own feelings about becoming king. Hal has been trying to escape not only his awareness of the heavy responsibilities that await him, but also the narrowing of his life and personality that will accompany his full acceptance of his adult role. He has been rebelling against the demand of his father and the court that he be nothing but the Prince of Wales. He has been the prince when he has had to, but he has held on to his last chance to have a private life, to be a person apart from his role—more and more desperately, perhaps, as his father's end approaches. His taking up the crown signifies his acceptance of his duties, and his upbraiding it for what it has done to his father is an expression of his anxiety about what it will do to him.

The crown does not kill Hal as it does his father, but the total identification with his role that follows upon his accession turns him into a rigid, one-dimensional man who reminds us of Hotspur. Something, indeed, dies in Hal when he becomes King, as he himself proclaims:

> My father is gone wild into his grave;
> For in his tomb lie my affections,
> And with his spirits sadly I survive,
> To mock the expectation of the world.

> (5.2)

The madcap prince who had rebelled against his fate as an adult is now to be totally suppressed and the part of him that had identified with his father is to be dominant. His complete immersion in his role is the product also of his guilt and his need for vindication. If he is to convince himself and others that he is not degenerate, he must be a model of wisdom, sobriety, and responsibility; he must be totally righteous. His dissolute youth does prepare him to be a perfect king, or at least a perfectionistic one—but not in the way that is usually thought.

The rejection of Falstaff is not only a political, it is also a psychological necessity for Hal. He rejects Falstaff so harshly because he is profoundly threatened by the part of himself that is still attracted to Falstaff and all that he represents. He is doing unto Falstaff what he is doing unto the self-indulgent, impulsive, escapist side of himself, a side that has dominated him heretofore, that he has been unable to relinquish in any permanent way, and that he therefore must reject with vehemence. He must shatter Falstaff's dream of freedom from the laws of reality and morality in order to affirm his own acceptance of an adult perspective:

> I know thee not, old man. Fall to thy prayers.
> How ill white hairs become a fool and jester!
> I have long dreamt of such a kind of man,
> So surfeit-swell'd, so old, and so profane;
> But being awak'd, I do despise my dream.
> Make less thy body, hence, and more thy grace;
> Leave gormandizing. Know the grave doth gape
> For thee thrice wider than for other men.
>
> (5.5)

Hal here confronts Falstaff with the harsh realities of age and death, mocks the disparity between his years and his behavior, condemns his self-indulgence, and urges him to reform. He is externalizing his self-condemnation, rejecting his escapism, and reinforcing his commitment to reality, maturity, and repression. He reduces his guilt by showing himself and others how much he despises his "former self" and by blaming Flastaff for his riotous living. His banishment of Falstaff is, again, a sign of the extent to which he is afraid of the temptation that Falstaff represents. It would be fatal to his project if he should ever allow his former self to surface.

The interpretation of Hal that I have presented not only sheds light upon some of the puzzling aspects of his character, such as his opening soliloquy, his behavior toward his father, his relapse in part 2, and his harshness toward Falstaff; it also helps us to understand the critical controversies that have surrounded *1 and 2 Henry IV* and to appreciate the plays' strengths and weaknesses. Critics cannot agree whether Hal's is a story of vindication or of reformation. It is both. The rhetoric encourages us to view Hal as a model prince who is being misconstrued by his fellows, while the mimesis presents a troubled young man, full of inner conflicts, who needs to turn away his former self if he is to become a good king. The relation between part 1 and part 2 is confusing when we follow the rhetoric, for part 1 creates expectations that part 2 disappoints. At the level of mimesis the plays seem quite unified. This also creates a problem, since we cannot fully understand Hal's earlier behavior, especially his opening soliloquy, until we receive the information about him that is contained in part 2. The rhetoric in both parts gives us a misleading view of Hal and tends to obscure the brilliance of Shakespeare's psychological portrait. Prince Hal is a much more interesting character than the rhetoric suggests. Analyzing his motives helps us to recover Shakespeare's psychological intuitions and to do justice to his mimetic achievement. Though it undermines our sense of the organic unity of the plays by showing how the portrait of Hal subverts the rhetoric of vindication, it also reveals the integration, indeed, the strong interdependence, of the two parts; for it is the character of Hal, with his conflicting compulsions, that, more than anything else, binds the two plays together. It can, in fact, bind all three plays about Hal together by enabling us to see the connection between the apparently flexible, easygoing, many-sided prince and the stern, perfectionistic, one-dimensional king of *Henry the Fifth*.

5
Henry V

I

Shakespeare's presentation of Henry the Fifth has been even more controversial than his presentation of Prince Hal. There are debates about whether Henry is the same person as Hal or an entirely new character, about whether he is realistically drawn or a cardboard figure, and about whether he is a unified conception or a "patchwork character" (Tillyard 1944, 308) whose behavior is so inconsistent as to make no sense. The fiercest debate has to do with whether or not Henry is, as the Chorus proclaims him in act 2, "the mirror of all Christian kings." For some critics, observes Karl Wentersdorf, "the play presents the story of an ideal monarch and glorifies his achievements; for them the tone approaches that of an epic lauding the military virtues. For others, the protagonist is a Machiavellian militarist who professes Christianity but whose deeds reveal both hypocrisy and ruthlessness; for them, the tone is predominantly one of mordant satire" (1976, 265).[1]

As in my discussion of Prince Hal, I shall approach the controversies generated by *Henry V* through an analysis both of Shakespeare's rhetoric and of the protagonist's character. I think that Henry is continuous with Prince Hal, that he is realistically drawn, and that his behavior is consistently inconsistent when we understand his personality structure. The debate over whether Henry is admirable or not is generated, in large part, I believe, by a disparity between the play's rhetoric, which celebrates him as "this grace of kings" (2, Chorus), and its mimetic portrayal of Henry, which subverts that rhetoric by its inclusion of unsavory traits.[2] Some critics respond to the rhetoric and see the play as glorifying Henry, and some respond to the mimesis and see the play as undercutting his heroic pretensions. Of those who are aware of the tension between rhetoric and mimesis, some feel that

Shakespeare was confused or "didn't believe what he was trying
to say" and that he "left us a mess" (Rabkin 1981, 34); and some try
to integrate the conflicting signals that the play sends out. Norman Rabkin argues, for example, that "Shakespeare seems
equally tempted by both [of the play's] rival gestalts" and that he
deliberately creates an ambiguous structure that "forces us . . . to
share his conflict" (1981, 62). I tend to side with those who believe
that Shakespeare left us a mess; but I think that it is a very
interesting mess because of the complexity of Henry's character,
which is more fully developed here than it was in the earlier
plays, and because of the authorial conflicts and fantasies that it
expresses.

To me it seems quite clear that Shakespeare presents Henry as
the "exemplary monarch," the "flawless ruler," the "fully heroic"
king whom so many critics celebrate (Rabkin 1967, 98). There is a
powerful and continuous rhetoric of vindication, of justification,
and of glorification. The vindication motif appears here as an
important but subordinate pattern. In discussing the King at the
beginning of the play, the Bishops of Ely and Canterbury at first
present his change as a process of reformation, but they then
decide that he has been developing his newly displayed virtues all
along and has merely "obscured his contemplation / Under the
veil of wildness" (1.1). Henry presents a similar interpretation of
himself to the French ambassador when he says that he understands the Dauphin well, "How he comes o'er us with our wilder
days, / Not measuring what use we made of them" (1.2); and the
Constable of France tells the Dauphin that Henry's

> vanities forespent
> Were but the outside of the Roman Brutus,
> Covering discretion with a coat of folly;
> As gardeners do with ordure hide those roots
> That shall first spring and be most delicate.
>
>   (2.4)

In presenting Hal as a misunderstood young man who has been
noble all along and whose apparent dissipations are actually advantageous, the rhetoric of this play is similar to that of *1 and 2
Henry IV.*

As the play opens, Henry has vindicated himself to the English,
but he still has a detractor in the person of the Dauphin, who
mocks him, much as Hotspur had done, because of his light
behavior. He adds a final insult by sending Henry a cask of tennis
balls as "meeter for [his] spirit" than the dukedom he claims. As he
had done in the earlier plays, Henry predicts his vindication ("I

will rise there with so full a glory / That I will dazzle all the eyes of France"—1.2); and once again his predictions are borne out by the action. After Henry lands in France, the Dauphin maintains his scornful attitude, dismissing England because "her scepter is so fantastically borne, / By a vain, giddy, shallow, humourous youth" (2.4). From this point on, the deprecation of Henry and the deprecation of the English go hand in hand, so that the vindication of Henry is made to appeal to the patriotic emotions of the audience. While they underestimate the English, the French greatly overestimate their own courage and prowess. The battle of Agincourt is the day of reckoning toward which the play has been building; the English and Henry are vindicated while their detractors are defeated and converted. The true worth of the English is revealed, beneath their unimpressive appearance, while the false claims of the French are exposed. The Herald Montjoy, who has been demanding Henry's ransom, addresses him now as "great King" (4.7), and Henry is treated with deference and awe henceforth by the French.

There is a rhetoric not only of vindication, but also of justification surrounding Henry. His riotous youth, his claim to the throne of France, and his decision to go to war are all justified by the highest authorities. An archbishop and a bishop urge him to fight and tell him that his "brother kings and monarchs of the earth / Do all expect that [he] should rouse [him]self, / As did the former lions of [his] blood" (1.2). He is spurred on not only by the expectations of his subjects and fellow monarchs and the precedent of his glorious ancestors, but also by the Dauphin's insult, which is an affront to the national honor and entitles him to revenge. His aggressiveness is justified in the name of national pride and glory.

Much of the rhetoric of justification is put into Henry's own mouth. He justifies his execution of the traitors on the grounds of their own lack of mercy and his "kingdom's safety" (2.2), his threatened devastation of Harfleur on the grounds of its guilty resistance (3.3), and the hanging of Bardolph on the grounds of military policy (3.6). He defends himself against Williams's charge that "it will be a black matter for the King" if his men "do not die well" both in his direct reply and in his subsequent soliloquy (4.1). Many critics feel that Williams gets the better of the argument, but Williams himself assents to Henry's position without knowing that he is talking to the King: "'Tis certain, every man that dies ill, the ill upon his own head; the King is not to answer it" (4.1).

When Henry does something that may shock the sensibility of the audience, his justification is often put into the mouths of other characters who have been established as sound in their judgment, as when Fluellen refuses to intercede on Bardolph's behalf: "for if, look you, he were my brother, I would desire the Duke to . . . put him to execution; for discipline ought to be used" (3.6). It is Fluellen again who responds to Hostess Quickly's comment that "the King has killed [Falstaff's] heart" (2.1): ". . . as Alexander killed his friend Cleitus, being in his ales and his cups, so also Harry Monmouth, being in his right wits and his good judgments, turned away the fat knight" (4.7). When Henry orders his men to kill their prisoners, his action is defended by Gower, who concludes that "the King most worthily hath caused every soldier to cut his prisoner's throat. O, 'tis a gallant king!" (4.7). In passages such as these Shakespeare seems to be strengthening his celebration of Henry by confronting directly the possible charges against him. We may still be more responsive to the charges than to the rhetoric, but we should not confuse our personal feelings with the play's rhetorical intentions.

Henry is justified above all by his victory at Agincourt. All the horrors of war for which many blame Henry are the fault of the French, whose wrongs have brought about the conflict. Shakespeare treats the battle as a trial by combat in which the greatly outnumbered English defeat the French because God is on their side. When Henry, in disguise, says that the King's "cause [is] just and his quarrel honourable," Williams replies, "that's more than we know" (4.1). All doubts are resolved by the near-miraculous quality of the victory. Henry is perfectly right from Shakespeare's perspective when he responds to Burgundy's plea for an end to the devastation by saying, "you must buy that peace / With full accord to all our just demands" (5.2).

There is, finally, a rhetoric of glorification that is generated in large part by the Chorus, which describes this "mirror of all Christian kings" as "free from vainness and self-glorious pride" (5). This view of Henry is sustained in the dramatic portions of the play by the praise of other characters. The Archbishop of Canterbury celebrates his transformation, his knowledge, and his eloquence:

> . . . when he speaks,
> The air, a chartered libertine, is still,
> And the mute wonder lurketh in men's ears
> To steal his sweet and honeyed sentences.

(1.1)

Henry is chiefly celebrated, of course, for his great feats of military conquest. The famous opening lines of the play ("O for a Muse of fire") present him as an epic hero whose grandeur cannot be adequately conveyed by dramatic representation. The inadequacy of the playwright, of the stage, of the actors, and of the audience attests to the greatness of the subject, which is not only Henry, of course, but the conquest of France that he brings about. There is a reluctance to accept the jingoism of this play and its glorification of war as a direct expression of the author's attitudes, but it is essential to recognize that Shakespeare celebrates aggressive behavior when it is placed in the service of national glory, however much he may condemn it when it is an expression of self-interest and leads to disruptions within the state. For Henry, as for Macbeth and Othello, the big wars make ambition virtue. Modern critics may have negative or ambivalent feelings about Henry's conquest of France; Shakespeare, I think, did not.

Henry is glorified, then, as a great military hero by the Chorus, by his men (Fluellen compares him to Alexander the Great), and even by his enemies after they have been defeated. On his return to England, the people welcome him as "the conqu'ring Caesar" (5, Chorus). Henry proclaims himself covetous of honor, and he receives as much of it as he could possibly wish. He predicts not only that he will triumph over France but also that he will be a world-historical figure, that with his victory at Agincourt he and his men will be remembered "From this day to the ending of the world" (4.3). Indeed, the play itself is a confirmation of his prediction. The play ends as it began, with the Chorus celebrating Henry ("This star of England") and lamenting the inability of the author to do justice to the "mighty men" who have been depicted. It is true that the last lines of the play remind us that Henry's successors soon lost what he had won; but this does not indicate, as many critics contend, that Shakespeare is calling into question the greatness of Henry's accomplishment. Their loss of France is a reflection on Henry's successors, not on Henry himself. The play ends not with a satiric undercutting of Henry but on a note of nostalgia for lost glory.

II

It must be remembered that I have been trying to describe not the view of Henry that emerges from the play as a whole, but the view that is advanced by the rhetoric. One of the problems of the play is that the Chorus presents Henry as such a grandiose being that it is almost impossible for Shakespeare to create a character who can live up to that image. This problem is compounded by the fact that the dramatized Henry is not merely an idealized or illustrative figure but is, like Prince Hal, a mimetic character with inner conflicts who subverts his illustrative functions. If Henry were the cardboard character that some critics claim him to be, he would be too good to be true. The difficulty, however, is that he is too true to be as good as the rhetoric proposes.

This sort of difficulty is quite common in realistic fiction, where the mimetic portrait of a hero or heroine is often in conflict with the author's analysis and judgment (see Paris 1974). It is less striking in Shakespeare's plays because the dramatic form tends to reduce the amount of rhetoric and to make it more oblique. Because of the presence of the Chorus, however, *Henry V* is like a novel with an editorializing narrator, and it generates, therefore, interpretative problems similar to those found in realistic fiction. It is not surprising that some critics solve these problems by seeing Shakespeare's treatment of Henry as ironic, for this permits them to account for the disparity between rhetoric and mimesis in a way that preserves the play's artistic unity. The hypothesis of deliberate ambiguity also presents the play as an integrated work.

Having examined the view of Henry that emerges from the rhetoric, let us now look at Henry as a creation inside a creation who may be inharmonious with the whole of which he is a part. Many critics feel, of course, that Henry is not a realistically drawn character at all but is a patchwork figure who lacks internal consistency. Henry's character *is* full of contradictions. He wages a cruel war against a nation that has done him no real harm, and he does so for obvious political reasons; yet he seems obsessively concerned with the justness of his cause, and he repeatedly disclaims responsibility for his warlike behavior. He is an ambitious man who is so driven by a thirst for glory that even though he is badly outnumbered at Agincourt, he does not wish "one man more" (4.3) because that would reduce his share of the honor. The Chorus describes him, however, as being "free from vainness and self-glorious pride" (5), and upon his return to England he will not allow himself to be treated like a hero. He insists, moreover, that all the glory for the victory belongs to God, and he is so anxious about this that he threatens death to anyone who boasts of the triumph. He has a strong tendency toward brutality, as is evidenced by his exhortation to his men before Harfleur (3.1), his threats to the inhabitants of the city (3.3), and his murder of his prisoners; yet he insists that his soldiers pay for their provisions, he punishes stealing with death, and he proclaims that "when lenity and cruelty play for a kingdom, the gentler gamester is the soonest winner" (3.6).

These and similar inconsistencies make Henry at once a very puzzling and an extremely interesting character. Those who do not see him as either a cardboard or a patchwork character tend to see him as a hypocrite. They explain his contradictions by seeing his idealistic utterances as a Machiavellian facade and his aggressive words and deeds as a revelation of the real Henry. From a psychological point of view, however, Henry is not a Machiavel, but a man whose inner conflicts result in inconsistent behavior.[3] In Horneyan terms, he has a mixture of perfectionistic, self-effacing, and arrogant-vindictive traits. His constant effort, and, indeed, that of the play as a whole, is to justify his aggression in such a way as to bring it into harmony with the demands of his perfectionistic and self-effacing tendencies. The conflict I have described exists not only in Henry, but also in the rhetoric, which both exalts Henry as "the mirror of all Christian kings" and celebrates him as "the warlike Harry" at whose heels "famine, sword, and fire / Crouch for employment" (1, Chorus).

In his portrait of Henry, Shakespeare did not, as Tillyard proposes, jettison "the character he had created" and substitute one that satisfies "the requirements both of the chronicle and of popular tradition" (1944, 306).[4] As I indicated earlier, there is a clear psychological connection between the compulsively madcap prince of *1 and 2 Henry IV* and the perfectionistic king of *Henry V*. As we saw at the end of *2 Henry IV*, once he becomes king, Henry needs to allay the anxieties of his people and to prove to himself that he really was virtuous all along by fulfilling the demands of his role. Any backsliding now, any taint upon the new image he is determined to create, would exacerbate the doubts he is trying to allay and would threaten him with self-hate. As prince he may have been rebelling against his own perfectionism out of a fear of becoming enslaved by it. As king he *is* enslaved by it, so much so that he cannot lift a hand to save his old friends.

He needs to compensate not only for his own wayward youth, but also for the sins of his father, which are extremely threatening to him, since they call into question his right to the throne and activate his fear of divine retribution. In *Henry V*, he seeks to reduce his anxiety on this account by honoring the memory of Richard, by engaging in acts of contrition, and by maintaining his own rectitude. He hopes in this way to compensate for his father's crime and to distinguish himself from the guilty parent who paid such a high price for the throne.

   Henry's perfectionism manifests itself in his concern for the
righteousness of his cause. He has many motives for going to war.
What better way to prove himself worthy of the throne, to uphold
the honor of his lineage, and to win the fame and adulation he
craves than by the conquest of France? The Archbishop tells him
what he wants to hear, but I do not think that he is cynically
exploiting the Archbishop's desire for the war, as many critics
contend. He seems to be afraid of political motives and exhorts
the Archbishop in very strong terms to give him a truthful response:

> My learned lord, we pray you to proceed,
> And justly and religiously unfold
> Why the Law Salique, that they have in France,
> Or should or should not bar us in our claim.
> And God forbid, my dear and faithful lord,
> That you should fashion, wrest, or bow your reading,
> Or nicely charge your understanding soul
> With opening titles miscreate, whose right
> Suits not in native colours with the truth;
> For God doth know how many now in health
> Shall drop their blood in approbation
> Of what your reverence shall incite us to.
> Therefore take heed how you impawn our person,
> How you awake our sleeping sword of war.
> We charge you in the name of God, take heed;
> For never two such kingdoms did contend
> Without much fall of blood, whose guiltless drops
> Are every one a woe, a sore complaint
> 'Gainst him whose wrongs gives edge unto the swords
> That makes such waste in brief mortality.
> Under this conjuration, speak my lord:
> For we will hear, note, and believe in heart
> That what you speak is in your conscience washed
> As pure as sin with baptism.

                                                              (1.2)

If this speech is insincere, then Henry is a hypocrite indeed!
   I think that Henry is sincere because there is much evidence in
the play that he has the perfectionistic "conviction of an infallible
justice operating in life" (Horney 1950, 197). What is important to
him is not the appearance of virtue, but its reality. His response to
the conspiracy against him is a good illustration of his perfectionism. Scroop shares (or appeared to share) many of Henry's
own characteristics, and his fall "hath left a kind of blot / To mark

the full-fraught man and best indued / With some suspicion" (2.2). It threatens Henry's belief in man's power to resist evil and undermines his trust in his fellows. Though his accounting system is threatened by the treachery of those he had treated so well, it is validated by the providential revelation of their conspiracy. The traitors themselves attribute their "prevention" to God and give thanks for it. Henry has not been treated fairly by others, but he has by Providence, and his mournfulness gives way to buoyancy as his bargain with fate is confirmed: "We doubt not of a fair and lucky war, / Since God so graciously hath brought to light / This dangerous treason" (2.2).

Henry's conviction of an infallible justice operating in life is nowhere more evident than in his reliance on God for his victory. Critics doubt the strength of his claim to the French throne and the morality of his going to war even if the claim is sound, but the perfectionistic person tends to have a legalistic conception of justice, and in Henry's mind, since his claim is good, his cause is just. In his scheme of things, the guilt for the war attaches to those who are in the wrong, and he feels completely justified, therefore, in attacking France. Being convinced that he is in the right, he is ready to leave it to God to "dispose the day" (4.3). He is confident before the battle of Agincourt, despite the overwhelming odds against him, because he believes that right makes might; his strength is the strength of ten because his heart is pure. We can understand now, I think, why he lets the French know of his weakness and thereby insures the confrontation. After the battle, he insists that credit for the victory belongs entirely to God: "O God, thy arm was here! / And not to us, but to thy arm alone, / Ascribe we all!" (4.8). The Chorus sees this as evidence of his humility, and it *is* part of his self-effacing bargain, but it is also a sign of enormous pride on Henry's part. By refusing to ascribe the victory to his martial prowess, he turns it into a miracle that God has performed on his behalf. His success is therefore a proof of his virtue and of the justice of his claim to both the English and French thrones.

In Henry's belief system a corollary of the triumph of right is the inevitable defeat of the wrong. He exhorts the Archbishop to tell him the truth because if his claim to the throne is not good, God will fight on the side of the French. As it is, he fears that God will punish him for "the fault / [His] father made in compassing the crown" (4.1), and he prays before the battle of Agincourt that God will not think upon the fault that day. He has taken many measures to expiate his father's guilt; but, being a predominantly perfectionistic person, he relies mainly on righteousness as his means of controlling fate and does not have great faith in penitence and forgiveness: "More will I do: / Though all that I can do is nothing worth; / Since that my penitence comes after all, / Imploring pardon" (4.1). We see here a self-effacing side of Henry also, of course, since he does not presume that God has accepted his offerings and hopes to impress Him by his humility. Contrasted with Henry's humility is the pride of the French, which is crushed by their overwhelming defeat.

In the perfectionistic belief system, those who are in the wrong deserve the terrible things that happen to them. This may help us to understand Henry's threats against the people of Harfleur if they persist in their "guilty" resistance (3.3) and his lack of compassion for his defeated enemies. Henry has a double set of standards. Outside of battle he has a code of behavior that is extremely strict and that he imposes on his men, with severe penalties for violators. He is so rigid about this code in part because his claims to divine favor are based upon behavioral perfection. In battle, however, anything goes—from the rape of maidens to the murder of old men, infants, and prisoners; and the horrible violence is all the fault of those who guiltily resist his legally justified claims.

The understanding of Henry developed so far will help to illuminate the much discussed scene in which Henry visits his men incognito on the eve of the battle. Many critics feel that Henry comes off poorly here, that he fails to respond adequately to Williams's challenge; but that, I think, is because they have misread the scene. When Henry says that he "could not die anywhere so contented as in the King's company, his cause being just and his quarrel honourable," Williams replies, "That's more than we know"; and he goes on to say that "if the cause be not good, the King himself hath a heavy reckoning to make, when all those legs and arms and heads, chopped off in battle, shall join together at the latter day and cry all, 'We died at such a place'" (4.1). Henry does not reply to this for two reasons: (1) he believes in the justice of his cause and feels no need to defend it; and (2) he agrees with what Williams says about the culpability of those whose "cause be not good," for he had said virtually the same thing himself to the Archbishop.

What Henry quarrels with is Williams's charge that it will be "a black matter for the King" if his men do not die well in battle, that is, if they die in a state of sin and suffer damnation as a consequence. Henry's reply to this is interesting and is very much to the point:

> . . . there is no king, be his cause never so spotless, if it come to the arbitrament of swords, can try it out with all unspotted soldiers: some (peradventure) have on them the guilt of premeditated and contrived murder; some of beguiling virgins with the broken seals of perjury; some, making wars their bulwark, that have before gored the gentle bosom of peace with pillage and robbery. Now, if these men have defeated the law and outrun native punishment, though they can outstrip men, they have no wings to fly from God. War is his beadle, war is his vengeance; so that here men are punished for beforebreach of the King's laws in now the King's quarrel. . . . Then if they die unprovided, no more is the King guilty of their damnation than he was before guilty of those impieties for the which they are now visited. Every subject's duty is the King's, but every subject's soul is his own. Therefore should every soldier in the wars do as every sick man in his bed—wash every mote out of his conscience; and dying so, death is to him advantage.
>
> (4.1)

Williams's charge is very threatening to Henry because it holds him responsible for what happens to his men "be his cause never so spotless." Henry defends himself by arguing that if his men die in a state of grace, then their deaths are advantageous and that if they do not, the responsibility is entirely their own.

He comes very close to suggesting, indeed, that their deaths themselves, and not merely the state of their souls, are the men's responsibility, that they are being punished by God for earlier crimes. Man's justice is imperfect, but God's is infallible, and it is most fitting that men should meet their punishment as a consequence of their efforts to escape it. For Henry, men's fortunes, even in battle, are never unjust. Some deaths are punishments, some are advantageous, and some, as the dying words of York suggest, are sources of eternal glory (4.7).

Henry is a predominantly perfectionistic person, then, who believes that he can control destiny by means of his rectitude. He has a magical bargain with fate in which if his cause is just and he obeys the rules, he will be assured of victory, whatever the material circumstances. He has also, as we have seen, a self-effacing side that manifests itself in a variety of ways. He has strong taboos against pride and vindictiveness. He punishes the conspirators because of their threat to the commonwealth, but says that "Touching our person, seek we no revenge" (2.2). Before battle, he feels that his fate is in the hands of God; and after his triumph at Agincourt, he ascribes the victory entirely to God, refuses to play the role of "conqu'ring Caesar" (5, Chorus), and threatens death to anyone who boasts of their accomplishment (4.8). His self-effacing side manifests itself most strongly, of course, in relation to his father's crime. Since his rectitude is of no avail in expiating his father's guilt, he turns to prayer, to submission, and to acts of contrition and penitence. He says that these acts are "nothing worth" both because, being predominantly perfectionistic, he is still afraid of being punished by God's infallible justice and because, being also self-effacing, he would undo their magical efficacy if he allowed himself consciously to believe in their power.

Henry has, in effect, a double bargain with fate, a perfectionistic one in which he controls God through his rectitude and a self-effacing one in which he controls God (and escapes His infallible justice) through his penitence, submission, and humility. His self-effacing bargain is that fate will favor him because of his efforts to honor Richard's memory and atone for his death (magical acts of undoing) and because he refuses to take pride in his victories but gives all the credit to God. He is so anxious about any show of pride, either on his own part or on the part of his men, because that would violate his bargain. Then his claims would not be honored and he would be exposed to divine retribution.

If Henry had only a combination of perfectionistic and self-effacing traits, he would come much closer to living up to the glorifying rhetoric, and he would not be such a controversial figure. He has also, however, many aggressive traits that are at variance with the other components of his personality and that have led some critics to feel that he is a hypocrite and others that he is a patchwork character. He is engaged in a search for glory by means of conquest, he is vindictive, and he has a penchant for extreme forms of violence. These traits are difficult to reconcile with much of the rhetoric and with the rest of his personality, but they make sense, I believe, as part of a structure of inner conflicts. As I have said, Henry's constant effort is to justify his aggressiveness in such a way as to bring it into harmony with the demands of his perfectionistic and self-effacing tendencies.

Of Henry's many motives for invading France, the most powerful, perhaps, is his need for glory. Glory is a recurrent theme in his speeches. He tells the French ambassador that he "will rise there with so full a glory / That [he] will dazzle all the eyes of France, / Yea strike the Dauphin blind to look on us" (1.2). He promises glory to those who accompany him to France: "Now, lords, for France; the enterprise whereof / Shall be to you as us, like glorious" (2.2) His speech to his men before the battle of Agincourt expresses his own and plays upon their desire for a place in history. He does not care about such trivial things as gold or distinction in dress:

> But if it be a sin to covet honour,
> I am the most offending soul alive.
> No, faith, my coz, wish not a man from England.
> God's peace! I would not lose so great an honour
> As one man more methinks would share from me
> For the best hope I have.
>
> (4.3)

We might dismiss this as battlefield rhetoric if it did not echo sentiments Henry had expressed earlier. Though after the battle Henry gives all the credit to God, the adulation of his people is important to him, and he receives all the more of it because of his humility.

We cannot help wondering why Henry has such a powerful need for glory that he would sacrifice the best hope he has (can he mean his salvation?) rather than lose some honor by having more soldiers with him at Agincourt. It is not possible to arrive at a totally satisfying answer to this question, but if we consider the three plays in which Henry appears together, we can understand some of the factors that make him so compulsively ambitious. Henry's search for glory arises out of his need to vindicate himself in the eyes of others, out of his need to live up to the arrogant-vindictive component of his idealized image, and out of his need to compensate for the negative feelings he has about himself.

As a madcap Prince, Henry generates extremely negative attitudes toward himself on the part of his father and members of the court. Though he has numerous ways of defending himself against this, he is deeply disturbed by the doubts, fears, and criticisms to which he is exposed; and he has elaborate fantasies of self-vindication. One way of vindicating himself, especially in the eyes of his father, is to become a great warrior, like Hotspur. *1 Henry IV* opens with King Henry praising Hotspur as "A son who is the theme of honour's tongue," while "riot and dishonour stain the brow / Of my young Harry." Because his father, and, indeed, his culture, measure him against Hotspur, Hotspur's values become incorporated into Henry's idealized image (along with much else); and his competition with Hotspur persists, in an intrapsychic way, after the deaths of both his rival and his father. He can feel good about himself, and be sure of the approval of others, only when he is surpassing Hotspur at winning Hotspur's kind of honor.

As we have seen, despite his apparent self-assurance, Henry has negative feelings about himself that surface from time to time in the *Henry IV* plays and that are manifested in expressions of self-dissatisfaction and in promises to himself and others that he is going to change. In *Henry V,* his negative feelings about himself are revealed in his scene with Katherine, in the course of which he says a number of self-deprecating things about his abilities as a courtier and his attractiveness to the opposite sex. He has "no cunning in protestation," he "never looks in his glass for love of anything he sees there," and he frightens ladies when he comes to woo them. He will be a constant husband, he assures Katherine, "because he hath not the gift to woo in other places" (5.2). It is surprising to see the man who was once a witty, many-sided Prince present himself as nothing but a blunt, plain soldier who has "neither words nor measure" and who can only woo a lady through feats of arms and horsemanship.

One source of the kind of insecurity Henry displays here may be his earlier withdrawal from the normal life of a young man of his station. As Prince, he developed such skill in relating to the denizens of the tavern that they dubbed him the "king of courtesy," but he seems not to have developed equal skill in dealing with members of his own class. His relationships with lower-class women did not prepare him for wooing a Princess. Since there is no other mention made of Henry's being physically unattractive, his statement that his face "is not worth sunburning" may be more an indication of his negative self-image than of his actual appearance. He compensates for his feelings of undesirability through his athletic prowess and military feats. He wins Katherine, in fact, through his conquest of France—she is one of the spoils of victory; and even in this wooing scene he is preoccupied with martial glory. Since he gets her "with scrambling," she should be "a good soldier-breeder," and he has visions of their son conquering the Turks.

Henry has, it is clear, both an idealized and a despised image of himself, and he must actualize the one in order to avoid feeling like the other. He has an all-or-nothing scenario for his life:

> Or there we'll sit,
> Ruling in large and ample empery
> O'er France and all her (almost) kingly dukedoms,
> Or lay these bones in an unworthy urn,
> Tombless, with no remembrance over them.
> Either our history shall with full mouth
> Speak freely of our acts, or else our grave,
> Like Turkish mute, shall have a tongueless mouth,
> Not worshipped with a waxen epitaph.
>
> (1.2)

Henry feels that he must be great if he is to be worth anything at all. As his speech to his men before Agincourt indicates, his aspiration is to achieve immortal fame: "And Crispin Crispian shall ne'er go by, / From this day to the ending of the world,/ But we in it shall be remembered" (4.3). Either he will become a legendary figure, or he deserves no respect whatsoever and will be totally forgotten. Henry is not as different from Richard II as we at first might think.

Henry says that "if it be a sin to covet honour," he is "the most offending soul alive" (4.3). This gives us a good indication of the immensity of his ambition. It is clear, however, that in this speech Henry does not feel his pursuit of glory to be a sin, nor does Shakespeare treat it as such, even though his villains are often characters who resemble Henry in their need to be great. As we have seen, Henry defends himself against feelings of sinfulness in a variety of ways. He justifies his invasion of France on the grounds that his cause is just, making the Archbishop of Canterbury responsible for the legitimacy of his claims and the French responsible for the ensuing slaughter. He has a powerful craving for glory, but a considerable anxiety about pride. He devotes himself to the pursuit of military honor, but when he wins it he avoids the charge of vanity by giving all the credit to God. It is when he feels pride, vaunts his prowess, or experiences triumph that he is most insistent upon his humility. He at once feeds his pride and gets around the taboo against it by transferring his pride to God and experiencing it through him. This strategy also confirms his sense of rectitude, since it makes his good fortune a sign of divine approval.

Henry is motivated in his assault on France not only by his desire for glory, but also by vindictive and sadistic impulses. He is outraged by the tennis ball insult and responds to it with threats of violence:

And tell the pleasant prince this mock of his
Hath turned his balls to gunstones, and his soul
Shall stand sore charged for the wasteful vengeance
That shall fly with them; for many a thousand widows
Shall this his mock mock out of their dear husbands;
Mock mothers from their sons, mock castles down;
And some are yet ungotten and unborn
That shall have cause to curse the Dauphin's scorn.
But this lies all within the will of God,
To whom I do appeal, and in whose name,
Tell you the Dauphin, I am coming on
To venge me as I may, and to put forth
My rightful hand in a well-hallowed cause.

(1.2)

The various sides of Henry's personality all manifest themselves in this speech. The Dauphin's jest is threatening to him because it implies that he is still an irresponsible youth who is not to be taken seriously, and this is precisely the image of himself that Henry is attempting to overcome. He needs to show everyone that he is no longer a madcap prince but a powerful king who is not to be laughed at, and he vows to crush the nation that has insulted him. As he boasts of what he is going to do to the French, he becomes anxious about manifesting pride and hastens to submit himself to the will of God, who will decide the outcome. God is sure to be on his side, however, because he comes "in a well-hallowed cause" and has a right to revenge. Henry does not decide to go to war because of the tennis ball incident, of course; he had made that decision before he gave audience to the French ambassador. He allows himself to react so violently to the Dauphin's "jest" because it provides an additional justification for his aggression and frees him to inflict horrible suffering upon the French without having to feel guilty about it. It is not he, but the Dauphin's mock that will deprive so many wives of their husbands, children of their fathers, and mothers of their sons.

Henry seems drawn to war because it permits the innocent enjoyment of a kind of primitive behavior that is forbidden under all other circumstances. As he explains to his men at the siege of Harfleur, "In peace there's nothing so becomes a man / As modest stillness and humility"; but "when the blast of war blows in our ears," we should "imitate the action of the tiger; / Stiffen the sinews, conjure up the blood, / Disguise fair nature with hard-favoured rage" (3.1). In war the kind of savagery against which there are powerful taboos in peace becomes a virtue, a tribute to our valiant forbears, a proof of our mother's honor (3.1) The most terrible images of violence in the play, and perhaps in all Shakespeare, occur in Henry's speech to the people of Harfleur. If the city gives in, he will show mercy; but

> If not—why, in a moment look to see
> The blind and bloody soldier with foul hand
> Defile the locks of your shrill-shrieking daughters;
> Your fathers taken by the silver beards,
> And their most reverend heads dashed to the walls;
> Your naked infants spitted upon pikes,
> Whiles the mad mothers with their howls confused
> Do break the clouds, as did the wives of Jewry
> At Herod's bloody-hunting slaughtermen.
> What say you? Will you yield, and this avoid?
> Or, guilty in defense, be thus destroyed?
>
> (3.3)

It is not he but the people of Harfleur who will be responsible for such demonic behavior on the part of his troops because of their guilty resistance.

Henry's defenders argue that his threats are a tactic, and a successful one at that, but the ferocity of his lines suggests that Henry derives a sadistic enjoyment from the thought of such an orgy of lust and aggession: "What is it then to me if impious war, / Arrayed in flames like to the prince of fiends, / Do with his smirched complexion all fell feats / Enlinked to waste and desolation?" (3.3) Henry once again disowns responsibility for the horrors he is prepared to inflict on his enemies: it is not he but war that is impious and satanic. War is for him a state of morally justified anarchy in which mercy and conscience are suspended. If Harfleur does not yield,

> The gates of mercy shall be all shut up,
> And the fleshed soldier, rough and hard of heart,
> In liberty of bloody hand shall range
> With conscience wide as hell, mowing like grass
> Your fresh fair virgins and your flow'ring infants.
>
> (3.3)

We do not see Henry or his men actually engage in such brutal behavior, except in the killing of prisoners; but it is clear that he feels that they have a right to do so, especially when the enemy angers him by refusing to honor his claims. "France being ours,"

he proclaims to his court, "we'll bend it to our awe, / Or break it all
to pieces" (1.2). It is not difficult to understand why Hazlitt saw
Henry as a man who is resolved "to destroy all that he cannot
enslave" and to lay "all the blame of the consequences of his
ambition on those who will not submit tamely to his tyranny"
(1965, 212).

III

Like many of Shakespeare's protagonists, then, Henry is a man
with inner conflicts. Instead of being caught in a crossfire of
conflicting shoulds that paralyzes him or makes him hate himself
whatever he does, Henry is able to harmonize his conflicting
trends, to feel righteous and humble while satisfying his need for
aggressive triumph. He gains at once the glory of being a great
conqueror and the glory of being a man who is free from vanity
and pride. He is able to indulge his vindictive and sadistic impulses while remaining noble and innocent. The reconciliation of
his conflicting needs is made easier for Henry by certain social
factors that we should not overlook. The pursuit of military honor
is not a sin within the feudal code of chivalry that is clearly
operative in this play, and it is sanctioned all the more for Henry
by virtue of the fact that he is king. Personal ambition is usually
treated as an evil by Shakespeare, who shows it again and again
as leading to treachery, chaos, and civil war. National ambition is
an entirely different matter. It has a unifying effect and is a source
of legitimate pride and glory. Since Henry is king, his personal
ambition is identical with that of the state, and his glory is also the
nation's. His position, then, sanctifies his aggressiveness.
Whereas his father's ambition led him to become a usurper and
ultimately a regicide, Henry's leads him to become a national
hero, in whose conquests Shakespeare takes a great deal of
pride.[5]

The conflicts we have observed in Henry occur also in the
author, who celebrates Henry's righteousness, aggressiveness,
and humility. The play as a whole is a fantasy of justified aggression. Through Henry, Shakespeare is able to release ambitious,
belligerent, and sadistic impulses in a way that does not conflict
with his need to be modest, noble, and innocent. Though Henry's
solution appears to work for the author, it fails to work for those
critics who are aware of the aggressiveness in the play but do not
feel that it has been reconciled with the claims for righteousness

and humility. The controversy surrounding the play has been sponsored in part by the disparity between rhetoric and mimesis, in part by a failure to understand the dynamics of Henry's personality, and in part by the author's inner conflicts, which lead him to glorify incompatible values.

It has been sponsored in part, also, by our uncertainty about what kind of a play this is and about how we should respond to it. Because of its historical basis and its rich mimetic portrait of Henry, it belongs with the realistic plays; but in some respects it is closer to the comedies and romances than it is to the histories and tragedies. The power of the realistic plays derives in part from the fact that they show magical bargains failing and characters being destroyed by their inner conflicts. Desire is subjected to reality. By virtue of their unrealistic conventions, the comedies and romances permit conflicting needs to be harmonized and magical bargains to be honored; and this, of course, is what happens in *Henry V*. Desire seems to triumph over reality. The realistic and the unrealistic elements in the play arouse different sets of expectations, both of which cannot be satisfied. The aim of the play, I believe, is to celebrate a fleeting moment in English history when reality and desire coincided; but Shakespeare's presentation of Henry contains too much idealization to seem real and too much reality to seem ideal.[6]

6
Julius Caesar

I

Julius Caesar was written soon after *Henry V,* and many critics have pointed to the similarities between its thematic concerns and those of the preceding history plays. It is difficult to establish Shakespeare's exact attitude toward Caesar, Brutus, and the republican cause, in part because the rhetoric of this play is less explicit than that of the histories; but it seems evident that he shares the belief of Faonius, quoted in Plutarch's *Life of Marcus Brutus,* "that civill warre [is] worse than tyrannicall government usurped against the lawe" (Bullough 1964, 97). Though he does not clearly present Caesar's as a tyrannical government, he does show that the consequences of killing Caesar are far worse than Caesar's reign was likely to be.

While its political themes connect *Julius Caesar* to the history plays that preceded it, its characterization links it to the tragedies that follow. Brutus's inner conflicts are similar to those of Macbeth, and the relationship of Brutus and Cassius is the first of Shakespeare's great studies of the destructive interaction of different personality types. Though much attention has been given to the play's political aspect, it is essentially a tragedy of character, the outcome of which is dictated by the interplay of Cassius, Brutus, and Caesar. The motives of these characters are more personal than political, and Shakespeare presents them as such. As R. A. Foakes points out, commentators have found it difficult to determine "what the play is about and in what sense, if any, it has unity" (1963, 193). Foakes suggests that its unity "lies in the birth and completion of the rebellion" (1963, 200). I propose that the play is essentially about the Cassius-Brutus-Caesar relationship, which generates the rebellion and determines its outcome.[1] These characters are so closely interconnected that it is impossible to understand them individually without examining their relations with each other. This is especially true of Cassius and Brutus. Much is revealed about these men by their reactions to the rise of Caesar, and Brutus and Cassius have hidden sides to their personalities that are manifested in the susceptibility of each to the influence of the other.

"How came Brutus," asks J. I. M. Stewart, "to join the conspirators?" (1949, 52). This is the central mystery of *Julius Caesar*. Brutus is often compared to Hamlet. He is, says E. M. Forster, "an intellectual who can do things, who is not (like Hamlet) hampered by doubts" (1969, 63). Hamlet and Brutus are not only both intellectuals, they are also both men of honor who care very much about their moral nobility. Despite his concern for his innocence, it is difficult to understand why Hamlet, with such strong inducements to act, cannot proceed to his revenge. In view of his concern for his honor, it is difficult to understand why Brutus, with such weak and nebulous motives, participates in the murder of Caesar. "There is," says Stewart, "an element of unresolved mystery here, strongly underlined in that groping soliloquy in the orchard. . . . there is a great blindness in the deed to which he gives his name and arm" (1949, 51).

Brutus is usually assumed to have been motivated by political idealism, and that is clearly the way he sees himself: "If it be aught toward the general good," he tells Cassius when the latter has something to "impart" to him, "Set honour in one eye and death i' th' other, / And I will look on both indifferently" (1.2). At Caesar's funeral, he informs the people that he "slew [his] best lover for the good of Rome," so that they could "live as freemen" (3.2). The problem is that before the murder we do not see Brutus being very much concerned about the general good or with republican ideals.

Cassius says that "honour is the subject of [his] story," but the speeches that follow have nothing to do with honor but rather with Cassius's personal sense of rivalry with Caesar and his bitterness at being an underling. Yet Brutus is moved by Cassius's appeal and arrives, on his own, at the conclusion that Caesar must die. Cassius knows that Brutus is not being motivated by lofty ideals but that he has been "seduc'd," that his "honourable mettle" has been "wrought / From that it is dispos'd" (1.2). In the "groping soliloquy" to which Stewart refers, Brutus develops a notoriously flimsy tissue of rationalizations for killing Caesar, and it should be noted that even his rationalizations have little to do with republican ideals. He decides to kill Caesar because of what *might* happen if Caesar became king, even though he has no complaints against Caesar at present. Since Cassius has provided no ideological reasons for conspiring against Caesar and Brutus offers none, even to himself, it is difficult to see the tragedy as "created by the actions of a young idealist in the fulfillment of the highest principles" (Schanzer 1963, 34); and we are left with Stewart's question, "How came Brutus to join the conspirators?"

Stewart feels that Brutus's behavior is the product of "obscure emotions at play behind the stoic mask" (1949, 51), and Leo Kirschbaum says that "all commentators . . . regard Brutus as a man who does not understand himself or others" (1968, 34). Kirschbaum is wrong about the commentators but right, I think, about Brutus's lack of self-understanding. Shakespeare's problem was to present a character who has a powerful need to deceive himself in such a way that he will not deceive the audience. That Shakespeare did not entirely succeed is evidenced by the fact that so many critics have accepted Brutus's version of himself, despite Cassius's clear statement that he has been seduced. Brutus's behavior is much more difficult to fathom than is that of Macbeth, who is his closest counterpart in the canon. Macbeth and Brutus have similar inner conflicts, but Macbeth is sharply aware of his, whereas Brutus senses his conflicts only through their symptomatic manifestations. Macbeth knows why he kills Duncan and what the consequences will be; Brutus does not know why he kills Caesar or the price he will have to pay for doing so. Macbeth can be understood from his own speeches, but Brutus's motives must be inferred from the words of others. While we do not have direct insight into Brutus's motives for joining the conspiracy, we know that he is moved by the speeches of Cassius. We must analyze those speeches, which have mainly to do with Cassius's feelings toward Caesar, in order to understand Brutus.

I shall proceed, then, by examining the relationship between Cassius and Caesar, keeping in mind that much which is conscious in Cassius is unconscious in Brutus. In order to understand the relationship, it will be useful to look first at Caesar so that we can see exactly what it is to which Cassius is reacting so strongly at the beginning of the play. Indeed, the precipitating event in this play is Caesar's rise to preeminence. Cassius, Brutus, and Caesar all respond to this event in ways that are highly irrational and that have tragic consequences.

II

As the play opens, Caesar's dream of glory has been almost completely realized. He has just defeated the last of his rivals and has been appointed dictator for life. His only frustration is that there is opposition to his desire to be king. He not only wants the crown; he also wants everyone to want him to have it. When the people cheer his refusal, he expresses his sense of rejection by offering them his throat. He is showing the people how badly they have hurt him and is trying to make them feel guilty about it. His rage is so great that he falls into a fit; but when he recovers, he apologizes for his behavior, indicating his awareness of its irrationality. He remains upset, however; there is an "angry spot" upon his brow, and his companions "look like a chidden train" (1.2).

Caesar is so enraged because his claims are not being honored and his idealized image is being called into question. With his final "triumph over Pompey's blood" (1.1), he has come to feel that he *is* his grandiose self, and his claims escalate accordingly. One of his claims is that his preeminence should be confirmed by the title of king. Another is that he should be feared by others while being immune to fear himself. It is his need to flaunt his greatness that arouses the resentment of the conspirators and his need to prove his fearlessness that makes him an easy victim of their plot.

Caesar has excellent insight into Cassius's psychology, as his remarks to Mark Antony indicate: "Such men as he are never at heart's ease / While they behold a greater than themselves, / And therefore are they very dangerous" (1.2). He understands Cassius so well because he and Cassius have similar personalities, and he knows how he would feel if he were in Cassius's place. Caesar is a shrewd observer, but his idealized image requires that he be above the ordinary vicissitudes of life, and he must therefore ignore the threat that Cassius represents: "I rather tell thee what is to be fear'd / Than what I fear; for always I am Caesar" (1.2). He should not have to take the usual kinds of precautions because he possesses a magical potency that comes with being Caesar. To pay attention to reality, to fear Cassius, is to give up his claims, and with them his exalted status.

Caesar's taboos against fear are very much in evidence on the Ides of March and are more responsible than anything else for his destruction. He is disturbed by Calphurnia's dream, the portents and prodigies she describes, and the findings of the augurers; but he cannot allow these things to keep him home, for to do so would expose him to unbearable self-hate. He defends himself against his anxieties and maintains his courage by reaffirming his claims. He is more dangerous than danger; the things that threaten him will vanish when they see his face (2.2). His fatalistic attitude toward death is another means by which he dismisses fear and preserves his idealized image of himself. When the augurers do not want him to go forth because there is no heart within the beast they have sacrificed, Caesar reinterprets their findings in such a way as to reinforce his determination to demonstrate his courage: "The gods do this in shame of cowardice. / Caesar should be a beast without a heart / If he should stay at home to-day for fear" (2.2). He drives himself to live up to his shoulds by reminding himself of the self-contempt he would feel if he should fail. That he actually is afraid is indicated by his yielding to Calphurnia when she provides him with a face-saving device: "Call it my fear / That keeps you in the house and not your own."

Caesar's mind is changed once again by Decius Brutus, who understands him well and who works upon him both by feeding his pride and arousing his anxiety. Decius reinterprets Calphurnia's dream in such a way as to have it signify that Caesar will be the savior of Rome from whom great men will seek "tinctures, stains, relics, and cognizance" (2.2). Caesar's deepest desire is to become such an object of worship. Decius says that the Senate "have concluded / To give this day a crown to mighty Caesar," but they may change their minds if he does not appear. "If Caesar hide himself," moreover, "shall they not whisper / 'Lo, Caesar is afraid'?" Decius makes Caesar feel that if he goes to the Senate, he will receive the confirmation of his idealized image that he so desires, whereas if he remains at home, he will not only be in danger of losing that, but he will become an object of contempt to himself and others. Caesar is unable to resist this kind of pressure.

While Caesar's ascendancy intoxicates him, it depresses Cassius. If Cassius cannot be one of the great men of the age, he feels like a worthless wretch. One of his chief complaints to Brutus is that Caesar has taken all the glory for himself and has left none for anyone else: "When went there by an age since the great Flood / But it was fam'd with more than with one man?" (1.2). Caesar's preeminence shatters his pride and makes him feel like his despised self. Caesar is a Colossus and Cassius one of the "petty men" who "Walk under his huge legs and peep about / To find [themselves] dishonourable graves" (1.2). Cassius says that honor is the subject of his story, but he is actually talking about the injury Caesar has done to his pride and the rage that he feels as a consequence. His rage is intensified by his sense of injustice; for he feels that he is as good a man as Caesar—indeed, in the swimming match, he was better. It is intolerable to Cassius that "this man," whom he had once saved from drowning, "Is now become a god, and Cassius is / A wretched creature and must bend his body / If Caesar carelessly but nod on him" (1.2). As the play opens, Cassius is in a state of psychological crisis. He feels that he has no chance of winning the glory he deserves, and he would "as lief not be" as live "In awe" of Caesar (1.2).

Cassius desperately needs to restore his pride. One method he employs is to tear Caesar down, to remember things to his discredit, as in his account of the swimming match and of Caesar's illness in Spain. The story of the swimming match is especially satisfying to Cassius, since it takes him back to a time when he was triumphant in his competition with Caesar and had the power of life and death over him. Both men are driven into foolhardy behavior by their fiercely competitive natures and by their common obsession with proving themselves to be fearless. In the next scene, while Casca stares and is breathless at the menace of the storm, Cassius must show that he is not afraid of anything, even of the gods (1.3). He presents himself to others as physically and psychologically undauntable, while Caesar almost drowned in the Tiber and behaved feebly during his illness in Spain.

These stories assuage Cassius's injured pride by reaffirming his superiority to Caesar, but they also feed his bitterness by intensifying his sense of the unfairness of Caesar's predominance.

> Ye gods, it doth amaze me
> A man of such a feeble temper should
> So get the start of the majestic world
> And bear the palm alone.
>
> (1.2)

Since, according to Cassius's philosophy, the stronger man ought to win, the triumph of Caesar means either that Caesar is stronger or that Cassius's beliefs are incorrect, that rewards are not necessarily distributed according to his notions of merit. Neither of these conclusions is tolerable to Cassius. He rejects the first by tearing Caesar down and the second by attributing the rise of Caesar to the shameful weakness of the Romans. There is a kind of justice in Caesar's triumph not because he has been properly rewarded, but because the Romans have gotten what they deserve. It is important for Cassius to feel that what has happened to him is not the result of caprice or of forces beyond his control: ". . . the fault, dear Brutus, is not in our stars, / But in ourselves, that we are underlings" (1.2). If the fault is in themselves, there is something they can do about it; they can still hope to master their fate.

Cassius does not see the fault as in himself, of course, but as in his countrymen, who have invited Caesar's domination by their submissiveness:

> [Caesar] would not be a wolf
> But that he sees the Romans are but sheep;
> He were no lion, were not the Romans hinds.
> Those that with haste will make a mighty fire
> Begin it with weak straws. What trash is Rome,
> What rubbish and what offal, when it serves
> For the base matter to illuminate
> So vile a thing as Caesar!
>
>   (1.3)

This way of viewing the situation at once diminishes Caesar and brings him under control. Since the problem is the sheepishness of the Romans, the solution is to exorcise those "womanish" qualities that have led them to accept their "yoke and sufferance" and to rouse up "those sparks of life / That should be in a Roman" (1.3). Cassius does this by heaping scorn upon their subservient behavior and by holding before them an arrogant-vindictive idealized image of what it means to be a Roman, an image that is personified by himself. To accept Caesar's rule is to be contemptible, whereas to revolt is to be one of the "noblest-minded Romans" who, having still alive in them the spirit of their fathers, are prepared "to undergo . . . an enterprise / Of honourable-dangerous consequence" (1.3).

The conspiracy against Caesar is the means, then, by which Cassius attempts to cope with his psychological crisis. His plot, like that of Iago, serves a number of purposes. If it succeeds, it will prove his superiority to Caesar and the correctness of his world view: the stronger man will have triumphed. It will show that he is not an underling but is one of the great men of the age— as leader of the conspiracy, perhaps, indeed, the greatest. It will demonstrate that he is not a weak, submissive, womanish creature, like the great mass of Romans, but a powerful man who is master of his fate. Even if the plot fails, it will still have great value for Cassius. What he fears most is being afraid, is being in awe of Caesar. His plot, the danger of which he likes to emphasize, will demonstrate his daring. He can still master his fate, moreover, by killing himself. Cassius's plot, then, is the means by which he attempts to escape his self-hate, to restore his pride, and to actualize his idealized image. If it succeeds, his dream of glory will have come true; and if it fails, he will have demonstrated his courage and his refusal to submit to Caesar's rule and the capriciousness of fate.

Now that we have examined Cassius's motives for wanting to bring Caesar down, we are ready to answer J. I. M. Stewart's question: "How came Brutus to join the conspirators?" The dominant view of Brutus is that he is a misguided idealist. "The tragedy of Brutus springs," according to Maurice Charney, "from his complete sincerity in preferring his duty to Rome to his personal friendship with Caesar" (1963, 49). "He was simply an upright man," says L. C. Knights, "who made a tragic mistake . . . a man who thought that an abstract 'common good' could be achieved without due regard to the complexities of the actual" (1965, 51). I side with the darker view of Brutus that has been set forth most tellingly by Harold Feldman and Gordon Ross Smith. Ernest Schanzer observes that most of Cassius's "arguments seem misdirected, while he leaves unsaid all the things that could have moved Brutus. No reference is made to the welfare of the people. From first to last he treats Brutus as if he were another Cassius" (1963, 39). Harold Feldman understands that Brutus *is*, in some respects, another Cassius, that his response to Cassius's arguments indicates that he shares Cassius's emotions (1952, 377). Cassius's speeches have, after all, the desired effect. "We can surmise that Brutus agreed upon the assassination," concludes Gordon Ross Smith, "because he could not bear the thought of anyone's being able to rule over him" (1959, 374).

I have suggested that Brutus's conflicts are similar to those of Macbeth. This has been noted also by G. Wilson Knight, who observes that Brutus, "like Macbeth, embarks on a line of action . . . directed against the symbol of established authority; at root, perhaps, selfish. For, though he may tell himself that his ideals force him to a work of secrecy, conspiracy, and destruction, he is not at peace. He suffers a state of spiritual or mental division" (1965, 120). That division, in the psychological terms I have been using, is between his dominant perfectionistic tendencies, which demand that he live up to a strict code of honor, and his repressed vindictive side, which pushes him in the direction of murdering Caesar. "The instigation in both plays comes," as Knight says, "partly from within, partly from without. . . . Both Brutus and Macbeth find their own vague mental suggestions brought to rapid growth by outside influences" (1965, 122). Just as Macbeth would never have murdered Duncan without the influence of his wife, so Brutus would never have moved against Caesar without the instigation of Cassius. But Macbeth had thoughts of regicide before he rejoined his Lady, while Brutus tells Cassius that he has been "Vexed . . . / Of late with passions of some difference" (1.2); and he is very disturbed by the shouts of the people, which he takes to mean that "new honours" are being "heap'd on Caesar" (1.2).

The major difference between Brutus and Macbeth is that Macbeth's inner conflicts are to a large degree conscious, whereas Brutus's are not. Brutus speaks of being "at war" with himself, but he displays no distinct awareness of what his internal strife is about. Macbeth is torn between perfectionistic and arrogant-vindictive conceptions of manhood and can move against Duncan only after Lady Macbeth has converted him, for the moment at least, to her system of values. In order to be at peace with himself after the murder, he tries to kill his perfectionistic side and to inure himself to violence. When Cassius begins to sound him, Brutus immediately lets him know that he should couch his appeal in terms of "honour" and "the general good"; and even though Cassius does not do this, Brutus persists in thinking that he is acting from lofty motives. Like Macbeth, Brutus is driven to violate his code of honor by the force of his aggressive impulses; but, unlike Macbeth, he never acknowledges to himself what he has done. This is what makes Brutus such a fascinating and elusive character. Through a massive repression of awareness, he wards off conscious self-hate and maintains his idealized image to the end.

Gordon Ross Smith says that Brutus's "virtue" fools everyone, even himself (1959, 368). Does this include Shakespeare? Harold Feldman feels that Shakespeare's mimetic portrait of Brutus escaped his rhetorical intentions, that he probably meant "to exalt his hero," but that "the subsequent process of character intuition forced his honest pen to draw in the darker, more contradictory features to the bitter end" (1952, 335). I believe that Shakespeare presents Brutus as self-deceived from the beginning and that he confuses our perception of Brutus at the end by having Antony confirm Brutus's idealized image of himself:

This was the noblest Roman of them all.
All the conspirators save only he
Did that they did in envy of great Caesar;

He, only in a general honest thought
And common good to all, made one of them.

(5.5)

This speech has become a crux in Shakespeare, but it presents difficulties mainly to those who cannot believe Antony's version of Brutus, which is Brutus's version of himself. The one person in the play whom Brutus does not fool is Cassius, who understands that he has succeeded with Brutus by appealing to motives that have nothing to do with Brutus's conception of honor. Brutus's soliloquy in 2.1 reinforces our sense that Shakespeare is presenting a man who is deceiving himself. The very feebleness of his rationalizations makes it difficult for even the friendliest critics to believe that Brutus is in touch with his own motives, or that they are noble.

Given Cassius's personality, it is not surprising that he exults in having "seduc'd" Brutus; for this triumph gives him a sense of power and the comforting feeling that, whatever their pretensions to disinterestedness, all men are competitive creatures like himself. As I have indicated, observing how Cassius accomplishes this seduction is one of our chief sources of information about the hidden side of Brutus. One of Cassius's obvious techniques is to flatter Brutus by insisting that he is the equal of Caesar and by speaking of his "hidden worthiness" (1.2). He will make Brutus aware of that worthiness by acting as his mirror: "I, your glass, / Will modestly discover to yourself / That of yourself which you yet know not of" (1.2). This is exactly what Cassius does, only it is not his hidden worthiness that Cassius discovers to Brutus, but his hidden envy, competitiveness, and aggression. Brutus cannot become consciously aware of this side of himself, of course, for that would threaten his idealized image; but, as we have seen, it has already been activated by Caesar's triumphs, and it is powerfully reinforced by his encounter with Cassius.

What transpires between Brutus and Cassius has been best described by a critic who has totally misunderstood it. According to Ernest Schanzer, Cassius can comprehend "people sufficiently like himself," such as Casca and Antony,

but with a man whose mental landscape is so remote from his own as that of Brutus, he is entirely adrift. Throughout this scene he tries to arouse in Brutus emotions toward Caesar identical with his own, feelings compounded of envy and resentment of Caesar's greatness, of thwarted ambition and neglected merit. He has clearly much in common with Milton's Satan. Both resent the domination of one above them in authority, assert their equality with him, mask as a campaign for liberation what is essentially one for self-aggrandisement, and try in their seduction-scenes to arouse in their victims the same feelings that motivated their own rebellion. (1963, 38–39)

What Schanzer fails to see, of course, is that Cassius does arouse in Brutus emotions toward Caesar similar to his own.

Cassius succeeds with Brutus despite the fact that, as Schanzer correctly observes, he is not terribly skillful as a seducer. He does not leave "unsaid *all* the things that could have moved Brutus" (Schanzer 1963, 38; my italics), but he leaves unsaid a good many. He makes some calculated appeals to Brutus's ancestry, pride, and competitiveness; but he makes no effort to address the perfectionistic side of Brutus by presenting his objections to Caesar in idealistic terms. Mostly, he pours out his own feelings in a compulsive, uncontrolled way. He tells his stories about the swimming match and Caesar's illness because these are the sorts of things that have been obsessively whirling about in his brain. They are not carefully selected for their effect upon Brutus. They affect Brutus as they do because they happen to correspond to the sorts of things that have been whirling about in *his* brain, much more dimly but just as obsessively; because Brutus's mental landscape is not, in fact, all that remote from Cassius's. Cassius succeeds with Brutus not because he possesses the skill of a Satan, an Iago, or a Lady Macbeth, but because Brutus is predisposed to be moved against Caesar and is therefore easy to seduce. Brutus indicates as much himself: "What you would work me to, I have some aim. / How I have thought of this, and of these times, / I shall recount hereafter" (1.2).

As a result of his encounter with Cassius, certain feelings that were already there, vexing Brutus and causing him to feel "at war" with himself, are reinforced: "Look how great Caesar has become. He is just an ordinary mortal, with failings like the rest of us, but he is being treated like a god. I am as good a man as he, in some ways better, but now I am one of the little men who must show him deference. If he becomes king, I shall always be an underling. He will have all of the glory, and there will be none left for me. This is an intolerable situation, and I will be a contemptible creature if I don't try to do something about it. I am the descendent, after all, of Lucius Junius Brutus, a great Roman hero who helped to drive the Tarquins from Rome when they tried to establish a monarchy. If I am to be worthy of my name, I must show as much daring as he." It is thoughts such as these, not so coherent, of course, and accompanied by the appropriate affects, rather than a concern for "the general good," that induce Brutus to join the conspiracy.

Brutus is also induced to join the conspiracy by the opportunity it offers him to be a great man. Cassius begins to feed Brutus's pride immediately by speaking of his "hidden worthiness"; and after he feels that Brutus is almost his, he plans to have writings thrown in at his windows, "all tending to the great opinion / That Rome holds of his name: wherein obscurely / Caesar's ambition shall be glanced at" (1.2). Cassius gets Brutus to kill Caesar for his ambition by playing upon Brutus's own desire for power and recognition. His last words to Brutus when they part in 1.2 are "think of the world," and the first thing he tells Brutus when the conspirators gather at his home is that they all honor him and wish "You had but that opinion of yourself / Which every noble Roman bears of you" (2.1). These crude devices are effective because they confirm Brutus's idealized image and encourage his dream of glory. The conspirators want Brutus because, as Casca says,

> he sits high in all the people's hearts;
> And that which would appear offence in us,
> His countenance, like richest alchemy,
> Will change to virtue and to worthiness.

> (1.3)

Brutus understands this and relishes this role, which is a tribute to his moral nobility. That is why he rejects the idea of approaching Cicero, whose "silver hairs," says Metellus Cimber, "Will purchase us a good opinion / And buy men's voices to commend our deeds" (2.1). As Harold Feldman observes, "there cannot be two popes in Rome. He and no other must be the one by whose virtue's light the black deed is to appear white" (1952, 320). As has been frequently noted, Brutus is a masterful person. Once he joins the conspiracy, he insists upon being its leader. Gordon Ross Smith counts "at least fourteen occasions in which Brutus proceeds to dominate or to domineer over his fellows" (1959, 368) and concludes that he has a "psychological necessity to exercise control" (369).

III

When we recognize the ambitious, competitive, recognition-hungry side of Brutus, it is no longer difficult to understand why he is so disturbed by the honors being heaped on Caesar and why he is so moved by Cassius's seemingly misdirected arguments. As the play proceeds, Cassius, however, becomes something of a puzzle. Given his vehement response to the idea of being subordinate to Caesar, why does he accept the domination of Brutus? Again and again, he allows the mistaken judgments of Brutus to govern the behavior of the conspirators, despite his invariably accurate prevision of the consequences. The explanation usually given for his disastrous concessions is that Cassius values Brutus's friendship so much that he does not want to risk it by opposing him on matters of policy. There may be some truth to this version of Cassius, but it is certainly not congruent with the picture of Cassius presented in the first act, where he sets out deliberately to seduce Brutus and then exults in his success. He seems clearly to be an arrogant-vindictive person for whom power and glory, rather than love and friendship, are the paramount values.

We must explain, then, not only the ability of Cassius to induce Brutus to join the conspiracy, but also the ability of Brutus to dominate Cassius once he embraces his cause. The arrogant-vindictive Cassius and the perfectionistic Brutus seem to be opposites—and, indeed, their differences often lead them to disagree; but they have complementary inner conflicts in which the dominant side of each appeals to the subordinate side of the other. Cassius thinks that he needs Brutus for purely political reasons, to gain the approval of the people, but he also has personal reasons for wanting to win Brutus to his cause. He has an underlying uneasiness about his aggressive behavior, and it is reassuring to him to feel that the noble Brutus is, at bottom, very much like himself. But, while he needs to overcome Brutus's virtue in order to reinforce his cynical view of human nature, he also needs to believe in it in order to satisfy his conflicting need to think of himself as honorable. He not only wants the people to feel that his actions are virtuous because of Brutus's participation; he wants also to feel this himself.

Cassius is undone by his inner conflicts. The shrewd, power-seeking part of him that planned the assassination and could have brought it to a successful issue is undermined by the part of him that hungers for Brutus's approval. When Brutus insists that they must let Antony live and let him speak at the funeral in order to demonstrate their righteousness, Cassius knows that these are serious mistakes; but he cannot resist because he, like Brutus, cannot give up the claim to virtue. To go along with Brutus is to be a "sacrificer," while to oppose him is to be a "butcher" (2.1). Brutus's rationalizations have a power over Cassius because they satisfy his own needs. We do not see Cassius being haunted by Caesar's ghost, as is Brutus, but his sense of guilt is evident in his deference to the moral authority of his fellow conspirator.[2]

Cassius hungers not only for Brutus's approval, but also for his love. One of his grievances against Caesar is that Caesar loves Brutus but does not like him: "Caesar doth bear me hard; but he loves Brutus. / If I were Brutus now and he were Cassius, / He should not humour me" (1.2). The implication of these lines is that Cassius would not have turned against Caesar if Caesar had loved him and that Brutus is a fool to do so. Cassius is engaged in a contest with Caesar for the love of Brutus, partly out of competitiveness and partly out of a powerful need for affection. His love need is largely hidden by his aggressive behavior early in the play, but it emerges quite vividly later. He submits to Brutus in part because he is fearful of losing his affection.

Cassius's need for Brutus's love and approval is most dramatically displayed in the great quarrel scene in act 4. Brutus's assault on Cassius is devastating. He tells him that he was wrong to have supported Lucius Pella, that he himself is "much condemned to have an itching palm" (4.3), and that he has escaped "chastisement" because "The name of Cassius honours this corruption." When Cassius expresses his outrage at being spoken to in this way and warns Brutus to "tempt him no farther," Brutus dismisses him contemptuously—"Away, slight man!"—and continues his attack.[3] Cassius is enraged by Brutus's insults, which strike at his most vulnerable points and exacerbate many of the feelings that had led him to murder Caesar. He has an impulse toward violent retaliation, but he does not strike back, either physically or verbally. Given the intensity of his rage, he is remarkably restrained in his response. This restraint is the result, I think, of his need of Brutus, which is even stronger than his desire to retaliate.

Cassius seems to be afraid that he is no good and that nobody loves him. He needs Brutus's love and approval to allay this fear, but when Brutus turns on him, his insecurity is greatly increased. He is tempted to restore his pride by attacking the man who has injured him, but to do so would leave him with no way to escape the feelings that have been intensified by Brutus's rejection. Instead of retaliating, therefore, he seeks reassurance. He tries to arouse Brutus's guilt and compassion by accusing Brutus of not loving him and showing how deeply he has been hurt. He endeavors to cope with the loss of Brutus's approval by making an appeal for unconditional acceptance, such as a child might seek from a parent. When Brutus refuses to overlook his faults, Cassius presents himself as a pathetic victim, "hated by one he loves," who "is aweary of the world" (4.3). He offers Brutus his dagger and his naked breast:

> within, a heart
> Dearer than Pluto's mine, richer than gold.
> If that thou be'st a Roman, take it forth.
> I, that denied thee gold, will give my heart.
> Strike as thou didst at Caesar; for I know,
> When thou didst hate him worst, thou lov'dst him better
> Than ever thou lov'dst Cassius.
>
>   (4.3)

This reminds us of Richard III's wooing of Lady Anne, and to some extent Cassius's speech may also be a tactic, but there is genuine emotion here, as there was not with Richard. Cassius's relationship with Brutus has become the most important thing in his life, and he is in despair at the thought that Brutus no longer loves him. He feels that Brutus cared more for the man he murdered than he does for him and that he is once again the least loved member of the triangle.

Brutus cannot resist Cassius's appeal, and he gives him the reassurance he seeks. He has enough love, he tells Cassius, to "bear with" him when his "rash humour" makes him "forgetful" (4.3). Cassius eagerly seizes upon Brutus's confession that he "was ill-temper'd too," for it permits him to be reconciled to Brutus without an undue loss of pride for having swallowed his insults. The news that Portia is dead also helps Cassius save face: "How scap'd I killing when I cross'd you so?" (4.3). Cassius is highly gratified when Brutus turns from thoughts of Portia to "bury all unkindness" with a bowl of wine: "My heart is thirsty for that noble pledge. / Fill, Lucius, till the wine o'erswell the cup. / I cannot drink too much of Brutus' love" (4.3). It is understandable that, when soon after this Brutus and Cassius have their disagreement about marching to Philippi, Cassius cannot make an effective resistance. The fate of the rebellion is less important to him than the fate of his relationship with Brutus. His compliance is rewarded when he and Brutus retire for the night: "Noble, noble

Cassius, / Good night and good repose" (4.3). He is once again the noble Cassius and he remains so until the end. Brutus's tribute to Cassius upon his death is just what he would have wanted: ". . . the last of all the Romans, fare thee well! / It is impossible that ever Rome / Should breed thy fellow" (5.3).

A number of critics have noted the shift in Shakespeare's treatment of Cassius. In act 1, Cassius is presented as the villain, the seducer, the Machiavel; but as the play progresses, he becomes an increasingly sympathetic figure. The reason for the shift in Shakespeare's treatment is, I think, the alteration that occurs in Cassius's personality. At the beginning of the play, he displays the kind of arrogant-vindictive traits that Shakespeare always treats negatively, but he becomes increasingly compliant as his needs for love and approval emerge and make him dependent upon Brutus. The very vulnerability that destroys him by making him unable to stand up to Brutus also makes him a more appealing figure. As Cassius changes, so does the play. It becomes less a play about the fate of the conspiracy and more a play about the fate of the Cassius-Brutus relationship. This accounts, I think, for the puzzling quality of the ending, which depicts not only the just defeat of the conspirators, but also their triumph. Cassius loses the war, but he wins the battle for Brutus's love. He is punished for the murder of Caesar, "even with the sword" with which he had killed him (5.3); but he seems triumphant in death. Through his suicide he achieves a kind of mastery of fate, and he is surrounded by loyal, affectionate companions who pay him tribute. When Titinius discovers him dead, he proclaims that "the sun of Rome is set" (5.3) and kills himself. Cassius gets us, like Brutus, to love him despite his faults. He does this in part, I think, by showing his emotions, whether it be his need for Brutus's love or his fear of being killed on his birthday. He seems appealing by contrast with Brutus, who is so much more tightly controlled and so out of touch with his feelings.

IV

Once Cassius whets him against Caesar, Brutus, no less than Cassius, is in the grip of his inner conflicts, which manifest themselves both before and after the assassination. After his conversation with Cassius, he cannot sleep, he feels himself to be living in "a hideous dream," and he compares his state to that of a kingdom suffering "an insurrection" (2.1). Because of his disturbed behavior, Portia concludes that Brutus has "some sick offense within [his] mind" (2.1). Brutus's state is similar to that of Macbeth once he thinks of murdering Duncan; but Macbeth knows, as Brutus does not, that he is in such turmoil because he is about to violate his moral ideals and to expose himself to self-hate. Macbeth's inner conflicts are revealed in great detail in his soliloquies, but Brutus is so busy disguising his feelings that even his soliloquy in the orchard provides only an indirect access to his inner state. His primary object in this soliloquy is to assure himself that he is not going to kill Caesar for any "personal cause" but "for the general" (2.1), though his reasoning is so weak that it is difficult to believe it gives him much comfort. Brutus's need to maintain his idealized image is so great that it is impossible for him to be aware of what is going on inside of him. At the same time, he is a man, as J. I. M. Stewart observes, "over the threshold of whose awareness a terrible doubt perpetually threatens to lap" (1949, 52).

We can see that doubt, and the need to suppress it, at work in Brutus's behavior toward his fellow conspirators. As he awaits their entrance, his true horror of what he is about to do rises momentarily to the surface:

> O conspiracy,
> Sham'st thou to show thy dang'rous brow by night,
> When evils are most free? O, then by day
> Where wilt thou find a cavern dark enough
> To mask thy monstrous visage? Seek none, conspiracy.
> Hide it in smiles and affability!
> For if thou path, thy native semblance on,
> Nor Erebus itself were dim enough
> To hide thee from prevention.
>
> (2.1)

Brutus recoils from the conspiracy here as a monstrous, hellish thing; but when Cassius proposes that they "swear [their] resolution," Brutus objects because taking an oath would make their plot seem like a shady enterprise:

> unto bad causes swear
> Such creatures as men doubt; but do not stain
> The even virtue of our enterprise,
> Nor th' insuppressive mettle of our spirits,

To think that or our cause or our performance
Did need an oath.

(2.1)

They must do what they do not just because they have sworn an oath, since oaths have been sworn for bad reasons by cowardly men, but because of their nobility of spirit and the virtue of their enterprise. Brutus's lengthy and passionate speech in response to Cassius's proposal is clearly defensive, a sign not of his firm belief in the justice of their cause, but of his need to deny his misgivings about it.

Brutus's need to oppose the taking of an oath does no real harm to the conspiracy, but his need to spare the life of Antony dooms it to ultimate failure. Here, too, he is governed by his inner conflicts. He needs to kill Caesar, but he also needs to see himself as a "purger" rather than as a "murderer." If they kill Antony, their "course will seem too bloody." Brutus needs to idealize the deed, to emphasize its spiritual significance, to turn it into a thing of beauty:

Let us be sacrificers, but not butchers, Caius.
We all stand up against the spirit of Caesar,
And in the spirit of men there is no blood.
O that we could come by Caesar's spirit
And not dismember Caesar! But, alas,
Caesar must bleed for it! And, gentle friends,
Let's kill him boldly, but not wrathfully;
Let's carve him as a dish fit for the gods,
Not hew him as a carcass fit for hounds.

(2.1)

The bloodiness of the deed itself and Antony's later description of it (5.1) stand in ironic contrast to Brutus's conception. Brutus is driven by his psychological needs to construct a version of the assassination with which he can live and to impose it upon his fellow conspirators. His needs lead him also to deny the threat that Antony poses and to minimize his stature. Cassius is much more in touch with reality. He fears not only Antony's love for Caesar, but also his resourcefulness:

We shall find of him
A shrewd contriver; and you know, his means,
If he improve them, may well stretch so far

As to annoy us all.

(2.1)

Despite his knowledge of the consequences, Cassius accedes to Brutus's wishes, driven by his need for Brutus's affection and approval. The conspiracy is at once facilitated and destroyed by the interaction of the inner conflicts of these two men.

After the assassination, Brutus seems as much out of touch with reality as he was before. He persists in maintaining his idealized version of the conspirators' motives and the nature of their deed. They are "Caesar's friends," since they "have abridg'd / His time of fearing death" (3.1)—though Caesar had claimed that death was one thing he did not fear. Brutus tries to sanctify the act by having the murderers bathe their hands in Caesar's blood, and he expects everyone else to see the conspiracy as he intends. He has the illusion that he can control the meaning of events, both for himself and for others. He will give Antony good reasons why Caesar was dangerous, "Or else were this a savage spectacle" (3.1). His need to prevent the murder from seeming a savage spectacle leads to his second great tactical error, granting Antony permission to speak at Caesar's funeral. Once again Cassius accurately foresees the consequences—"Know you how much the people may be mov'd / By that which he will utter?" (3.1); but, because of his inner conflicts, he can do nothing about it. Brutus is confident that the people will believe him for his honor and accept his word that he slew Caesar for the good of Rome. Since it is essential to the credibility of his version of the assassination that Caesar "have all true rites and lawful ceremonies," Antony must be allowed to speak.

Brutus is living in a dream world, the nature of which is dictated by his need to preserve his image of himself as an honorable man. He is similar in some ways to Conrad's Lord Jim. Each character has an idealized image of himself that he violates, but neither can tolerate the self-hate that would result from acknowledging the true meaning of what he has done, and both follow Stein's advice on how to be: they live with their eyes shut and follow their dream to the end. Because of the doubt that perpetually threatens to lap over the threshold of their awareness, they are extremely touchy about anything that threatens their idealized version of events or of themselves (see Paris, 1974).

Brutus's touchiness is most vividly displayed in his quarrel with Cassius. He bristles immediately when Cassius accuses him of having done him wrong: "Judge me, you gods! wrong I mine enemies? / And if not so, how should I wrong a brother?" (4.2). Brutus is so disturbed by Cassius's charge because it threatens his image of himself as a man who could never do wrong, an image to which he clings more and more tenaciously as a defense against his guilt in relation to Caesar. He reacts to Cassius's accusation by appealing to the gods to clear him of the charge of having wronged his enemies (a charge that has not been made by Cassius) and by reaffirming his rectitude. Brutus is threatened also by the particular nature of Cassius's complaint, which is that he has condemned Lucius Pella for taking bribes even though Cassius had written in his support. Cassius wants Brutus to accept his own more pragmatic value system, but for Brutus to do so would mean giving up the claim to absolute rightness, without which he would feel like his despised self. The assassination of Caesar was justified only if it was done by honorable men for honorable motives:

> Remember March; the ides of March remember.
> Did not great Julius bleed for justice sake?
> What villain touch'd his body that did stab
> And not for Justice? What, shall one of us,
> That struck the foremost man of all this world
> But for supporting robbers—shall we now
> Contaminate our fingers with base bribes,
> And sell the mighty space of our large honours
> For so much trash as may be grasped thus?
> I had rather be a dog and bay the moon
> Than such a Roman.
>
> (4.3)

Any act that calls into question the honor of conspirators threatens to turn them into villains.

It is inconceivable that Brutus should yield in this quarrel, since Cassius is threatening his primary defense against guilt and self-hate. Indeed, Brutus must denounce Cassius in order to reaffirm his standards. As we have seen, this denunciation is devastating to Cassius, and he reacts at first with rage and threats of violence. Brutus responds by dismissing Cassius with contempt:

> There is no terror, Cassius, in your threats;
> For I am arm'd so strong in honesty
> That they pass by me as the idle wind,
> Which I respect not.
>
> (4.3)

For Brutus to be intimidated by Cassius is to doubt the power of his virtue, which should render him invulnerable. When his threats do not work, Cassius begins to plead for love and acceptance; and Brutus, once again in the superior position, responds with indulgence. They are able to make up because Cassius becomes self-effacing and takes the blame upon himself. Though it is Brutus who has been most unrestrained and violent in his behavior, it is Cassius who apologizes for his "rash humour." Once Cassius retreats, Brutus can concede that he has been "ill-temper'd too." Since this is one of the rare occasions on which Brutus admits to any failing whatsoever, Cassius appreciates its significance.

Brutus persists to the end in his haughtiness and self-delusion. When Octavius Caesar, in the parley before the battle of Philippi, says that he "was not born to die on Brutus's sword," Brutus's reply is absurdly self-aggrandizing: "O, if thou were the noblest of thy strain, / Young man, thou couldst not die more honourable" (5.1). He tells Cassius that he "bears too great a mind" ever to "go bound to Rome" (5.1), and he proclaims himself on the battlefield as "Marcus Brutus, I! / Brutus, my country's friend!" Before he commits suicide, he pays tribute to himself:

> Countrymen,
> My heart doth joy that yet in all my life
> I found no man but he was true to me.
> I shall have glory by this losing day
> More than Octavius and Mark Antony
> By this vile conquest shall attain unto.
>
> (5.5)

Much like Othello, Brutus is cheering himself up. His triumph derives not from self-knowledge or defiance, but from a persistent and determined blindness. He simply refuses to acknowledge that he is not the honorable man he proclaims himself to be and that his search for glory has failed—though if he refuses to recognize it, perhaps it has not.

Brutus is not without inner discomfort. He is visited twice by Caesar's ghost, which seems to be a manifestation of his own sense of guilt rising from the unconscious, and he interprets these visitations as a sign that his "hour is come" (5.5). He interprets Cassius's death as an indication that the conspirators are being punished by the spirit of Caesar: "O Julius Caesar, thou art mighty yet! / Thy spirit walks abroad and turns our swords / In our own proper entrails" (5.3). He utters similar sentiments as he is about to run upon his own sword: "Caesar, now be still. / I kill'd not thee with half so good a will" (5.5). His suicide is at once a means of escape, of triumph, and of self-punishment. He can relieve his sense of guilt by paying in this way for his crime. Some critics feel, indeed, that Brutus has "deep inner-longings for punishment and death" (Feldman 1952, 321) that account for his disastrous mistakes. "Caesar lives on," says Lynn de Gerenday, "in the guilt of the conspirators, projected into an expectation of, and desire for punishment which is present through much of the play in Brutus's self-destructive course of action" (1974, 30).

Brutus's guilt and expectation of punishment manifest themselves strongly at the end of the play, but, as we have seen, they are not primarily responsible for his earlier decisions to spare Antony and to allow him to speak at Caesar's funeral. As G. Wilson Knight observes, "both Brutus and Macbeth fail in their schemes not so much because of outward events and forces, but through the working of that part of their natures which originally forbade the murder" (1965, 128). That part of their natures manifests itself differently, however, in each. In Macbeth it manifests itself in self-hate and a fear of retribution that drive him to become a savage tyrant. In Brutus it manifests itself in his need to construct a version of himself and his deeds with which he can live and to blind himself to conflicting realities. He experiences some inner conflict both before and after the assassination, but he manages to ward off his guilt and self-hate through most of the play and to maintain his self-delusion to the end.

Shakespeare has given us a brilliant psychological portrait, not only of a remarkably well-defended man, but also of a man who is destroyed by the very success of his defenses. This portrait tends to be obscured, however, by the shift in his treatment of Brutus. Through most of the play he calls our attention to Brutus's self-deception, but toward the end the rhetoric seems to support Brutus's glorified version of himself. In an effort to protect his leader, Lucilius says that he is Brutus and seeks to be killed. When his identity is revealed, he declares that "no enemy / Shall ever take alive the noble Brutus," that when he is found, "alive or dead, / He will be found like Brutus, like himself" (5.4). Clitus, Dardanius, and Volumnius refuse to help Brutus kill himself, which testifies to their love for him and leads to Brutus's tribute to his ability to inspire fidelity in his fellows. Strato, who does assist him, proclaims to the enemy that "Brutus only overcame himself, / And no man else hath honour by his death" (5.5). "So

Brutus should be found," says Lucilius, who is glad that his "saying" has "prov'd . . . true" (5.5). Antony proclaims Brutus to be "the noblest Roman of them all," the only one of the conspirators who was motivated by the "common good" rather than by "envy of great Caesar"; and Octavius says that Brutus should be used "according to his virtues . . . / With all respect and rites of burial" (5.5)

Throughout the play, Shakespeare has juxtaposed Brutus's version of reality with other versions closer to the truth so that we will not be taken in by Brutus's exaltation of himself. It might be argued that he is doing the same thing here by juxtaposing this glorified version of Brutus with the evidence we have seen that Brutus is a haunted, guilty man who has a need to punish himself. This reading can explain the speeches of Brutus and his friends (whom Brutus has always taken in), but not those, I think, of Antony and Octavius, which leave us with an extremely positive final impression of Brutus. Kittredge says that Antony's speech is "a valediction emphasizing what Shakespeare has taken pains to keep before the audience from the outset—the patriotism of Brutus as contrasted with the mixed emotions of the other assassins" (1966, 102). In view of the pains Shakespeare has taken all along to emphasize the extent of Brutus's self-deception, it is puzzling that he has Antony at the end endorse Brutus's version of himself. The shift in Shakespeare's treatment of Cassius can be explained, as I have tried to show, by the alteration in Cassius's personality. The shift in his treatment of Brutus remains a mystery.

7
Antony and Cleopatra

I

The most puzzling thing about *Antony and Cleopatra* is the shift in its treatment of the protagonists that occurs in the fourth act. As George Bernard Shaw observes, "after giving a faithful picture of the soldier broken down by debauchery, and the typical wanton in whose arms such men perish, Shakespeare finally strains all his huge command of rhetoric and stage pathos to give a theatrical sublimity to the wretched end of the business, and to persuade foolish spectators that the world was well lost by the twain" (1934, 7). I do not agree with Shaw's characterization of the principals as a debauchee and a wanton; but it is true, I think, that, while most of the play presents Antony's bewitchment by Cleopatra as shameful and self-destructive, the ending glorifies their relationship and shows them to be the ones who are truly victorious. This disparity between the first three acts of the play and its conclusion makes it difficult for the interpreter to decide whether *Antony and Cleopatra* is "a tragedy of lyrical inspiration, presenting the relationship of its central figures as triumphant over adverse circumstance" or "a pitiless exposure of human frailties, of the dissipation of spiritual energies through wilful surrender to passion" (Traversi 1963, 79).

There have been four main responses to this problem. Some critics have insisted that the play is "a depiction of tragic folly and self-deception" throughout, while others have claimed that it is "a triumphant celebration of spiritual transcendence, a testament to the transforming power of love" (Kuriyama 1977, 326). The growing tendency among critics is to reject readings that choose one of these alternatives and to recognize that "either interpretation can be defended by reference to what Shakespeare has written" (Traversi 1963, 79). Such critics themselves, however, are split into two groups. Some see the apparently conflicting components of the play "less as contradictory than as complementary aspects of a unified artistic creation" (Traversi 1963, 79), while others contend that the play does indeed contain contradictions and is artistically flawed as a result. The best effort to subsume the play's contradictions into an artistic unity has been made by Janet Adelman (1973), while the best effort to account for its flaws, and its power in spite of those flaws, has been made by Constance Kuriyama (1977). My position is close to that of Kuriyama, who feels that "Shakespeare's ambivalence toward the characters" and their values "is extreme" (1977, 327) and that this ambivalence has not been brought under artistic control. Kuriyama offers a Freudian explanation of the ambivalence, while I shall attempt to account for it in Horneyan terms.

The problems in this play derive in large part, I believe, from its rhetoric, which is inconsistent with itself and, at times, with Shakespeare's mimetic portrait of the protagonists. Some critics feel that there are deficiencies in Shakespeare's characterization of Cleopatra, that she is illegitimately transformed from the strumpet of the opening scenes to the grand and faithful figure of the last two acts; but I believe that the mimetic portraits of both Antony and Cleopatra are consistent throughout and that the complaints about Cleopatra derive from a failure to understand the nature of her relationship with Antony. Though Shakespeare's characterization of his protagonists is consistent, his rhetorical treatment of them is not. Through the first three acts of the play, the rhetoric calls our attention to the self-destructiveness of Antony's behavior and the manipulativeness of Cleopatra's; but in the last two it obscures the responsibility of Antony and Cleopatra for their own fates and reinforces their self-glorification. In these acts, the characters subvert the rhetoric by which they are surrounded. The critics who see the play as "a depiction of tragic folly and self-deception" are responding to the rhetoric of the first three acts of the play and to the mimetic portrait of the protagonists throughout, but they tend to ignore or to rationalize away the glorifying rhetoric at the end. Those who see Antony and Cleopatra as triumphant at the end are justified by the rhetoric of that part of the play, but they allow it to blind them to the fact that the protagonists are cheering themselves up.

In the pages that follow I shall analyze first Shakespeare's rhetorical treatment of Antony and Cleopatra and then his mimetic portrayal of these characters. I shall pay particular attention to the dynamics of their relationship, to its inner contradictions, and to the way in which they manage to turn defeat into victory. After we have considered Antony and Cleopatra psychologically, we shall be able to see how the rhetoric moves from insight to blindness and how the mimetic dimension of the play supports a sense both of tragic folly and of transcendence. Finally, I shall attempt to account for the play's structural problems by seeing them as a manifestation of Shakespeare's inner conflicts.

II

Antony and Cleopatra begins as a tragedy of character in which the protagonist's flaws are directly responsible for his destruction and ends as a tragedy of fate in which responsibility for his downfall is placed upon forces beyond his control. In the first three acts of the play, Antony is condemned by the rhetoric, while in the last two acts he is glorified. Though the play clearly begins as a tragedy, the ending has such a powerful aura of wish-fulfillment that many critics have felt it to be more like a romance. I can find no way of accounting for these shifts in structure and rhetoric that preserves the play's artistic integrity.

As has often been observed, no simple choice can be made between Egypt and Rome, love and power, or the other sets of opposites within the play. Each term has its attractions and its limitations, its points of superiority and of inferiority to its opposite. As Norman Rabkin says, "the power of the play derives in good part from the full and satisfying reality Shakespeare gives to each of the poles between which the hero is drawn" (1981, 67). There is one question that must be exempted from this complementary view, however. The opening scenes of the play ask whether Antony can break away from Cleopatra, and the rhetoric leaves no doubt that he will be lost, not only as a Roman leader, but as a man, if he fails to do so.

There is an extraordinary amount of criticism of the hero in this play. It opens with Philo calling him a "strumpet's fool," and this is followed by assaults from such characters as Demetrius, Octavius, Pompey, Enobarbus, Canidius, and Scarus. Antony is not only criticized by others, but he is subject to recurrent bouts of self-condemnation. Whatever their relation to Antony, his critics say much the same things about him; and this, combined with the sheer bulk of the criticism, gives their commentary considerable thematic authority. They are all Romans, to be sure, and their view of Antony is conditioned by a set of values that is itself subject to question in the play, but there is no strong counterbalancing rhetoric or suggestion that Antony is being misjudged or misunderstood. If there is a positive way of looking at Antony, it is not very evident in the first three acts of the play.

From the Roman point of view, Antony's faults are numerous. He "fishes, drinks, and wastes / The lamps of night in revel," gives away kingdoms "for a mirth," tipples with slaves, and mingles with "knaves that smell of sweat" (1.4). He is like an adolescent who behaves in ways he knows to be foolish because he cannot give up "present pleasure" (1.4). This is the perspective of Octavius, who hopes that Antony will leave his "lascivious wassails" and come to Rome in order to help him fight Pompey; and it is also the perspective of Pompey, who describes Antony as an "amorous surfeiter" and who counts on his degeneracy to keep him in Egypt.

It is not Antony's pleasures by which the Romans are most disturbed, however, but his loss of manliness and self-control. They would not object to his amusing himself with Cleopatra—Caesar and Pompey the Great had done that; but they do object to his becoming so absorbed in his relationship with her that he is ignoring his public responsibilities. Love should be in man's life a thing apart; it has become Antony's whole existence. By seeking his glory in love rather than in battle, he is behaving according to a feminine rather than a masculine code of values, and this is why Octavius sees him as effeminate (1.4). Images of emasculation abound in the play. Cleopatra surrounds herself with eunuchs, puts her "tire and mantles" on Antony while she wears "his sword Philippan" (1.5), and wishes to "appear . . . for a man" (3.7) in the battle of Actium. Antony was once the greatest soldier in the world, but now his "captain's heart / . . . reneges all temper / And is become the bellows and the fan / To cool a gypsy's lust" (1.1).

The most serious charge against Antony is made by Philo in the opening lines of the play when he says that "this dotage of our general's / O'erflows the measure." Antony is excessively and foolishly in love. He is "the triple pillar of the world transform'd / Into a strumpet's fool" (1.1). His fall is all the greater because he has been such an epic figure and the object of his affection is so unworthy. Antony opposes to this a glorified version of his relationship with Cleopatra:

> Kingdoms are clay; our dungy earth alike
> Feeds beast as man. The nobleness of life
> Is to do thus [*embracing*]; when such a mutual pair
> And such a twain can do't, in which I bind,

On pain of punishment, the world to weet
We stand up peerless.

(1.1)

Antony answers the Roman criticism of him by saying that it is nobler to live for love than for power when the lovers are of such stature, but the Romans deny Cleopatra's nobility and Antony is not sure of it himself. In the next scene, he invites the messenger to "Name Cleopatra as she is call'd in Rome" (1.2). He blames himself for his idleness, wishes that he "had never seen her," and realizes that he will "lose [himself] in dotage" if he does not break his "Egyptian fetters" (1.2).

Antony seems to have broken his fetters when he leaves for Rome, and his marriage to Octavia seems to confirm his bond to his country. But through Enobarbus's descriptions in 2.2 Shakespeare keeps Cleopatra's charms before us and lets us know that Antony can never "leave her utterly." By 3.6, he has returned to "his Egyptian dish" (2.6), as Enobarbus had predicted, and the Romans are speaking of him as before: "Cleopatra / Hath nodded him to her. He hath given his empire / Up to a whore" (3.6).

Antony has not, then, broken his Egyptian fetters; and once he returns to Cleopatra, he makes a number of errors that fully demonstrate his dotage. Against all reason and good advice he determines to fight by sea, primarily because Cleopatra prefers it: "So our leader's led, / And we are women's men" (3.7). He allows Cleopatra to be present at the battle; and, when she flees, Antony "Claps on his sea-wing, and (like a doting mallard) / . . . flies after her" (3.10). With this act, he destroys his chances of defeating Caesar, for his has "given example" for the flight of his men "Most grossly by his own!" (3.10). When Cleopatra begs forgiveness, saying she "little thought" he "would have followed" her "fearful sails," Antony confesses his emasculation: "You did know / How much you were my conqueror, and that / My sword, made weak by my affection, would / Obey it on all cause" (3.10). When Cleopatra again begs pardon, Antony proclaims that her kiss "repays" him for "All that is won and lost," but set against this is Scarus's remark that "We have kiss'd away / Kingdoms and provinces" (3.10).

Through the end of the third act, the rhetoric of the play remains relentlessly critical of Antony. When Cleopatra asks Enobarbus who is at fault for the disaster at Actium, he replies, "Antony only, that would make his will / Lord of his reason. . . . /

The itch of his affection should not then / Have nick'd his cap-tainship" (3, 13). Shakespeare seems to subscribe to Plutarch's view of Antony:

> There Antonius shewed plainely, that he had not onely lost the corage and hart of an Emperor, but also of a valliant man, and that he was not his owne man: (proving that true which an old man spake in myrth, that the soule of a lover lived in another body, and not in his owne) he was so caried away with the vaine love of this woman, as if he had bene glued unto her, and that she could not have removed without moving of him also. For when he saw Cleopatraes shippe under saile, he forgot, forsooke, and betrayed them that fought for him, and imbarked upon a galley with five bankes of owers, to follow her that had already begon to overthrow him, and would in the end be his utter destruction. (Bullough 1964, 301)

Enobarbus now becomes Antony's chief critic. He sees Antony's challenge to fight Octavius in single combat as a sign that Caesar has "subdu'd / His judgment too" (3.13), and he wonders if he should remain loyal to so foolish a master. When Antony becomes furious and vows to "fight maliciously," Enobarbus regards this not as heroism, but as a form of bravado, born of desperation, that will have destructive consequences: "When valour preys on rea-son, / It eats the sword it fights with" (3.13). Shakespeare gives rhetorical support to this judgment by having Maecenas repeat it in the next scene: "When one so great begins to rage, He's hunted / Even to falling . . . / . . . Never anger / Made good guard for itself" (4.1).

The first three acts of the play present, then, a tragedy of character in which Antony's overwhelming passion for Cleopatra leads him to behave in shameful and foolish ways and results in his destruction. The protagonists are occasionally presented in a favorable light, but the rhetoric surrounding them is predomi-nantly negative. Cleopatra is a manipulative, emasculating woman, and Antony is the "noble ruin of her magic" (3.10). All of this changes in the last two acts, where Antony's destruction is blamed on fate, Cleopatra is vindicated, and the hero and heroine are consistently glorified.

In act 3, Antony is presented as an increasingly foolish, but also as an increasingly sympathetic figure. He behaves "like a doting mallard" at the battle of Actium, but he suffers greatly from his loss of honor and seeks some way to restore it. His rage when Cleopatra allows Thyreus to kiss her hand reveals that, with part of his mind at least, he sees her as a whore and himself as a strumpet's fool. He has lost the world for love, but can he be sure of Cleopatra? These are major issues in the remainder of the play. After Actium he has no chance of defeating Caesar, but it is very important to him to restore his manly honor and to preserve his grandiose conception of his love relationship. There is a sense of triumph at the end because Shakespeare allows him to do these things. He surrounds him with a favorable rhetoric that obscures his faults and turns him into a glamorous hero.

Much of this is accomplished in act 4, where Shakespeare emphasizes Antony's manliness and generosity. In scene 2, Antony declares that he "will live, / Or bathe [his] dying honour in the blood / Shall make it live again." He cannot control his fate, but he can live up to the soldier's code and prove his courage. He expresses gratitude to his servants and wishes that he might serve them as well as they have served him. In scene 4, his warlike image is refurbished. Whereas before he had been a man who would "make no wars without doors" (2.1), he now rises "betime" to business that he loves and declares war to be a "royal occupation." He leaves Cleopatra "like a man of steel," giving her "a soldier's kiss," rather than one of an amorous surfeiter. In scene 5, Enobarbus deserts and Antony demonstrates his magnanimity by sending "his treasure after." Enobarbus's rhetorical function is now to glorify Antony, and he performs this function all the more effectively for having been so critical earlier: "O Antony, / Thou mine of bounty, how wouldst thou have paid / My latter service, when my turpitude / Thou dost so crown with gold!" (4.6). Caesar's soldier calls Antony "A Jove," and Enobarbus, who feels himself to be the greatest traitor of all time, proclaims him "Nobler than my revolt is infamous" (4.9). The manner of Enobarbus's death is a further tribute to Antony. Meanwhile, Antony restores his honor by fighting valiantly. He receives a tribute from Scarus ("O my brave Emperor, this is fought indeed!"—4.7), and he is exalted by Cleopatra when he returns from "The world's great snare uncaught" (4.8). In Plutarch, the encounter after Actium is only an excursion, but Shakespeare makes it into a major battle in order to give Antony the opportunity to regain his heroic stature.

Antony is in danger of losing everything in the next day's battle when his fleet yields and he is convinced that Cleopatra has betrayed him. Once he is reassured of her love by the false news of her death, however, he begins to glorify himself, her, and their relationship. Since his "torch is out" (4.14) he is ready to die, but he envisions a glory in death far exceeding that of a Roman emperor. He and Cleopatra will be the most famous lovers in history, outdoing in Elysium even Dido and Aeneas. His suicide will be not only a means of reunion with Cleopatra, but also a proof of his courage and a triumph over Caesar, who would like to take him back to Rome and subject him to humiliation.

Antony receives tributes from others as well as from himself. Eros kills himself instead of his master in order to "escape the sorrow / Of Antony's death"; and, when Antony attempts suicide, the guards who discover him proclaim that "The star is fallen" and "time is at his period" (4.14). In his last speech, Antony asks us to ignore the "miserable change" now at his end and to remember his "former fortunes / Wherein I liv'd the greatest prince o' th' world" (4.15). There is nothing in the last two acts of the play to counteract this image, to remind us that he has not always been, in Cleopatra's words, "Noblest of men" (4.15).

It is Cleopatra, of course, who exalts Antony most extravagantly. She has done so throughout the play, as in 1.5 where she calls him "The demi-Atlas of this earth, the arm / And burgonet of men." When Antony dies, her language becomes even more hyperbolic. He was the "crown o' th' earth" without whom all distinctions are meaningless and "this dull world . . . is / No better than a sty" (4.15). Through Cleopatra's celebration of him, Antony becomes increasingly magnificent.

> His legs bestrid the ocean: his rear'd arm
> Crested the world. His voice was propertied
> As are all the tuned spheres, and that to friends;
> But when he meant to quail and shake the orb,
> He was as rattling thunder. . . .
>   In his livery
> Walk'd crowns and crownets. Realms and islands were
> As plates dropp'd from his pocket.
>
>   (5.2)

Usually imagination can create forms more wonderful than those produced by nature, but Antony was beyond anything imagination could create. He was "nature's piece 'gainst fancy, / Condemning shadows quite."

No one else has such an exalted view of Antony, but even his enemies are extraordinarily moved by his death, which they regard as a cosmic event that should have been marked by disruptions in the natural order: "The breaking of so great a thing should make / A greater crack" (5.1). "It is tidings," says Caesar, "To wash the eyes of kings!" Antony's suicide is treated as an act of courage and honor, and his faults are minimized:

> MAECENAS.   His taints and honours
>   Wag'd equal with him.
> AGRIPPA.   A rarer spirit never
>   Did steer humanity; but you gods will give us
>   Some faults to make us men.
>
>   (5.1)

Antony is no longer "the abstract of all faults / That all men follow" (1.4). Caesar laments that they "could not stall together / In the whole world" because their "stars" were "unreconcilable" (5.1). This complements Cleopatra's view that Antony is the victim of "the injurious gods" and "the false huswife Fortune" (4.15).

Cleopatra's point of view dominates the last act of the play and becomes one of the chief vehicles of Shakespeare's rhetoric. In its presentation of Cleopatra, the play follows a vindication pattern. From the outset, there are two views of Cleopatra—the Roman view of her as a strumpet and Antony's view of her as a majestic woman who is worthy of his devotion. Whereas the Romans see a "ne'er-lust-wearied Antony" under the spell of "salt Cleopatra" (2.2), Antony sees himself and Cleopatra as "peerless" lovers in whose relationship lies "The nobleness of life" (1.1). As the play unfolds, Antony's view of Cleopatra comes more and more to prevail. At the beginning, Cleopatra is an unsympathetic figure who is trying to manipulate Antony into demonstrating his love for her while she conceals the depth of her own feelings. After Antony leaves, however, Shakespeare shows us how much Cleopatra adores him. Antony feels that "every thing becomes" Cleopatra—"to chide, to laugh, / To weep" (1.2); and Cleopatra feels the same way about Antony: "Be'st thou sad or merry, / The violence of either then becomes, / So does it no man else" (1.5). We see that Antony is the love of Cleopatra's life—"Did I, Charmian, / Ever love Caesar so?"—and we are assured of her devotion. Our sympathies are with her when she hears of Antony's marriage (2.5) and when she hopes that she can win him away from Octavia (3.3). When Antony's faith in her is shaken in acts 3 and 4, the Roman view of her emerges; but the audience knows that she has been true, and his belief in her is quickly restored.

Cleopatra's vindication is completed in acts 4 and 5, in which she demonstrates her loyalty to Antony and proves herself, through the manner of her death, to be most royal. In 3.12, Caesar sends Thyreus to win her away from Antony: "Promise, / And in our name, what she requires. . . . / Women are not in their best fortunes strong, but want will perjure / The ne'er-touch'd Vestal." By being truer to Antony than many of his men, Cleopatra disproves Caesar's view of her and thwarts his desires. She thwarts him also by committing suicide so that he cannot display her in his triumph. Just as Antony regains the honor he lost at Actium by his bravery in battle, so Cleopatra redeems her act of cowardice and earns her royal status by the courage with which she confronts death. Cleopatra is, at the end, an exceedingly glamorous figure. She is so beautiful in death that even the prosaic Caesar imagines her as ready to "catch another Antony / In her strong toil of grace" (5.2).

The most powerful tribute to Antony and Cleopatra is put into the mouth of Caesar, the man who had been their greatest detractor. Even though Antony was married to his sister, Caesar recognizes that he and Cleopatra belong together in death:

> She shall be buried by Antony.
> No grave upon the earth shall clip in it
> A pair so famous. High events as these
> Strike those that made them; and their story is
> No less in pity than his glory which
> Brought them to be lamented.

>   (5.2)

Cleopatra has been regarded through most of the play as a strumpet and Antony as a fool, but this speech confirms Antony's view of himself and of Cleopatra. Caesar sees his own glory as a derivative of theirs. The highest event that has occurred is not his victory but their deaths, and his glory lies in having "Brought them to be lamented."

As Cleopatra is vindicated, so, too, is Antony, for we see that she is not an unworthy object of devotion. The difficulty is that the play never resolves the problem of Antony's dotage. However majestic or loyal Cleopatra may be, Antony's behavior has been truly shameful; and though he redeems himself to some extent in act 4, he does not do enough to wipe out the disgrace of Actium or to counteract the negative rhetoric of the first three acts. While Cleopatra seems more and more to deserve the tributes she receives, Antony seems her peer only because of the greatness he had achieved before his passion for her destroyed him. Antony remains the doting lover, but his absorption in Cleopatra is now glorified. The contribution his mistakes have made to his destruction is deemphasized; he is presented as the victim of the gods, or fortune, or the stars. Antony no longer blames himself, and no one else blames him. The gods have given him faults to make him human, and Shakespeare's rhetoric has given him a stature he does not seem to deserve.

III

The tensions in *Antony and Cleopatra*, and the resulting critical controversies, are created not only by inconsistencies in the rhetoric, but also by disparities between rhetoric and mimesis. Shakespeare's characterization of Antony and Cleopatra is consistent throughout, but he seems less clearsighted about his protagonists toward the end than he had been at the beginning. Their self-exaltation and evasion of responsibility make good sense in psychological terms, but Shakespeare seems to have no critical perspective upon their behavior. Those who see the play as "a depiction of tragic folly and self-deception" throughout are responding correctly, I think, to Shakespeare's mimetic portrait of Antony and Cleopatra, though they are ignoring the rhetoric of the last two acts. That rhetoric is disturbing to many because it seems to be in conflict with the earlier rhetoric of the play and with the characters whom Shakespeare has actually created.

It is time, now, to look at those characters. Cleopatra is perhaps Shakespeare's most fascinating portrait of a woman, and the tormented Antony is a marvelous creation. The relationship between them is one of the most complex and fully drawn in all of Shakespeare. Most of the critical attention given to this play has been devoted to other matters, but the play is very much about Antony and Cleopatra as imagined human beings and about their interaction with each other (see Barroll, 1984). It is only when we have understood the protagonists in motivational terms that we can see how they relate, often in a subversive way, to other aspects of the drama. Both Antony and Cleopatra have contradictory needs that produce inconsistent, often self-destructive behavior. In the first three acts of the play, their contradictory needs put them at odds with themselves and each other; but after their defeat, Antony and Cleopatra are able to resolve their conflicts, to rebuild their defenses, and to restore their sense of themselves as glorious beings.

It is important to recognize that Antony and Cleopatra glorify themselves and their relationship not only at the end of the play, but from the very beginning. The Romans see Antony as motivated by the pursuit of sensual pleasure, but he sees himself as pursuing "The nobleness of life" (1.1), which lies in love when the lovers are "such a mutual pair" as he and Cleopatra.[1] Antony and Cleopatra see themselves as the most glamorous man and woman in the world; and it is this sense of glamor, and not simply sensual intoxication, that accounts for the romantic intensity of their relationship. When Antony seeks to leave, Cleopatra reminds him of his words when he "su'd staying":

> Eternity was in our lips and eyes,
> Bliss in our brows' bent, none our parts so poor
> But was a race of heaven. They are so still,
> Or thou, the greatest soldier of the world,
> Art turn'd the greatest liar.

(1.3)

Even their physical attraction is experienced by them as part of a search for glory.

I do not wish to deny the importance of that physical attraction, but for Cleopatra it derives, in part at least, from Antony's being "the greatest soldier of the world." We can see how important Antony's power is to her when, after his departure, she wants to have Herod's head, but asks, "how, when Antony is gone / Through whom I might command it?" (3.3). Antony, to sooth her feelings, sends her an "orient pearl" and promises "to mend the petty present" by piecing "Her opulent throne with kingdoms. All the East, / . . . shall call her mistress" (1.5). As queen of Egypt, Cleopatra has an exalted station but relatively little power; through Antony, she becomes not only the most majestic, but also the most potent woman in the world. When she wonders where Antony is now, she clearly identifies with the horse on whom she imagines him sitting:

> "O happy horse, to bear the weight of Antony!"
> Do bravely, horse! for wot'st thou whom thou mov'st?
> The demi-Atlas of this earth, the arm
> And burgonet of men.

(1.5)

The sexual overtones of this passage are obvious. For Cleopatra, the thrill of bearing the weight of Antony is related to his greatness.

It has been the pattern for Cleopatra to attach herself to great men; Caesar and Pompey preceded Antony. She derives from this more than political power; it feeds her pride in her feminine wiles, in her sexual prowess and irresistibility. She dreams of passing the time while Antony is away by betraying "Tawny-finn'd fishes" and imagining "every one an Antony" (2.5). Cleopatra's idealized image of herself as the most desirable woman in the world can be confirmed only by capturing the most desirable man. This is the main reason for her magnification of Antony; she exalts herself by glorifying him, just as a fisherman inflates his accomplishment by exaggerating the size of his catch.

Cleopatra describes herself as "morsel for a monarch" (1.5), but she wants to be more than a prized possession. She wants, rather, to dominate the man who loves her. As we have seen, there is much imagery of emasculation and of Cleopatra's wanting to play the male role. She remembers with delight the time she put her "tires and mantles" on Antony whilst she "wore his sword Philippan" (2.5). If Antony is the "Herculean Roman" (1.3), Cleopatra is his Omphale. As the play opens, we see how Cleopatra manipulates Antony by keeping him on the defensive, by questioning his love and urging him to heed the summons of "the scare-bearded Caesar" or the "shrill-tongu'd Fulvia" (1.1). She is trying to make him feel how shameful it would be for him to be controlled by a boy or a woman. What she wants is to control him herself. She is fearful of his Roman side, which threatens always to remind him of duty, and she seeks continual reassurance of her power over him. She gains this when he dismisses Rome, glorifies their relationship, and immerses himself in the pleasures she is so adept at providing. She wants him to drown his Roman conscience in riotous living and in "the love of Love and her soft hours" (1.1).

By conquering "the greatest soldier of the world," Cleopatra masters the world that Antony has conquered. The problem is that the more Cleopatra succeeds in dominating Antony, the more she destroys the qualities that had made him worth conquering. Cleopatra has contradictory needs of Antony. She needs him to prove his love, but she also needs him to be a source of power. Antony is such a romantic figure because he is "the triple pillar of the world" who is ready to "let Rome in Tiber melt" out of love for her. But if he sacrifices his exalted position in order to prove the grandeur of their love, the basis of that love's grandeur will be destroyed. He will no longer be the greatest soldier in the world, and they will no longer "stand up peerless."

Cleopatra needs both to worship Antony as a great man and to

enslave him. Her contradictory needs are reflected in her inconsistent behavior in act 1. After using her cunning to keep Antony
with her, or at least to make him uncomfortable about leaving, she
capitulates gracefully:

> Your honour calls you hence;
> Therefore be deaf to my unpitied folly,
> And all the gods go with you! Upon your sword
> Sit laurel victory, and smooth success
> Be strew'd before your feet!
>
> (1.3)

This is more, I think, than making the best of a bad situation.
Antony's honor and martial success are important to Cleopatra,
and she feels, with part of her being at least, that it is wrong to
keep him from pursuing these things and that he should be deaf
to her folly. If she had succeeded in keeping Antony with her, he
would have been less worthy of her love.

Antony's inner conflicts are considerably more complicated
than Cleopatra's. Cleopatra has contradictory needs of Antony,
but she seems to feel no ambivalence toward him or toward their
relationship. She glorifies him consistently and continues to want
him even after he betrays her by marrying Octavia. Antony,
however, is ambivalent about Cleopatra from the beginning, and
he experiences a great deal of self-hate as a result of their relationship. He is not sure which version of her is correct, and he is
torn between his intoxication and his sense of duty. He cannot live
without Cleopatra, but he cannot live with himself as long as he is
under her spell.

Just as Cleopatra sees Antony as the greatest soldier in the
world, so he sees her as the world's most desirable woman,
embodying as she does both majesty and exotic eroticism. Her
glamor is evoked most vividly by Enobarbus:

> The barge she sat in, like a burnish'd throne,
> Burned on the water. . . .
>   For her own person,
> It beggar'd all description. She did lie
> In her pavilion, cloth-of-gold of tissue,
> O'er picturing that Venus where we see
> The fancy outwork nature.
>
> (2.2)

These are not Antony's words, of course, but they convey what must also have been his impression. Just as Cleopatra later describes Antony as "nature's piece 'gainst fancy" (5.2), so Cleopatra is described here as "O'er picturing" fancy. She is more alluring than the most alluring female that men have been able to imagine. For Antony, it is glorious to love and to be loved by such a woman.

Antony is drawn to Cleopatra not only by her glamor and desirability, but also by an affinity of temperament. Among his fellow Romans, he has been a disciplined soldier who has performed great feats of endurance, but there is a sybaritic side of him that responds to the life of sensuous delights Cleopatra offers. Under her influence, he throws off his Roman restraint and indulges in epicurean feasts, amorous surfeits, and "lascivious wassails" (1.4).[2] Together, they are perfect playmates, which may be one reason Cleopatra prefers him to her earlier lovers. Having experienced life with Cleopatra, Antony could never be content with a woman like Octavia:

> ENOBARBUS. Octavia is of a holy, cold, and still conversation.
> MENAS. Who would not have his wife so?
> ENOBARBUS. Not he that himself is not so; which is Mark Antony.
>   He will to his Egyptian dish again.
>
> (2.6)

Antony is drawn to Cleopatra also by the fact that in some ways they are opposites. She is a masterful woman who wants to manipulate the man who loves her. He is aggressive as a soldier, but he has a self-effacing side that is susceptible to her manipulation. Some of his self-effacing traits are well described by Plutarch: "And furthermore, being given to love: that made him the more desired, and by that meanes he brought many to love him. For he would further every man's love, and also would not be angry that men should merily tell him of those he loved. But besides all this, that which most procured his rising and advauncement, was his liberalitie, who gave all to the souldiers, and kept nothing for him selfe" (Bullough 1964, 257). Shakespeare's Antony likewise desires love and is given to liberality. After his defeat at Actium, he offers treasure to his followers and bids them fly; and when Enobarbus deserts, he is not angry, but sends his treasure after him. Following his death, Cleopatra celebrates his generosity: "For his bounty, / There was no winter in't; an autumn 'twas / That grew the more by reaping" (5.2). It is Antony's self-effacing side that explains, I think, the curious scene in which he wishes that all of his servants could be "clapp'd up together in / An Antony, that I might do you service / So good as you have done" (4.2). He is not only expressing gratitude here; he is uncomfortable in his position of superiority and wants to be beneath those who have served him. The fact that his servants are disturbed by his behavior ("The gods forbid!") makes clear its inappropriateness.

Because of his self-effacing tendencies, Antony is prone to being dominated by a more masterful personality, whether it be Octavius or Cleopatra. He flees from each to the other, but he can hold his own with neither. Cleopatra also displays a self-effacing side in her tendency to worship and merge with Antony, but she keeps it concealed from him and controls him as a result. She is deliberately wrangling and perverse:

> CHARMIAN. Madam, methinks, if you did love him dearly,
>   You do not hold the method to enforce
>   The like from him.
> CLEOPATRA.   What should I do, I do not?
> CHARMIAN. In each thing give him way, cross him in nothing.
> CLEOPATRA. Thou teachest like a fool. The way to lose him!
>
>   (1.3)

Given Antony's personality, Cleopatra knows exactly the way to make him love her dearly. Antony is completely unmoved by a self-effacing woman, as we can see from his indifference to Octavia, who does not even become angry when he returns to Cleopatra. But he is spellbound by Cleopatra, and under her influence he gives up his Roman values and finds the nobleness of life in love.

Antony cannot do this wholeheartedly, however. He carries within him a Roman code of behavior that he is violating by his life with Cleopatra. A Roman soldier does not live for love or present pleasure; he does not neglect his duties; and, above all, he does not allow himself to be enslaved by a woman. The Romans despise Antony for his unmanliness, and their attitudes are echoed by Antony in his expressions of self-contempt. While he is in Egypt he feels at once that he has found the nobleness of life and that something terrible is happening to him. When he arrives in Rome, he acknowledges to Caesar that "poisoned hours had bound [him] up / From [his] own knowledge" (2.2).

Antony's inner conflicts are acted out upon a vast geographical stage, as the various sides of his nature propel him from Egypt to Rome, from Rome to Athens, and then back again to Egypt. As the play opens, Antony's conflicts are activated by the arrival of a messenger whose presence threatens to arouse the Roman side of his nature. By saying "Let Rome in Tiber melt," Antony is trying not only to placate Cleopatra, but also to assure himself that he has made the right choice, that he has not sacrificed his nobility by living for love. Part of Antony believes these things, and part of him believes the opposite. To escape his conflict, he refuses to see the messenger and plunges himself into the distraction of "sport." Indeed, he may have been throwing himself into the Egyptian revels with such abandon all along because he has been trying to drown out his Roman thoughts.

His Roman thoughts are uppermost the next day, however, when he hears of "the ills" that his "idleness" has hatched (1, 2). He urges the messenger to

> Speak to me home. Mince not the general tongue.
> Name Cleopatra as she is call'd in Rome.
> Rail thou in Fulvia's phrase, and taunt my faults
> With such full license as both truth and malice
> Have power to utter. O, then we bring forth weeds
> When our quick minds lie still, and our ills told us
> Is as our earing.

(1.2)

Antony is full of self-hate because of his derelictions, and he wants the messenger to taunt his faults because that will satisfy his need for punishment and shame him into doing his duty. He asks to hear what the Romans say not only of him, but also of Cleopatra because he hopes that seeing her as a strumpet will help him to tear himself away from her.

In the first two scenes of the play, Antony's feelings about Cleopatra swing from one extreme to the other. In the first scene, the nobleness of life lies in her embrace, while in the second scene, Antony wishes he "had never seen her." Antony's ambivalence toward Cleopatra is the product both of her reputation and of his inner conflicts. When his self-effacing side is uppermost, he is dazzled by her glamor and masterfulness, but when his Roman side is uppermost, all his doubts about her are activated. In scene 2, Antony tries to relieve his guilt by blaming Cleopatra—"She is cunning past man's thought"—and by working himself up to a clean break.

When the time comes to part, however, Antony's behavior reflects continuing inner conflicts. As in the opening scene, Cleopatra is on the offensive and Antony is on the defensive. He is trying both to leave and to placate her: "The strong necessity of time commands / Our services awhile; but my full heart / Remains in use with you" (1.3). When Cleopatra says that his lack of grief for Fulvia shows how her death shall be received, Antony flares up but retreats almost immediately:

> Quarrel no more, but be prepar'd to know
> The purposes I bear; which are, or cease,
> As you shall give the advice. By the fire
> That quickens Nilus' slime, I go from hence
> Thy soldier, servant, making peace or war
> As thou affects.
>
>   (1.3)

Antony gains control of the situation only when Cleopatra's taunts anger him so much that he stops trying to soothe her and threatens to storm out. Then Cleopatra retreats and gives him her blessing.

Octavius hopes that Antony's "shames" will "Drive him to Rome" (1.4), and this is precisely what happens, but Antony remains full of inner conflicts. After apparently breaking his Egyptian fetters, he sends Cleopatra an orient pearl covered with "many doubled kisses" and promises "To mend the petty present" by piecing "Her opulent throne with kingdoms" (1.5), a promise he keeps when he makes her "Absolute queen" of lower Syria, Cyprus, and Lydia (3.6). It is clear that he is still bound to Cleopatra. When he gets to Rome, he condemns his "poisoned hours" in Egypt (2.2) and tells Pompey that he has "gain'd" by having been forced to return sooner than he had intended (2.6). He wants to make peace with Octavius, who is the voice of the Roman side of his nature, and to place additional obstacles between himself and Cleopatra. He marries Octavia in hopes of accomplishing these things, but, given his inner conflicts, this is a catastrophic decision. He thinks he can engage himself wholeheartedly, but he is lacking in self-knowledge. Shakespeare calls this to our attention immediately by having Enobarbus describe the appeal of Cleopatra and predict that Antony will never "leave her utterly" (2.2).

Antony's conflicts rise to the surface in the next scene. He begins by promising Octavia that henceforth all shall "be done by th' rule," but by the end of the scene he decides to return to Cleopatra: "I will to Egypt; / And though I make this marriage for my peace, / I' th' East my pleasure lies" (2.3). Antony's behavior here is puzzling, especially since he has not yet married Octavia.

Does he really think that he can make his peace by marrying her and then returning to Cleopatra? And why the radical shift from Roman to Egyptian values within thirty-five lines? Shakespeare does not present his motivation in much detail here; but if we understand the dynamics of Antony's conflicts, we shall see that his behavior is compatible with his personality.

While he lives with Cleopatra, Antony hates himself for his neglect of duty, for his self-indulgence, and for his submissiveness to a woman. When he gets to Rome, he condemns the soft beds of Egypt (2.6) and his poisoned hours there, is penitent about his past, and promises to reform. These measures alleviate his self-hate, and this, ironically, permits his desire for Cleopatra to re-emerge. Antony is so inconsistent because neither side of his conflict can be deeply repressed; as soon as one set of needs is partially satisfied, the other set begins to emerge. When he is with Cleopatra, he feels guilt for his violation of Roman values; and when he relieves that guilt in Rome, he feels a renewed desire for Cleopatra, which will lead, of course, to more self-contempt.

Antony is motivated in 2.3 not only by a desire for Cleopatra, but also by a fear of Caesar. Between his promise to keep his square at the beginning of the scene and his decision to return to Egypt at the end comes his conversation with the soothsayer, who tells him that his spirit is "o'erpow'r'd" when he is near Caesar but "noble" when he is away: "Therefore, O Antony, stay not by his side!" Antony is driven from Egypt to Rome by his shame at his submission to Cleopatra and is driven from Rome to Egypt by his need to free himself from Caesar's domination. He is trying, vainly, to escape the contempt that he feels for his own self-effacing trends. His foolishness in marrying Octavia and his dishonesty with her and with Caesar are the result of his inability to assert himself in Caesar's presence. He is dishonest also with himself. Because he can neither disappoint Caesar nor stay away from Cleopatra, he convinces himself that he can make the marriage for his peace and still return to Egypt. His conflicting needs result in self-destructive behavior while inducing him to believe, in a muddle-headed way, that everything will somehow work out.

Ironically, then, Antony leaves Rome in an effort to live up to his Roman ideal of manhood, which he cannot do while he is under Caesar's influence. He is too full of conflict to proceed directly to Egypt, so he settles in Athens, which is roughly midway, where he nurses his grievances against Caesar and convinces himself that he must go to war in order to preserve his honor (3.4).

Away from both Caesar and Cleopatra, and in the presence of the meek Octavia, Antony can be his bellicose self. When Octavia returns to Rome on a peace-making mission, Antony immediately goes to Egypt, where he pieces Cleopatra's throne with kingdoms and levies "the kings o' th' earth for war" (3.6).

In defying Caesar, Antony falls under Cleopatra's spell again and behaves in ways that lead to his ultimate downfall. Earlier, his subjection to Cleopatra had kept him from conducting any "wars without doors" (2.1); now it leads him to wage war in a foolhardy way. Antony knows that love and war should be kept separate, but he mixes them because of his inner conflicts. He fights at sea partly because Caesar dares him, forcing him to prove a manhood about which he is insecure, and partly because that is Cleopatra's preference and he cannot refuse her. He allows Cleopatra to be present at the battle and then "flies after her" (3.10) when she flees.

Once again Antony's subjection to Cleopatra has led him to violate his Roman values, and he is overwhelmed with self-hate. He feels that the land is ashamed to bear him and that he has "lost [his] way for ever" (3.11). He reproves himself for "fear and doting" and "is unqualitied with very shame." He has become his despised self, and it seems as though he can never recover his self-esteem.

It is striking, therefore, that within a single scene of seventy-five lines he moves from self-hate and despair to an attitude of affirmation:

CLEOPATRA.   Pardon, pardon!
ANTONY. Fall not a tear, I say. One of them rates
    All that is won and lost. Give me a kiss.
    Even this repays me. . . .
                          Fortune knows.
    We scorn her most when most she offers blows.

                                                        (3.11)

By begging for pardon, which she does three times in this scene, Cleopatra accepts part of the blame for Antony's flight from battle. This eases his self-contempt and casts him in the role of comforter. Having lost half of the world, Antony reaffirms the attitude that "Kingdoms are clay" (1.1) and that the nobleness of life lies in his relation with Cleopatra. He exalts her in order to justify his intoxication and to reaffirm the grandeur of their love. At the end of his speech, he shifts the blame for their defeat to Fortune, whose blows he scorns. Antony restores his pride by externalizing responsibility for his downfall and by glorifying love and resignation.

In order for his solution to work, Antony must maintain his belief in Cleopatra's splendor and in her love for him. That is why he reacts so strongly when she permits Thyreus (Thidias in some editions) to kiss her hand. Since Thyreus is an underling, this act diminishes Cleopatra's stature, and since he is an emissary of Caesar, it casts doubt upon her loyalty:

> To let a fellow that will take rewards,
> And say "God quit you!" be familiar with
> My playfellow, your hand, this kingly seal
> And plighter of high hearts!

(3.13)

Cleopatra consistently idealizes Antony, but Antony has both an idealized and a despised image of her. When he thinks that "To flatter Caesar" she mingles eyes "With one that ties his points," his despised image of her as a strumpet and a "boggler" emerges. Because she is so important to him, he is enraged by his disillusionment, and he attacks her viciously, describing her as "a morsel" that he found "cold upon / Dead Caesar's trencher" (3.13). Since his belief in Cleopatra is his defense against self-hate, the collapse of that belief leads him to turn against himself as well. He berates himself for having "Forborne the getting of a lawful race, / And by a gem of women" in order "to be abus'd / By one that looks on feeders" (3.13), and he sees his lack of judgment as a punishment for his viciousness. Without Cleopatra, Antony has no way of coping with his situation. When Cleopatra restores his faith by calling down terrible curses upon herself if she does not love him, Antony rallies his courage and determines to restore his reputation as a soldier.

Antony has been torn from the beginning of the play by a conflict between love and honor, between his need for Cleopatra and his need to live up to the Roman ideals of duty and manly behavior. Up to this point the conflict has seemed to be irreconcilable. It has led to his inconsistent behavior, to his political blunders, and to his disgrace at Actium. Once he has lost the world, Antony invests his pride almost entirely in his relationship with Cleopatra, but he also makes one last effort to restore his image of himself as a soldier. He can regain his honor even if he loses the battle as long as he fights bravely. Antony's conflict between love and honor has reflected a conflict between himself and Cleopatra, and this, in turn, has reflected a conflict within Cleopatra, since she has needed him to be both a great man and her slave. These conflicts are now resolved. The lovers know they are doomed and it is important to both that Antony die well. Antony's ferocity restores Cleopatra's pride in him and allows her to be her grandiose self once again: "It is my birthday. / I had thought t' have held it poor; but since my lord / Is Antony again, I will be Cleopatra" (3.13). The psychological conflicts that could never have been resolved in victory are resolved by the defeat they have brought about. This is one reason why the play ends on a positive note.

Antony is thrown into crisis once more by the defection of the Egyptian fleet, which he attributes to Cleopatra. His self-effacing bargain seems to have failed. He "made these wars" (4.14) for Cleopatra, whose "bosom" was his "crownet," his "chief end" (4.12); but, instead of rewarding his devotion, she has "Beguil'd [him] to the very heart of loss!" (4.12). Antony's greatest loss is not the battle, but the exalted version of Cleopatra and of their relationship through which he has relieved his self-hate and fulfilled his search for glory. He also feels betrayed by his followers: "The hearts / That spaniel'd me at heels, to whom I gave / Their wishes, do discandy, melt their sweets / On blossoming Caesar" (4.12). Again Antony's bargain has failed; his generosity has not been repaid by the loyalty and gratitude he feels he deserves.

The breakdown of Antony's bargain leads to a psychological crisis similar to Othello's; but unlike the crises of the major tragic heroes, it occurs late in the play and is resolved in a rapid and positive manner. When he feels himself betrayed by Cleopatra, he is full of rage and despair and sees nothing left but to revenge himself upon her and then to end his own life. Everything changes, however, when Mardian tells him that Cleopatra died speaking his name. His belief in her is restored, and with it his belief in himself and in the grandeur of their relationship. His self-effacing bargain has been confirmed by Cleopatra's fidelity; he has had her heart, just as she has had his. Suicide is now not an act of despair but a means of rejoining Cleopatra: "I will be / A bridegroom in my death and run into 't / As to a lover's bed" (4.14). In death he will find a confirmation of his vision of himself and Cleopatra as a peerless pair of lovers:

Where souls do couch on flowers, we'll hand in hand
And with our sprightly port make the ghosts gaze.

Dido and her Aeneas shall want troops,
And all the haunt be ours.

(4.14)

Instead of being a defeat, death will be the consummation of their search for glory.

Antony has a very happy death. Mardian says that Cleopatra loved him and mingled her fortunes with his "entirely" (4.14), and Antony remains persuaded of this even after he learns that Cleopatra is still alive. He dies in her arms in one of the most beautiful and romantic scenes in Shakespeare. Cleopatra now has no motive for concealing her feelings from Antony, and she lavishes upon him the tenderness and admiration that she has always felt. She wishes she had "great Juno's power" so that she could order the "strong-wing'd Mercury" to fetch him up and set him "by Jove's side" (4.15). She assures him that she will never adorn "th' imperious show / Of the full-fortun'd Caesar" (4.15) but will join him in death. She rails at the "false huswife Fortune," reinforcing the feeling that they are the victims not of their own flaws but of fate. Blame has vanished from Shakespeare's rhetoric and Antony seems free of guilt and self-hate. Through most of the play he has been worried about his honor, but now his suicide secures it: "Not Caesar's valour hath o'erthrown Antony, / But Antony's hath triumph'd on itself" (4.15). Indeed, his valor triumphs over Caesar by depriving him of the opportunity to inflict a public disgrace. Antony has undergone a "miserable change," it is true; but he consoles himself by thinking of his "former fortunes, / Wherein [he] liv'd the greatest prince o' th' world, / The noblest" (4.15).

Antony dies with his defenses working well and the previously incompatible components of his idealized image all being realized. He is the peerless lover, the valiant Roman, and the greatest prince of the world (in retrospect). Death is his solution; it permits him to achieve an inner peace, a secure sense of glory, and a harmonious relationship with Cleopatra that were impossible in life.

Cleopatra also dies with her idealized image intact and her search for glory successfully consummated. As we have seen, she needs Antony to be great and to be hers, and these things are in conflict with each other. When he goes to Rome to regain his honor, he marries Octavia; and when he returns to Egypt, his slavish devotion leads to his disgrace at Actium. Cleopatra is assured of his love, but he is no longer the Antony she has admired. In the Thyreus episode, Cleopatra is in danger of losing everything she values, as is Antony; but when she convinces him of her love, he rallies his courage, and she can be Cleopatra again. Her sense of her own greatness depends upon his love and grandeur, just as his depends upon hers. From this point on, the lovers want the same thing: to restore Antony's honor and to maintain their idealized version of themselves. Cleopatra no longer tries to intrude upon Antony's masculine territory, as she had done at Actium, but subsides into a proper femininity. She gives him moral support, helps him put on his armor, and celebrates his victory. This harmony is destroyed by the desertion of her fleet, for which Antony holds her responsible, but it is restored by his response to the news of her "death." His suicide demonstrates his courage and proves his love for her.

After his death Cleopatra glorifies him even more than she had done before: he was "nature's piece 'gainst fancy, / Condemning shadows quite" (5.2). Since Cleopatra has invested her pride in Antony, her magnification of him is a magnification of herself. His courage at the end wipes out his disgraces and permits her imagination to adorn him with godlike attributes. His death is a great loss, but, since this noblest of men has sacrificed everything for her, it is also a great triumph.

Cleopatra has other triumphs as well. She is aware of the Roman view of her as a boggler, a witch, and a triple-turned whore. Through her constancy, she proves the Romans to be incorrect and Antony's faith to have been warranted. She has aspired, as we have seen, to certain masculine prerogatives. Through her suicide, she undoes the womanly weakness of her flight from Actium and earns a kind of masculine status. As she approaches the act, she has "nothing / Of woman" in her and is "marble-constant" (5.2). Like Antony, she does "what's brave, what's noble / . . . after the high Roman fashion" (4.15). She sees Antony rousing himself "To praise [her] noble act" (5.2) and feels that her courage gives her the right to call herself his wife. This suggests a discomfort with her status as mistress from which she has finally gained relief. Through her suicide she realizes both masculine and feminine aspects of her idealized image.

For Cleopatra, as for Antony, suicide is a means of turning defeat into victory. Their loss to Caesar brings certain consequences that cannot be reversed. Antony will never again be the triple pillar of the world, and Cleopatra's desire for power through him cannot be fulfilled. The greatest threat to Antony and

Cleopatra, however, is not the loss of empire, or even of life, but the humiliation involved in being displayed by Caesar as part of his triumph. Antony speaks of this to Eros when he urges him to kill him (4.14), as does Cleopatra to Iras when she prepares to commit suicide. "Mechanic slaves, / With greasy aprons" will hold them up to view; "Saucy lictors / Will catch at [them] like strumpets"; and "scald rhymers [will] ballad [them] out o' tune" (5.2):

> The quick comedians
> Extemporally will stage us and present
> Our Alexandrian revels. Antony
> Shall be brought drunken forth, and I shall see
> Some squeaking Cleopatra boy my greatness
> I' th' posture of a whore.
>
> (5.2)

Antony and Cleopatra are threatened, in effect, with becoming their despised selves should they allow Caesar to capture them. By committing suicide, they can avoid this terrible fate and become their idealized selves once and for all. As she prepares for death, Cleopatra is more and more regal: "Show me, my women, like a queen" (5.2). After her death, she receives tribute from Caesar for both her courage and her beauty; and she is buried with Antony, whom even Caesar seems to recognize as belonging to her. This is quite a contrast to her vision of her reception in Rome.

Through her suicide, then, Cleopatra is successful in thwarting Caesar's efforts to debase her. She not only maintains her idealized image; she also experiences a deeply satisfying vindictive triumph at the thought of fooling his "preparation" and conquering his "most absurd intents." She wishes the asp could speak that she might hear it "call great Caesar ass / Unpolicied!" (5.2). Caesar acknowledges her victory and admires her for it: "Bravest at the last! / She levell'd our purposes, and being royal, / Took her own way" (5.2).

Cleopatra triumphs over Caesar in yet another way, and that is by conquering the fate to which he is still subject:

> My desolation does begin to make
> A better life. 'Tis paltry to be Caesar.
> Not being Fortune, he's but Fortune's knave,
> A minister of her will. And it is great
> To do that thing that ends all other deeds,
> Which shackles accidents and bolts up change,

Which sleeps, and never palates more the dung,
The beggar's nurse and Caesar's.

(5.2)

By killing herself, Cleopatra will remove herself from the
vicissitudes of the human condition. She will not be the plaything
of fortune, or an agent of its will, but will have taken her fate into
her own hands and will have ended her life in such a way as to
preserve her glory. Caesar, on the other hand, by remaining alive,
will be subject to accident and change and the limitations of an
earthbound existence. He seems triumphant now, but his is the
luck "the gods give men / To excuse their after wrath" (5.2), a
wrath to which Cleopatra will no longer be subject. The "injurious
gods" (4.15) will not be able to hurt her anymore. Her loss of
empire is an irreversible consequence of her defeat by Caesar, but
empire turns out to be insignificant. It is more glorious to kill
oneself than to be the ruler of the world, who, like the most
humble of human beings, must palate the dung.

At the beginning of the play, Antony had proclaimed that
"Kingdoms are clay: our dungy earth alike / Feeds beast as man"
(1.1). He finds his "space" in his love for Cleopatra, to which he
attributes a glory greater than empire. As he prepares to commit
suicide, he envisions that glory attained, as he imagines himself
and Cleopatra being reunited in Elysium, where they will be more
famous than Dido and Aeneas. In a similiar way, Cleopatra imagines herself going to Antony as she applies the asp. She sees her
death as a means of becoming a purely spiritual being: "I am fire
and air; my other elements / I give to baser life" (5.2). At the end,
both lovers find the nobleness of life in suicide, which permits
them to resolve their conflicts, to wipe out their faults, and to
achieve immortality as their idealized selves. Though apparently
victims of Caesar and of fate, they are able through their deaths to
transcend the limits of the human condition and to defeat the
forces that seem to have defeated them. In the grave that clips the
famous pair, they find their space at last.

IV

Now that I have examined the protagonists in motivational
terms, let me consider their relation to the structure and rhetoric
of the drama. The play begins, as we have seen, as a tragedy of
character and concludes as a tragedy of fate. Antony is sur-

rounded by a rhetoric of condemnation in the first three acts and
by a rhetoric of glorification in the last two. When we look at
Antony in psychological terms, we find the structure and rhetoric
of the first three acts to be harmonious with the mimetic protrait.
Antony *has* lost himself in dotage. He is compulsively tied to
Cleopatra and is unable to resist her psychological domination. At
the same time, he hates himself for not living up to his Roman
ideals, and his inner conflicts result in a series of tragic mistakes.
A tension develops between structure and rhetoric on the one
hand and mimetic characterization on the other in the last two acts
of the play. Given the protagonists' responsibility for their downfall, it seems inappropriate to present them as victims of the
injurious gods. Once they have brought about their own destruction, they employ a variety of defenses that permit them to evade
responsibility and to maintain their sense of grandeur; but the
rhetoric, instead of calling our attention to what they are doing,
reinforces their self-glorification. Shakespeare's intuitive understanding and mimetic portrayal of his characters is splendid
throughout, but his rhetoric moves from insight to blindness.
This is why many critics feel that we are being asked to respond to
Antony and Cleopatra in ways inappropriate to their actual fates
and characters. The rhetoric of the last two acts of the play is
subverted by the characterization.

In the first three acts of the play, Antony fails in all of his
objectives. He does not break his Egyptian fetters, he does not
make peace with Caesar or succeed in standing up to him, and he
does not restore his Roman honor. At the battle of Actium, his
intoxication with Cleopatra leads to an overwhelming disgrace.
This seems to confirm the Roman view of their relationship as
demeaning, destructive, and pathologically intense. After Actium, Antony tries to relieve his guilt by holding fortune responsible for his downfall, to restore his honor by fighting bravely, and
to compensate for his loss of empire by seeking glory through
Cleopatra. The rhetoric supports Antony's sense that he has
achieved these objectives; but when we look at him from a psychological perspective, he seems to be deluding himself.

After his flight from Actium, Antony is full of shame, self-hate,
and despair. He deals with these feelings by blaming Cleopatra,
and, when she begs pardon, by shifting the responsibility for his
defeat to Fortune. Given the intensity of his guilt and the scope of
the disaster, it is understandable that he would resort to this kind
of externalization. It seems to work for him psychologically, but
he gains his relief by denying the truth about himself. Through

his rhetoric, Shakespeare supports Antony's version of reality and thus participates with him in covering up the moral and psychological deficiencies that were criticized so severely in the first three acts. Antony deceives himself in order to avoid being overwhelmed by self-hate, and Shakespeare tries to get the audience to accept his self-deception as truth.

His externalization of responsibility not only permits Antony to escape his feelings of guilt, but also to restore his pride and to gain a sense of control over his destiny. By scorning fortune "when most she offers blows" (3.11) he is showing that fate cannot break his spirit. Instead of having a sense of failure, he can feel triumphant because he is the master of his emotions. After he has wounded himself in his suicide attempt, he tells his lamenting guards not to "please sharp fate" by gracing "it with [their] sorrows. Bid that welcome / Which comes to punish us, and we punish it, / Seeming to bear it lightly" (4.14). Instead of having to blame himself for his plight, Antony holds fate responsible and then defeats fate by being indifferent to or pretending to welcome his destruction.

After Actium, Antony feels himself to be "Stroy'd in dishonour" (3.11). He has, in Plutarch's words, "betrayed them that fought for him"; and it is difficult to see how he can wipe out his shame. Antony restores his image of himself as a soldier by fighting bravely in the next battle, and the rhetoric reinforces his self-perception. It is true that he has proved himself not to be a coward, as he had seemed at Actium, but has he really made up for his disgraceful behavior? He is very hard on himself immediately following Actium, but he is too easy on himself thereafter, and his self-deception is indulged by the author.

Antony feels that he restores his honor completely through his suicide, which proves his courage and thwarts the will of Caesar. When he is told that Cleopatra has ended her life, he condemns himself for remaining behind: "Since Cleopatra died / I have liv'd in such dishonour that the gods / Detest my baseness" (4.14). His sense of baseness derives not from Cleopatra's suicide, but from his own shameful behavior, which has not really been redeemed. By experiencing his dishonor as the result of being alive, he can purge himself of it by killing himself. Through suicide, moreover, he can replace his despised with his idealized self, since he glorifies the act. Antony sees himself as triumphant, and he is presented that way by Shakespeare; but, as Traversi says, his suicide is "the logical end of a process which folly, weakness, and dissolution have made inevitable" (1963, 178). He perceives himself as conquering Caesar, but he is driven to self-destruction by the "inevitable prosecution of / Disgrace and horror" (4.14) that awaits him if he lives.

After Actium Antony tries to compensate for his defeat by seeking his glory through Cleopatra, one of whose tears "rates / All that is won and lost" (3.9). A relationship that the first three acts have shown to be destructive is now celebrated as grandly romantic. Antony and Cleopatra have mutually dependent pride systems; each sees the other as the other wants to be seen. This is often the basis of what we call "romantic love," being told we are wonderful by someone we have glorified and whose judgment, therefore, counts. As is common in such relationships, Cleopatra is not a real person for Antony, but is either an idealized or a despised being. When he despises her, he loses his own sense of worth, but when he idealizes her, then he, too, is a glorious person. He needs to exalt her also to cope with his guilt, since his violation of Roman values can be justified only if she is worth the sacrifice. He can die happy when he thinks she has committed suicide because this restores his idealized version of her and thus his belief in himself. His vision of their reunion in Elysium dwells less upon exchanges of tenderness than upon the glory of competitive triumph, and even his death scene focuses largely upon exaggerated claims for his grandeur. Antony is no more real for Cleopatra, of course, than she is for him. Her need to glorify him is so powerful that it overrides reality. In her mind, he is no longer the weak man who vacillated between Egypt and Rome, who kissed away kingdoms and provinces, and who disgraced himself at Actium, but a colossus who is "past the size of dreaming" (5.2).

The pride systems of the protagonists are working perfectly at the end. Their relationship is so grandly romantic because it embodies the very appealing fantasy of being loved by an extremely glamorous person who finds life meaningless without us and whose devotion will show the world how much we are worth. The relationship is all the more romantic because it ends in defeat and death. Antony's behavior at Actium testifies to Cleopatra's "full supremacy" over his spirit (3.11), and when he hears that she is dead, he has no wish to go on living. Cleopatra's suicide is, among other things, a proof of her devotion. As we have seen, both lovers have inner conflicts that produce tensions in their relationship and that are bound to lead to their downfall. After their defeat, their conflicts disappear and their contradictory needs are fulfilled. Antony gains both love and honor, and Cleopatra possesses completely a man she perceives to be great.

This resolution can be maintained, however, only by their deaths. By dying, they can have their moment of glory and imagine it lasting forever.

My argument has been that a psychological study of the protagonists supports those critics who feel the play to be a depiction of tragic folly and self-deception throughout, while those who see Antony and Cleopatra as triumphant are responding to the rhetoric of the last two acts but are failing to see how that rhetoric is subverted by the characterization. I should like to qualify this argument by observing that it is not only the rhetoric but also the mimesis that sustains a sense of transcendence.

We can respond to the mimetic characterization from more than one perspective. When we look at it from a detached, analytical point of view, we see Antony and Cleopatra as having a pathologically intense relationship and a shared delusional system. Our understanding of their motivation leads to both a greater appreciation of Shakespeare's intuitive insight and a greater resistance to his rhetoric, which seems to identify with the protagonists too much. It is not only they, but the play as a whole that seems to be making exaggerated claims for their grandeur and to be celebrating resignation, morbid dependency, and death. The result is quite different when we approach the mimesis from a phenomenological perspective, a perspective, that is, from which we experience Antony and Cleopatra as they experience themselves. From this perspective, they clearly are triumphant and the rhetoric is appropriate to their sense of transcendence. Indeed, by fostering our engagement with the protagonists, the rhetoric induces us to adopt a phenomenological perspective, which then leads us to feel that the rhetoric is valid. Once we have adopted such a perspective, rhetoric and mimesis reinforce each other.[3] The rhetoric confirms the protagonists' sense of reality by having other characters support their view of themselves, whereas earlier in the play they found no confirmation except through each other. Since everything conspires to present their glory as real, it is no wonder that the end of the play casts such a powerful spell.

Antony and Cleopatra is, then, a story neither of tragic folly nor of transcendence, but of both. The protagonists' thirst for glory and their inner conflicts lead to their destruction, but once they are doomed, their conflicts disappear and they attain the glory for which they have been searching. They seem more sublime as lovers because of their defeat. Their sense of success is real enough (see Kuriyama 1977, 345), but the price of success is death, the sting of which they remove by imagining a posthumous reunion and by glorifying the act of self-destruction. They could not find a way to live, but they do find a way to cope with defeat and to achieve a sense of transcendence in death. The neurotic intensity of their relationship, which led to so much of their self-destructive behavior, now permits them to achieve an extraordinary success, for they do become perhaps the most famous lovers in history, and this would not have happened had they continued to live. Their search for glory leads them to the grave, but it can be consummated only in death.

The preceding analysis has shown, I think, why *Antony and Cleopatra* has generated so much critical controversy. Many critics argue that Shakespeare somehow manages to balance conflicting points of view in this play. I feel that he presents Antony and Cleopatra first as self-destructive and then as triumphant and that there is nothing in the last two acts of the play to remind us of their earlier folly.[4] He is too close to his protagonists at the end to be able to judge them, and it is this closeness that produces his blindness to their continued self-deception. It also produces the lyricism and the inside views of Antony and Cleopatra that are responsible for much of the play's power and that have led so many critics to see it as "a testament to the transforming power of love."

Although I have found no way of accounting for the shift in Shakespeare's treatment of Antony in terms of the inner logic of the play, it makes sense, I believe, if we see it as the expression of an ambivalent attitude toward self-effacing behavior. As we have seen, the most serious criticism of Antony is that his "dotage . . . / O'erflows the measure." His devotion to love leads him to violate the Roman code, which demands aggressive and perfectionistic behavior. The Romans blame him for this, as they blame him for his sensuality, because his behavior represents a threat to both their political and psychological stability. They are tempted by Antony's life-style ("O rare for Antony"), but if they gave way to their sensual and self-effacing impulses, discipline would collapse and they would be subject to unbearable self-hate. It is the threat of this self-hate that makes them condemn Antony so severely; they reinforce their own repressions by attacking him. The author seems to share this need to attack Antony, either for the same reasons or, since the sonnets suggest that he has behaved like Antony (see Paris, 1991), as a form of self-condemnation or self-punishment.

If Shakespeare had maintained a consistent attitude toward Antony, the play would have been a tragedy of character throughout. But he is full of inner conflicts and is ambivalent toward every solution. He criticizes Antony and Cleopatra from the Roman point of view, but also Roman values from the perspective of the protagonists. As I observed earlier, the play never resolves the problem of Antony's dotage. It shows it leading to his destruction but then presents the world as well lost for love. Shakespeare seems to have a need both to criticize and to justify the self-effacing side of himself through Antony. Once Antony has been punished by losing the world, the author's justificatory impulses are released, and he provides both Antony and himself with a wish-fulfillment ending. Antony achieves immortal glory through love, while also living up to the aggressive and perfectionistic components of his idealized image. Through Antony, Shakespeare reimagines the experience of the sonnets. There he despised himself for being in love with a whore who betrayed his affection; here, through Cleopatra's fidelity, the self-effacing male is vindicated. His dotage makes him not a strumpet's fool, but the world's greatest lover. The fact that it leads to his destruction is obscured by the splendor of the poetry and the force of the rhetoric, which celebrates the lovers and blames fate for their downfall. Shakespeare has ambivalent feelings toward the self-effacing side of himself, but in this play the need to glorify it is ultimately uppermost.

8
Coriolanus

I

Although *Coriolanus* is not one of Shakespeare's more popular plays, it has received a great deal of critical attention, much of which has been devoted to the character of the protagonist. Indeed, the psychological analyses of Coriolanus are more numerous and more sophisticated than are those of any other character in Shakespeare except Hamlet.[1] The primary reason for this is that Coriolanus's behavior seems so extreme, so contradictory, and so out of control, even to those who sympathize with his politics, that it is difficult to interpret the play thematically (see Rabkin 1967, 120–44). The political conflict "is hopeless," as Bradley says, "not because the people, or even the tribunes, are what they are, but because [Coriolanus] is what we call an 'impossible' person" (1969, 85). Whereas it is often difficult for critics to see the ways in which likable protagonists contribute to their own downfall, neither Coriolanus's character nor Shakespeare's rhetoric induces much identification with this protagonist, and critics are widely agreed that the play is "pre-eminently a tragedy of personality" (Hofling 1957, 408).

Indeed, John Bayley feels that *Coriolanus* "may be Shakespeare's closest approach to a personal case history" (1976, 235). What is responsible for this perception of the play, and for the criticism to which it has given rise, is not only Coriolanus's compulsive and contradictory behavior, but also the fact that we are given an unusual amount of information about his upbringing. Charles Hofling contends that "in *Coriolanus* Shakespeare demonstrates, in addition to his undiminished intuitive, artistic genius, a *conscious* insight into the genesis of his hero's personality . . . which is in excess of that which he had demonstrated hitherto" (1957, 434). I am not sure that this is entirely true, since Richard III was also given a childhood that explained the genesis of his personality; but Shakespeare does seem to be aware of many of the forces that have shaped his protagonist's behavior. The chief of these is, of course, Volumnia, who has been widely recognized as having had a powerful impact upon her son's development. Her influence is such, says MacCallum, that "there is hardly a feature in him that cannot be traced to its origin in Volumnia" (1967, 555).

As in a number of other plays, there are precipitating events in *Coriolanus* that threaten the hero's bargain with fate and produce a psychological crisis that leads to his destruction. One of these occurs at the beginning, when the plebeians mutiny and are given five tribunes; and another occurs after the battle of Corioles, when Coriolanus is forced to seek the approval of the plebeians in order to become consul. His inability to do this in the customary way or to placate the plebeians after having offended them leads to his banishment, which is the final blow to his bargain. He responds by plotting revenge, but the switch in solutions is psychologically impossible for him, especially in the face of his family's appeals, and he finds himself in a position in which he is bound to lose whatever he does. He chooses mercy to Rome over both loyalty to Aufidius and his desire for revenge and is rewarded with an ending that satisfies his psychological needs.

We must understand Coriolanus's character if we are to comprehend the impact of the precipitating events upon him. No one else in the play is as disturbed by the plebeians' acquisition of political power, and no one else would have found it impossible to ask for the consulship kindly. His response to banishment and his inability to carry out his revenge are also products of his personality. I shall begin by examining Coriolanus's relationship with his mother and the motivational system to which it gives rise, and then I shall try to explain his response to the precipitating events. My analysis of his character will also help us to understand some of the other puzzling aspects of his behavior, such as his aversion to praise, his refusal to show his wounds, his relationship with Aufidius, and his invitations to both the plebeians and the Antiates to kill him.

II

It is evident from the conversation between Volumnia and Virgilia while Coriolanus is away fighting the Volsces that Volumnia is engaged in a search for glory of which Coriolanus is the instrument. She is an expansive woman who has embraced the ideal of military honor and who can pursue this ideal only through a male. She springs "in joy" when she gives birth to a "manchild" and when her son returns from his first battle with "his brows bound with oak" (1.3). She sends him "to a cruel war" at a tender age because she wants him to win "honour," "fame," and "renown." Indeed, the glory he can achieve is more important to her than his company, his safety, or his life. She is impatient with Virgilia's anxiety about Coriolanus because, as far as she is concerned, when he is fighting he is performing his primary function, which to bring glory to himself and his family. She is not afraid of his dying "in the business" as long as he does so nobly, for then "his good report" will be her son (1.3). She regards a noble death as preferable to a shameful life and would rather have eleven sons "die nobly for their country than one voluptuously surfeit out of action" (1.3).

Volumnia identifies with her son's achievements and experiences them as though they were her own. She feels that she is responsible for his greatness, partly because her "praises made [him] first a soldier" and partly because she has passed on to him her own heroic qualities—"thy valiantness was mine, thou suck'st it from me" (3.2). She is proud of her own courage as well as of his: "I mock at death / With as big a heart as thou" (3.2). One of her boasts is that if she "had been the wife of Hercules, / Six of his labours [she'd] have done, and sav'd / [Her] husband so much sweat" (4.1). She does not have a Hercules for a husband, but she has a Hector for a son, and she devotes herself to promoting his greatness, since it is through him that she will have her place in history. She takes delight in the bloody details of his battles, which provide a vicarious gratification of her own appetite for violence. His exploits correspond to her sense of what she would do if she were a man. She enjoys imagining the fear he strikes in his enemies and his relentless destruction of their ranks. His triumphs are hers not only because he is her son, but also because he is completely devoted to her. She proudly proclaims that "There's no man in the world / More bound to 's mother" (5.3).

Coriolanus receives a number of messages from Volumnia that profoundly affect his development. It is up to him to fulfill her dreams and to give meaning to her life. Honor and fame are more important than life itself, and he must be prepared to die in order to win these things. Honor is primarily military honor as defined by the patrician code of values that Coriolanus learns from his mother. The fact that her attitudes toward wounds, courage, bloodiness, martial ferocity, and service to the state are echoed by the culture intensifies their impact upon him. Coriolanus articulates the patrician code when he is seeking volunteers to follow him into battle:

> If any such be here
> (As it were sin to doubt) that love this painting
> Wherein you see me smear'd; if any fear
> Lesser his person than an ill report;
> If any think brave death outweighs bad life
> And that his country's dearer than himself . . .
> Wave thus to express his disposition,
> And follow Marcius.

                                                                        (1.6)

Coriolanus tries very hard to live up to this code in which "valour is the chiefest virtue" (2.2), but this is not enough to satisfy his mother. Volumnia needs him to be not only a virtuous man, according to the Roman standard, but also a hero of epic stature in a class with Hector and Hercules. She needs him to win "fame" in addition to "honour," to do memorable deeds that will make him a legendary figure. In this, as in other respects, Coriolanus fulfills his mother's expectations. His feats at Corioles are so extraordinary that Volumnia feels she has "liv'd / To see inherited [her] very wishes, / And the buildings of [her] fancy" (2.1). She is still not satisfied, however, for she wants him to be consul.

If Coriolanus's mission in life is to satisfy his mother's craving for glory, he is induced to accept this mission by her glorification of him. As Volumnia says, her "praises made [him] first a soldier" (3.2). She fosters in him a search for glory parallel to her own in which recognition from her is a major reward. Janet Adelman argues that Coriolanus has been deprived of nourishment by his mother and has transformed his "oral neediness" into "phallic aggression" as a way of discharging his anger and of "defending himself against vulnerability" (1980, 132). We cannot know whether or not his aggressiveness is the result of Volumnia's failure to nourish him, but there is ample evidence that it is the product of her reinforcement of aggressive behavior. G. Wilson Knight observes that Coriolanus loves Volumnia "in part for her idolization of him" (1963, 183). Mother and son are " 'in pride with each other' making honour the universal reality" (1963, 191). I think this is correct. Volumnia and Coriolanus have a symbiotic relationship in which each feeds the other's pride and adores the other for making him or her feel like a wonderful person. Exaltation of the other is a form of self-exaltation. The more she glorifies Coriolanus, the better Volumnia feels about herself; and, when

Coriolanus sees her as "the most noble mother of the world" (5.3), this heightens the value of her idolization of him. Matthew Besdine's work on "Jocasta mothering" suggests that Volumnia's glorification of her son may be partly responsible not only for his desire, but also for his ability to achieve what she wants (1968).[2] Freud observed, "A man who has been the indisputable favorite of his mother keeps for life the feeling of a conqueror, that confidence of success that often induces real success" (qtd. by Besdine 1969, 577).

Coriolanus is motivated not only by a desire for his mother's approval but also by a fear of disappointing her. Since he does not disappoint her, this fear is largely unconscious, but it is there and is heightened by the loftiness of her aspirations. Volumnia describes Coriolanus as going into battle "Like to a harvestman that's task'd to mow / Or all or lose his hire" (1.3). One of the messages that Coriolanus receives from his mother is that, if he does not do everything she expects of him, whatever he does will have little value. In order to feel successful, he must constantly perform extraordinary feats.

As a result of his upbringing, Coriolanus develops into a predominantly perfectionistic person. Like Shakespeare's other warrior heroes, he is a man for whom the big wars make ambition virtue. His aggressiveness is justified because it is in the service of the state. Volumnia is often compared to Lady Macbeth as a woman who imposes her conception of manliness upon the male through whom she seeks fulfillment of her own ambitions (see Kahn 1981, 151–55 and Harding 1969, 252–53); but it is important to recognize that she subscribes to the perfectionistic rather than to the arrogant-vindictive notion of what becomes a man. Coriolanus must achieve greatness in a way that is compatible with honor. His idealized image is based, in part, upon the Roman code, and his needs for glory drive him to live up to its standards. His sense of greatness is not unconditional, like that of a narcissist, but is contingent upon his performance. Coriolanus is motivated both by his relation to others and by his relation to his idealized image. The approval of those from whom he derived his standards remains very important to him, but once he internalizes those standards, they operate as shoulds that are independent of their external source.

Coriolanus's idealized image is based not only upon the Roman code but also upon Volumnia's dreams of his greatness. His search for glory involves the pursuit of both honor and fame. Honor is something he can attain, and his sense of having lived up to the code gives rise to his pride and his arrogance. The need for fame, however, generates demands of a more grandiose and indefinite nature, since it involves not simply acting in accordance with a prescribed set of principles, but surpassing all of his fellows and matching the exploits of legendary heroes. His need for fame makes it difficult for him to feel satisfied with himself. Along with his arrogance, therefore, we find behavior that is strangely humble and self-deprecatory.

Indeed, one of the reasons he shrinks from praise is that it makes him uncomfortably aware of how far his deeds, whatever they are, fall short of the demands he makes upon himself. After the battle of Corioles, in which he outdoes "his former deeds doubly" (2.1), Coriolanus minimizes his feats:

> I have done
> As you have done—that's what I can; induc'd
> As you have been—that's for my country.
> He that has but effected his good will
> Hath overta'en mine act.
>
>   (1.9)

He has fulfilled the demands of the code, as have his fellows, but this falls short of his aspirations; and when he measures his deeds against what he would like to achieve, they seem ordinary and the praise of them embarrassingly "hyperbolical" (see MacCallum 1967, 593 and Putney 1962, 381). He calls those who are praising him flatterers and liars. Since their acclaim is so far beyond the degree of approval he is able to bestow upon himself, they seem either to have an excessively low standard or to be guilty of exaggeration.

Coriolanus's discomfort in the presence of praise is the product in part, then, of his quest for fame, which makes him feel that, no matter what he has done, he has not "effected his good will" and therefore does not deserve adulation. It is the product also of his need for honor, since part of the Roman code is that a man fights for love of his country, which is "dearer than himself" (1.6), and not for the sake of reward. Coriolanus makes this clear when he refuses a tenth part of the spoils: "I thank you, General, / But cannot make my heart consent to take / A bribe to pay my sword" (1.9). For Coriolanus, praise is just as much a bribe as material rewards. Cominius understands this when he beseeches Coriolanus to hear his feats celebrated "In sign of what you are, not to reward / What you have done" (1.9). To accept a reward for what he has done, whether it be in the form of booty or of praise, threatens the purity of Coriolanus's motives by making it seem that he fought in order to be paid. To protect his honor, then, it is imperative for him not to appear to want or to enjoy praise; and so he must either deprecate his praisers (and himself), try to stop them, or leave if they insist upon proceeding, as he does when Cominius eulogizes him before the senate.

It must not be thought that Coriolanus is indifferent to recognition, though his aversion to praise, combined with his later remark about wanting to "stand / As if a man were author of himself" (5.8), has led many critics to arrive at this conclusion. As Janet Adelman observes, "most critics find Coriolanus' abhorrence of praise a symptom of his pride and of his desire to consider himself as self-defined and self-sufficient" (1980, 147). He is often seen as a man who wants to be *sui generis*, independent of "the community and its evaluative processes" (Fish 1976, 988). There is truth in these interpretations, since once Coriolanus internalizes the values of his mother and his culture, they become independent of external sanctions; but he is, nonetheless, very much concerned about getting his just deserts from the community. He has the perfectionist's "conviction of an infallible justice operating in life" (Horney 1950, 197) and expects his rectitude to be rewarded. His bargain is less with fate than with Rome and his mother; and his belief in its efficacy is encouraged by his culture, since part of the Roman value system, which even the plebeians seem to accept, is that the country should be grateful to those who risk their lives and incur wounds in its service.

There are conflicting attitudes in the Roman culture about rewarding martial valor. Citizens are supposed to fight for their country out of love and duty rather than from self-interested motives, and the state is supposed to be grateful to those who serve it so disinterestedly. They are not supposed to fight for a reward, but they are supposed to be rewarded for fighting. Thus we have the contradictory behavior of Cominius, who first urges Coriolanus to regard praise as a sign of what he is rather than as a reward for what he has done and then offers him a tenth part of the spoils. There is a tacit understanding between the state and its citizens that their unselfish devotion will be rewarded, and the state must perform its rituals of recognition in order to live up to its end of the bargain. Indeed, the rites in which Cominius engages after the battle of Corioles and in which the Senate engages when Coriolanus returns to Rome have a sacred quality, as one of Menenius's appeals to the plebeians makes clear:

> Now the good gods forbid
> That our renowned Rome, whose gratitude
> Towards her deserved children is enroll'd
> In Jove's own book, like an unnatural dam
> Should now eat up her own!
>
> (3.1)

Rome is renowned for her gratitude to her deserving children, which is noted and sanctioned by the gods. To fail of this gratitude is to reverse the natural order and to violate her compact with both her citizens and Jove.

Rome has a need to reward Coriolanus; and, despite his resistance, he has a need to be rewarded, since if he were not, he would be outraged, as Cominius well understands:

> MARCIUS. I have some wounds upon me, and they smart
>   To hear themselves rememb'red.
> COMINIUS.   Should they not,
>   Well might they fester 'gainst ingratitude
>   And tent themselves with death.
>
> (1.9)

Coriolanus needs both to resist the bestowal of recognition in order to protect the integrity of his motives and to have recognition bestowed upon him in order to validate his bargain. Praise makes him uncomfortable in part because it throws him into inner conflict; he wants it much more than he should. He looks for ways of receiving recognition without appearing to relish it, by fending it off, as he does after the battle of Corioles, or by allowing himself to be praised but refusing to be present, as he does when he is honored by the Senate. Perhaps because he is part of the same system, Cominius is not insensitive to Coriolanus's needs. After several false starts and some guidance, he offers forms of recognition—the garland, his steed, the name of Coriolanus—that are appropriately symbolic and that Coriolanus can therefore accept in good conscience:

> I will go wash;
> And when my face is fair, you shall perceive
> Whether I blush or no. Howbeit, I thank you.
> I mean to stride your steed, and at all times
> To undercrest your good addition
> To th' fairness of my power.
>
> (1.9)

This not ungracious acceptance indicates that the acknowledgement of his achievements is important to Coriolanus. Indeed, it is
essential to his solution, which breaks down when such acknowledgement is withheld.

Those who feel that Coriolanus regards himself as independent
of the community and its evaluative processes fail to distinguish
between his attitudes toward the patricians and the plebeians. His
scorn for the plebeians is such that he objects to needing their
approval to become consul, but he respects the patricians, whom
he describes as "the honour'd number, / Who lack not virtue"
(3.1). Coriolanus shares with the patricians a code of honor to
which they all subscribe, and though the achievements of his
fellows are inferior to his, their aspirations are the same. They,
too, do what they can, induced, as he is, by love of their country.
The plebeians, however, do not embrace the code: they are reluctant to defend their country, are cowardly in battle, and are eager
for spoils. Their value system is the opposite of Coriolanus's; from
his point of view, they have no principles but are "Time-pleasers,
flatterers, foes to nobleness" (3.1).

Coriolanus is not alone in his contempt for the plebeians; he
has imbibed it from his mother and his culture. When Volumnia
does not approve of his highly impolitic expressions of disdain
while he is trying to become a consul, he complains that she

> was wont
> To call them woollen vassals, things created
> To buy and sell with groats, to show bare heads
> In congregations, to yawn, be still, and wonder
> When one but of my ordinance stood up
> To speak of peace and war.
>
> (3.2)

The message Coriolanus has received from his mother is that the
plebeians are far beneath him in the hierarchy of being. They are
"vassals," "things," who are incapable of reasonable thought on
serious subjects. Their destiny is to devote their lives to petty
affairs and to show deference and wonder at the wisdom of the
patricians. Volumnia's attitudes are reinforced by the whole patrician culture, which makes them seem self-evident to Coriolanus.

We can get some sense of the patrician's contempt for their
inferiors by examining the attitudes of Menenius, whom the
plebeians regard as "worthy" and "honest" and "one that hath
always lov'd the people" (1.1). In the first scene of the play he

speaks of them as Rome's "rats," says that they "lack discretion" and are "passing cowardly," and tells them, through the parable of the belly, that "No public benefit which [they] receive / But it proceeds" from the patricians. In 2.1, he calls them "fools," "the beastly plebeians," and says that their "abilities are too infant-like for doing much alone." He informs their tribunes that, "in a cheap estimation," Marcius "is worth all your predecessors since De- ucalion." Coriolanus does not learn from his "father," Menenius, any greater respect for the plebeians than he had imbibed from Volumnia.

It is no wonder, then, that Coriolanus regards them not merely as inferiors, but as creatures of a different species. He holds them, as Brutus correctly observes, "Of no more soul nor fitness for the world / Than camels in the war" (2.1). It is not simply, as Bradley says, that the plebeians do not belong to the same community of virtue (1969, 87); they are *untermenschen* who outwardly resemble human beings but who have neither the same moral qualities nor the same rights as the patricians. The play abounds in imagery that associates them with the lower animals. The patricians regard them in much the same way that masters regarded their slaves or Nazis the gypsies and the Jews.

Important as it is, however, cultural influence cannot ade- quately account either for the degree of Coriolanus's hostility toward the plebeians or for his need to express it, since he is far more extreme than any of his fellows. The play opens with the plebeians wanting to kill Coriolanus because he is "chief enemy to the people" (1.1), and his subsequent behavior bears out this judgment. The other patricians wish he could temporize (4.6), that he could "speak 'em fair" (3.1); but, try as he might, Cor- iolanus cannot, even if it means disappointing his mother, pre- cipitating a civil war, or losing his life. The intensity of his feelings has a number of causes, among which are his perfectionism and his need to protect his idealized image.

Horney observes that the perfectionistic person "feels superior because of his high standards, moral and intellectual, and on this basis looks down on others. His arrogant contempt . . . , though, is hidden . . . behind polished friendliness, because his very standards prohibit such 'irregular' feelings" (1950, 196). We do not see Coriolanus behave with "polished friendliness" toward any- one, but he is never arrogant toward his fellow patricians, even when he vastly outdoes them in battle or attacks their policy toward the plebeians. He begins his most impassioned re- monstrance by addressing them as "good but most unwise patricians," "grave but reckless senators" (3.1). There are taboos against pride, arrogance, and disrespect in Coriolanus's culture, and he obeys them in his behavior toward other patricians. The checks on his expressions of arrogant contempt are not operative in relation to the plebeians, however, because they are not part of his community of values. He displaces some of his repressed feelings toward the patricians onto them and looks down upon them from the height of his standards. He takes pride in the openness of his scorn because it shows him to be a forthright person who is not afraid to speak his mind and who does not flatter.

Coriolanus's hostility to the people is motivated also by his need to protect his idealized image. He is not simply indifferent to the love of the people, which has no value because of their fickleness, but rather "he seeks their hate with greater devotion than they can render it him and leaves nothing undone that may fully discover him their opposite" (2.2). The height of his standards makes him feel insecure, and his contempt for the plebeians reinforces his sense of superiority.[3] He welcomes their deficiencies, since they prove him to be their opposite. Their approval would threaten his sense of difference, so he must seek their hostility. "Who deserves greatness," he tells them, "Deserves your hate" (1.1).

As several critics have observed, the mob represents to Coriolanus "unacceptable impulses in his own personality" (Hofling 1957, 420; Adelman 1980, 135–36; Barron 1962, 174, 180). There is no consensus about precisely what these impulses are, but there is some agreement that Coriolanus has been forced to repress childish hungers in order to gain his mother's approval and that it is a childish part of himself he fears and scorns in the people. This view of Coriolanus is quite compatible, I think, with the interpretation I have been developing.

Coriolanus has received a great deal of praise and support from his mother—and food, too, I suspect; but he has not been given the "unconditional positive regard," in Carl Rogers's phrase, that children need for healthy development. I think it is this for which he unconsciously hungers, rather than oral gratifications, and that he is angry at having been denied. In Abraham Maslow's terms (1970), Volumnia's is a "deficiency" rather than a "being" love; she is not concerned with his growth and well-being but with his ability to satisfy her neurotic needs. As some commentators have noted, Coriolanus has no opportunity to develop an authentic self but must conform to an ideal of manhood imposed upon him by his mother.[4] This may be another source of his rage: he has been forced to abandon his real self and with it his chances for genuine fulfillment. He has been taught that in order to get warmth and approval he must live up to the martial code and expose himself to injury and death. He develops taboos against wanting to be cared for, looked after, nurtured, mothered, indulged, since these longings have met with no response and are inimical to the pursuit of honor and renown. Along with these taboos, he develops an elaborate set of shoulds, one of which is that he should expect nothing from life except what he deserves.

To Coriolanus, one of the most disturbing things about the plebeians is their demand for benefits they have not earned but to which they feel entitled. They are asking, in effect, for what has been denied to him, an unconditional respect for their worth and concern for their human needs. Having never received this, Coriolanus cannot give it, nor can he feel it to be a legitimate expectation. If he has had to earn his rewards, so should they; he is enraged by their demands, which violate his sense of justice. He is so threatened in part because they are acting out his repressed longings for nurture. As Christopher Givan observes, "in the mob Coriolanus . . . sees an image of all the things he most despises and most fears he might become" (1979, 144). The plebeians are a personification of his despised self, and he heaps upon them the loathing he would feel toward himself, and that his mother would feel toward him, should he behave as they are doing. His verbal assaults at once satisfy his need for justice by giving them what they deserve and protect his idealized image by assuring him that he could never behave like these despicable creatures.

III

Having examined Coriolanus's upbringing, character structure, and feelings toward the plebeians, I now propose to show how character and event interact to produce the tragedy. The initial precipitating event is the plebeians' mutiny, which is deeply disturbing to Coriolanus. The people are supposed to be seen but not heard, to accept the decisions of the wise patricians with gratitude and humility. Instead, they are up in arms, complaining of unfair treatment and demanding "corn at their own rates" (1.1). Worst of all, in order to placate them the patricians have given them five tribunes, "of their own choice," "to defend their vulgar wisdoms" (1.1). Since Coriolanus sees the plebeians as being fickle, unpatriotic, lacking in the higher human faculties, it is intolerable that their voices should be heard, and his hostility is intensified by their new power and status. He fears that Rome will be destroyed by the division o'f authority.

The mutiny of the plebeians threatens not only Coriolanus's sense of hierarchy but his entire conception of how the world should be ordered. Having been taught that he must perform in order to be rewarded, he imposes the same demand upon others. He divides the world into those who are deserving and those who are not, and he sees the people as demanding rewards—food, respect, political power—they have not earned. As Maurice Charney observes, for Coriolanus "the formula for distribution can only be: 'to each according to his merits'" (1963, 152). He objects on principle to giving the people corn:

> They know the corn
> Was not our recompense, resting well assur'd
> They ne'er did service for't. Being press'd to th' war
> Even when the navel of the state was touch'd,
> They would not thread the gates. This kind of service
> Did not deserve corn gratis.
>
> (3.1)

He is afraid the people will interpret "the Senate's courtesy" as an act of fear and that this will encourage their ambitions. He is also afraid that the whole system of rewards by which he and his fellows are motivated will be destroyed. If the plebeians triumph by defying authority, what reason will there be for loyalty, or respect, or heroic service? We shall be left with a world in which honor and justice have no meaning.

Coriolanus reacts to this situation with a murderous rage that indicates the degree to which his solution is menaced:

> Would the nobility lay aside their ruth
> And let me use my sword, I'd make a quarry
> With thousands of these quarter'd slaves as high
> As I could pick my lance.
>
> (1.1)

He welcomes war with the Volsces as a "means to vent / Our musty superfluity" (1.1), apparently relishing the thought of the plebeians being slaughtered, and he threatens to "make [his] wars on [them]" if they should retreat (1.4). The violence of his verbal assaults is in part a substitute for the physical violence he would like to visit upon them. Later, he is ready to foment civil war against the plebeians, and it should not surprise us that he pursues their destruction after his banishment.

The rise of the plebeians would not have had tragic consequences without the second precipitating event, which is the Senate's choice of Coriolanus to be consul. This is a reward for his service that Coriolanus feels he has deserved and that his mother very much wants for him. When he returns to Rome in triumph after the battle of Corioles, Volumnia is exultant but still not quite satisfied:

> I have liv'd
> To see inherited my very wishes,
> And the buildings of my fancy. Only
> There's one thing wanting, which I doubt not but
> Our Rome will cast upon thee.
>
> (2.1)

Coriolanus does not object to the office, which in fact he desires, but, in order to obtain it, he must show his wounds to the people and seek their approval, and this is a most repugnant prospect. He beseeches the Senate to let him "o'er leap that custom" (2.2), but the tribunes insist, and he is caught in a crossfire of conflicting *shoulds*. He can neither disappoint his mother by declining to be a candidate nor perform the customary rituals. As a result of his conflict, he behaves in ways that lead to his banishment.

The pressure to stand for consul is immense. Coriolanus has been made to feel that his purpose in life is to realize Volumnia's dreams of glory, and he compulsively acts out her scenarios. The more he wins her praise, the more power she has over him, since he depends upon her for his feeling of greatness and would be deflated if she withdrew her favor. Her telling him now that he has almost fulfilled all her wishes puts him under additional pressure. When he is so close to total success, how can he deny her the "one thing wanting"? Coriolanus and Volumnia have always been in harmony, since her wishes and his *shoulds* have been identical. Her desire for him to be consul puts them into conflict, however, and threatens him with the consequences of her disappointment.

There are a number of reasons why Coriolanus does not want to seek the approval of the plebeians, most of which he articulates in the following lines:

> It is a part
> That I shall blush in acting, and might well

Be taken from the people. . . .
To brag unto them, "Thus I did, and thus!"
Show them th' unaching scars which I should hide,
As if I receiv'd them for the hire
Of their breath only!

(2.2)

His reluctance to show his scars is a puzzling piece of behavior that has attracted a good deal of attention. He seems to be at odds with his culture on this issue, since wounds are venerated as "marks of merit" (2.3) that entitle their bearers to respect. Volumnia "thank[s] the gods" (2.1) that her son has come home injured, delights in adding up his wounds ("Now it's twenty-seven"), and is pleased that "there will be large cicatrices to show the people when he shall stand for his place" (2.1). Cominius tries to command the attention of the plebeians by reminding them that he can show their "enemies' marks" upon him (3.3); and Menenius compares Coriolanus's wounds to "graves i' th' holy churchyard" (3.3). Coriolanus, however, consistently plays down his wounds, referring to them as "unaching scars" that he should hide or as "Scratches with briers, / Scars to move laughter only" (3.3). The need to display his wounds in order to claim the consulship clashes with his need to treat them as insignificant.

We can find a clue to Coriolanus's attitude, I believe, in the following lines of Volumnia:

> The breasts of Hecuba
> When she did suckle Hector, look'd not lovelier
> Than Hector's forehead when it spit forth blood
> At Grecian sword, contemning.

(1.2)

In the Kittredge-Ribner edition, "contemning" is glossed as "disdaining, holding in contempt." Coriolanus has learned from his mother that wounds are a sign of contempt for pain and for the power of his enemy really to hurt him. Minimizing his wounds serves this purpose, while making much of them defeats it. Though he has his arm bound in a scarf after the battle of Corioles, he treats his wounds as a mere nosebleed that he has not had time to wash. Since wounds are a sign of service to Rome and a basis of claims to recognition, they must be made much of, however. Others are supposed to glorify his wounds, but the courageous soldier is not. This conflict between the need to minimize and the need to magnify wounds does not prevent other

men from displaying their wounds, as it does Coriolanus, perhaps because their need to deny that they have been made to
suffer is not so powerful as his. Coriolanus needs to feel that he is
invulnerable. He insists that his scars do not ache, but they are
evidence that he, too, can be penetrated. Despite his twenty-
seven injuries, he wishes to project an image of himself as unhurt.
Hence his response to Cominius when his general offers to accompany him into exile: "thou art too full / Of the wars' surfeits to
go rove with one / That's yet unbruis'd" (4.1).

Another reason why Coriolanus does not want to show the
people his wounds is that doing so will make it seem as if he "had
receiv'd them for the hire / Of their breath only!" (2.2). I have
already examined his attitude toward accepting "a bribe to pay
[his] sword" (1.9). He is uncomfortable receiving praise and reward from his fellow patricians, since these things threaten to
impugn the purity of his motives and to deprive him of honor.
The same motives make him uncomfortable at the thought that he
might appear to have incurred his wounds in order to win the
approval of the plebeians and hence to become consul. His reluctance in this situation is greatly intensified by the fact that he
disdains the plebeians. He actually does want recognition from
his fellow patricians, whom he respects as "the honor'd number, /
Who lack not virtue" (3.1), though it must be conferred in a way
that circumvents his taboos against serving for self-interested
motives. He does not want the approval of the plebeians, however, since he has powerful motives for preferring their hatred. He
is being forced by the Senate, by custom, and by the wishes of his
mother to show the scars he feels he should hide to people whom
he disdains in order to gain an approval that threatens his need to
maintain his differentness from them.

Seeking the approval of the plebeians, moreover, gives them a
power and a status they should not have: "It is a part / That I shall
blush in acting, and might well / Be taken from the people" (2.2).
Coriolanus knows it is the custom, but he feels that in this case the
custom is wrong and should be discarded:

> Custom calls me to't.
> What custom wills, in all things should we do't,
> The dust on antique time would lie unswept,
> And mountainous error be too highly heapt
> For truth to o'erpeer.
>
> (2.3)

This rejection of custom on the part of an archconservative like Coriolanus indicates the intensity of his personal objections. Given his view of the plebeians as unthinking, unreliable, sub-human creatures, it is intolerable to him that they should have a say in the selection of consuls, and he wishes to strip them of this power.

It is intolerable too that he should be dependent on their good graces and should have to woo them. This disturbs his sense of hierarchy and justice and threatens his entire solution.

> Better it is to die, better to starve,
> Than crave the hire which first we do deserve.
> Why in this wolvish toge should I stand here
> To beg of Hob and Dick that does appear
> Their needless vouches? . . .
>   Rather than fool it so,
> Let the high office and the honour go
> To one that would do thus.
>
>   (2.3)

As an expansive person, Coriolanus is uncomfortable at being forced to "beg" and "crave" and wear "the napless vesture of humility" (2.1). He has contempt for such self-effacing behavior and feels like a "fool" when he engages in it. It arouses such self-hate that he feels it would be better to die than to humiliate himself in this way. The intensity of his reaction is the result also of the denial of his claims that is involved in having to "crave the hire which first we do deserve." According to his bargain, he should get what he deserves because he deserves it, because life is just. He should not have to do anything in addition to that, to brag, to beg, or to pretend to be humble. He should not even have "to ask it kindly" (2.3), especially of the plebeians. His claim is that they should respect and reward him because he deserves it, without his having to humor them in the least. He needs both to have them honor his bargain and to maintain his differentness from them, and he can achieve these objectives only if they give him what he deserves while he heaps scorn upon them. Ideally, of course, they should have no power whatsoever, and he should not be dependent upon them for anything.

For Coriolanus, then, to seek the approval of the plebeians is to violate his shoulds, to abandon his claims, and to betray his idealized image of himself. Since all of these things arouse self-contempt, he prefers to "Let the high office and the honour go."

The thought of doing that, however, activates the other side of his conflict, and he decides to proceed: "I am half through; / The one part suffer'd, the other will I do" (2.3). He is torn between his need for his mother's approval and his need to protect his pride, and he is bound to experience self-hate no matter what he does. The result of his inner conflict is an attempt at compromise in which he asks for the voices of the people but in a mocking way that barely disguises his scorn:

> Your voices! For your voices I have fought;
> Watch'd for your voices; for your voices bear
> Of wounds two dozen odd; battles thrice six
> I have seen and heard of; for your voices have
> Done many things, some less, some more. Your voices!
> Indeed I would be consul.
>
> (2.3)

Through the plebeians at first give their approval because he appears to have observed the custom, they soon realize that they have been treated with "contempt" and decide to "deny him" (2.3). Coriolanus's inner conflict and his resulting attempt at compromise have proved disastrous.

As we might expect, Coriolanus is enraged by the withdrawal of the people's approval, which he interprets as a "plot / To curb the will of the nobility" (3.1). He is incapable of entering into their perspective and of realizing how insulting his behavior has been. Indeed, since he feels that they deserve his scorn, he cannot appreciate their objections to it. The conflict is now not only between Coriolanus and the plebeians, but also between Coriolanus and the patricians, whom he attacks for their failure to exercise authority. His appeals to them to take their power back aggravate his conflict with the plebeians, who try to have him arrested and carried to the Tarpeian Rock.

Coriolanus wants the patricians to "Stand fast" (3.1); but they feel that "This must be patch'd / With cloth of any colour" and urge him to "Speak fair" (3.2) to the plebeians, who they are sure can be placated. This throws Coriolanus once more into inner conflict. He believes that resisting the plebeians is as much of a patriotic duty as fighting Rome's external enemies and that honor requires him to sacrifice his life in this cause, if necessary.

> Let them pull all about mine ears; present me
> Death on the wheel or at wild horses' heels;
> Or pile ten hills on the Tarpeian Rock,

That the precipitation might down stretch
Below the beam of sight—yet will I still
Be thus to them.

                                                                    (3.2)

Coriolanus is protecting his image of himself as a man who cannot
be frightened into giving up his principles by the prospect of pain
and destruction. Since he is behaving as he had been taught by his
mother, he cannot understand her lack of approval and is disturbed that she would have him "False to [his] nature" (3.2). He is
put under intense pressure to appease the plebeians, however,
and eventually capitulates.

On the one hand, Coriolanus needs to live up to his idealized
image of himself as a man who prefers "a noble life before a long"
(3.1); but on the other he is told that unless he takes back his harsh
words, the city will "Cleave in the midst and perish" (3.2). He
agrees to give his "noble heart" the lie, but protests that "were
there but this single plot to love, / This mould of Marcius, they to
dust should grind it / And throw't against the wind" (3.2). He is
trying to protect his pride by insisting that he is compromising
himself only for the sake of the city. Volumnia understands his
fear of incurring self-hate and argues that placating the plebeians
is just as acceptable as using policy in war to deceive the enemy.
Succumbing to the pressure of his mother and the patricians,
Coriolanus agrees to go to the market place to make peace with
the people.

Once he agrees to do this, however, his self-hate rises to the
surface, as he imagines himself fawning upon the plebeians. He
will be a "harlot," a "eunuch," a "knave," a "schoolboy," a "beggar" (3.2), and he will feel toward himself the contempt that he
feels toward such weak or dishonorable creatures. The image of
himself as a beggar is particularly disturbing since it clashes so
violently with his expansive pride:

                         A beggar's tongue
     Make motion through my lips, and my arm'd knees,
     Who bow'd but in my stirrup, bend like his
     That hath receiv'd an alms!

                                                                    (3.2)

It is his place to command the plebeians, not to be suppliant to
them. Instead of being a courageous warrior who is true to himself and who deals straightforwardly with others, he will turn into

a contemptible creature for whom he can have no respect. In the grip of these feelings, he withdraws his acquiescence:

> I will not do't,
> Lest I surcease to honor mine own truth,
> And by my body's action teach my mind
> A most inherent baseness.
>
> (3.2)

Coriolanus's refusal to compromise himself has been seen by many to be a sign of his integrity. His problem is that his "nature is too noble for the world" (3.1). There is something very stirring about his desire to "honor [his] own truth," but we can see this as an expression of integrity only if we feel that he is being true to his real self, as Sir Thomas More is, for example, in *A Man for All Seasons* (see Paris 1986a, 62–65). Given his upbringing, however, Coriolanus has had no chance to remain in touch with his authentic nature. There has evolved instead, as Coppelia Kahn says, a "warrior self" that "has a false, automatic, inhuman quality . . . because it has been implanted in him rather than being allowed to develop from within" (1981, 159; see also Stockholder 1970, 229). It is this idealized image of himself to which Coriolanus is being true when he refuses to placate the plebeians. He is defending not a healthy relationship to himself but a neurotic relationship to the plebeians, which is, as we have seen an integral part of his solution. Driven by his shoulds and his fear of self-hate, he would rather sacrifice his life than give up his search for glory.

Coriolanus's inner conflicts have not been resolved, however. After a few words from his mother, he does an about-face and agrees once more to go to the market place.

>   At thy choice then.
> To beg of thee, it is my more dishonour
> Than thou of them. Come all to ruin! Let
> Thy mother rather feel thy pride than fear
> Thy dangerous stoutness; for I mock at death
> With as big a heart as thou. Do as thou list.
> Thy valiantness was mine, thou suck'st it from me;
> But owe thy pride thyself.
>
> (3.2)

I do not believe Volumnia is motivated here primarily by a desire to change Coriolanus's mind, though her words have that effect. She has asked him to appease the plebeians because she is con-

cerned for the city and she wants him to have the consulship.
When he refuses on the grounds that he must be true to himself,
her pride is stung and she refuses to plead any longer. His refusal
makes her feel less noble than he and too much like a suppliant.
Coriolanus has said that he cannot beg of the plebeians, and she
responds that it is even more of a dishonor for her to beg of him.
He has indicated that his pride is more important than his life or
the survival of the city, and she replies that she would rather see
all come to ruin than humble herself further and that she mocks at
death with as big a heart as he. She is angry with Coriolanus, but
she is also proud of him. She takes credit for his "valiantness" and
turns defeat into victory by identifying with his solution: "Let /
Thy mother rather feel thy pride than fear / Thy dangerous stout-
ness." There is some criticism of his pride, which she says he did
not get from her, but more fellow feeling, and a pride in herself
for not being afraid of the consequences.

Coriolanus responds to this speech by saying he will go to the
marketplace. When he asks his mother to "chide . . . no more," he
is referring, no doubt, to the subtext of the speech, the references
to the city's "ruin," her "death," and his "pride." Having satisfied
one set of shoulds by saying that he must honor his own truth, he
now feels the claims of the opposing dictates of duty to mother
and city. Volumnia reminds him that he is choosing not only his
own death, but hers as well; and this is bound to have a powerful
effect, whether he actually wishes her death, as some critics feel,
or is protective toward her. He becomes conciliatory, asks her to
"be content," and vows to "return consul" (3.2). This submissiveness is triggered not only by his need to assuage her
anger, but also by her display of pride, which reinforces her image
as "the most noble mother of the world" (5.3), one who deserves
obedience, awe, and respect. There is a self-effacing side of
Coriolanus that is spellbound by Volumnia's aggressiveness.

Coriolanus cannot keep his promise, however. Because of his
psychological bond, he must try to do what Volumnia wants; but
because of his character structure, he cannot actually do it. She
feels that because her "praises made [him] first a soldier" (3.2), she
can get him to change his nature; but Coriolanus knows that she
has put him "now to such a part which never / I shall discharge to
th' life" (3.2). There is a conflict between her wishes and his
shoulds, and though her influence is powerful, his pride system
is more powerful yet. Like Lady Macbeth, Volumnia destroys the
man whose glory is so important to her through a failure of
psychological knowledge, by urging him to engage in a form of

behavior that violates his predominant solution. Like Macbeth, Coriolanus knows that he cannot do what is being asked of him without incurring self-hate. The difference is that Macbeth proceeds, whereas Coriolanus does not; but for Coriolanus the mischief has already been done, and he is going to be in trouble no matter which course of action he follows.

He means to proceed, to speak the plebeians fair, but he becomes enraged when they call him a traitor and denounces them immediately. Coriolanus is enraged at the name of traitor because it violates his claims. He has shed his blood in the service of the city, and he expects to be regarded as its benefactor. To be called a traitor by these people, who have mutinied in peace and refused to serve in war, is an intolerable injustice, and he must give them the lie in the strongest possible terms. When Sicinius says that he "Deserves th' extremest death," Coriolanus defies the plebeians to do their worst:

> Let them pronounce the steep Tarpeian death,
> Vagabond exile, flaying, pent to linger
> But with a grain a day—I would not buy
> Their mercy at the price of one fair word,
> Nor check my courage for what they can give,
> To have't with saying "Good morrow."
>
> (3.3)

Coriolanus is engaged here in defending his idealized image. He shows his scorn for the plebeians and demonstrates his courage by proclaiming his readiness to endure the worst possible fate rather than dignify their status by according them the barest form of civility. He invites martyrdom as a way of completing the scenario his mother had laid out for him. By choosing death before the dishonor of pleading with the people, he will gain the final victory.

The plebeians decide to banish Coriolanus rather than to kill him because they have inner conflicts of their own. They know that he wants to deprive them of power and that they must "stand to [their] authority / Or . . . lose it" (3.1). They know, too, that there is no solution to their problem but the death of Coriolanus: "To eject him hence / Were but our danger, and to keep him here / Our certain death" (3.1). Like the patricians, however, they believe that "Ingratitude is monstrous" (2.3), and they are moved by all the appeals to honor Coriolanus's wounds, his sacrifices, and his service to the state. Like Coriolanus, they are led by their inner conflicts to attempt an unworkable compromise that goes against their better judgment.

Coriolanus reacts to his banishment with rage and with massive efforts at self-defense. His scorn for the plebeians is fierce:

> You common cry of curs, whose breath I hate
> As reek o' th' rotten fens, whose loves I prize
> As the dead carcasses of unburied men
> That do corrupt my air, I banish you!
>
> (3.3)

By tearing down the plebeians, he reduces the importance of their acts. If he hates them and has no use for their "loves," he cannot be hurt by their rejection. By saying that he banishes them, he restores his sense of power and initiative. It is they who will suffer most from his departure. He will find "a world elsewhere," while they will be left vulnerable to their enemies and a prey to fear and despair. All of this restores his pride by denying that it has been hurt, by placing him in the superior position, and by portraying his banishment as something he is inflicting upon them— "Despising / For you the city, thus I turn my back" (3.3).

When he parts from his mother, he is similarly defensive. He tries to comfort her by citing her own precepts:

> You were us'd
> To say extremities was the trier of spirits;
> That common chances common men could bear;
> That when the sea was calm, all boats alike
> Show'd mastership in floating; fortune's blows
> When most struck home, being gentle wounded craves
> A noble cunning.
>
> (4.1)

Coriolanus has, no doubt, been repeating these precepts to himself, since their import is that the present occasion provides an opportunity to demonstrate his nobility of spirit. He envisions himself being "lov'd when [he is] lack'd" and more dreaded than before, "Like to a lonely dragon, that his fen / Makes fear'd and talk'd of more than seen" (4.1). He assures Volumnia that he'll "do well yet," that he'll "exceed the common," that she "shall / Hear from [him] still, and never of [him] aught / But what is like [him] formerly" (4.2). He is telling her, in effect, that his search for glory is still on, that he will find some way to make her proud of him.

He has received a crushing psychological blow, but he acts as though nothing has been lost.

IV

We do not see Coriolanus between his departure from Rome and his entry into Antium, but it is not difficult to imagine what has led him to seek out Aufidius. His defenses collapse when he is confronted with the actualities of exile. There is no world elsewhere, no way he can win honor and renown. His banishment has frustrated his claims, shattered his bargain, and left him without a sense of purpose. He copes with his psychological crisis by abandoning his perfectionistic solution, which can no longer work, and devoting himself to revenge. Turning against the city he has always served induces such guilt that he tries to minimize its significance in a strange soliloquy in which he reflects on how easily friends become enemies and enemies friends (4.4). He seeks out Aufidius in a mood of reckless desperation and offers his "revengeful services":

> But if so be
> Thou dar'st not this, and that to prove more fortunes
> Th'art tired, then, in a word, I also am
> Longer to live most weary, and present
> My throat to thee and to thy ancient malice;
> Which not to cut would show thee but a fool,
> Since I have ever followed thee with hate,
> Drawn tuns of blood out of thy country's breast,
> And cannot live but to thy shame, unless
> It be to do thee service.
>
>   (4.5)

Since life has no meaning other than revenge, Coriolanus wishes to die if Aufidius will not accept his services; and he seeks to assure this result by taunting Aufidius and stressing the "Great hurt and mischief" he has done the Volsces. This serves also to protect his pride, since it reminds everyone of his prowess and would give some meaning to his death should Aufidius decide to kill him.

From this point on, *Coriolanus* becomes a revenge play, with Coriolanus seeking revenge on Rome and then Aufidius seeking revenge on Coriolanus. Like other revengers in Shakespeare, Coriolanus tries to restore his pride by striking back at those who have injured him. He is now fully in touch with his sense of betrayal. The only reward he has received for "The painful service, / The extreme dangers, and the drops of blood / Shed for [his] thankless country" is the "surname Coriolanus" (4.6). He blames his humiliation on "the cruelty and envy of the people" and on the cowardice of the patricians, who have forsaken him. The patricians themselves seem to agree with his assessment of them: "If he could burn us all into one coal," says Menenius, "We have deserved it" (4.6).

Coriolanus has lived up to his shoulds, but Rome has not honored their bargain. He feels released from his civic obligations, free to show his "cank'red country" (4.5) that it cannot get away with what it has done to him. When his wife, mother, and child arrive, however, he is again thrown into conflict. To yield to their entreaties means to give up his revenge and to break his word to the Volsces. This would make him feel like "a gosling," a weak, foolish, contemptible creature. It is in this context that he tries to deny instinct, to "stand / As if a man were author of himself / And knew no other kin" (5.3). These words are not a sign that his "entire sense of himself depends on his being able to see himself as a self-sufficient creature" (Adelman 1980, 132) or that he wishes to be independent of "the community and its evaluative processes" (Fish 1976, 988). They are part of his struggle to avoid bringing shame on himself by giving in to his softer feelings.

If Coriolanus experiences such conflict at the mere sight of his family in supplicating postures, it is not surprising that he succumbs to their further entreaties. He is half won before a word is spoken. Critics have tried to identify which speech or action results in his capitulation, but there is no one cause of his about-face. For nearly a hundred lines his mother appeals to him, accompanied by pleading gestures from his wife and son; and although Coriolanus is for the most part silent, everything is registering upon him and undermining his resistance. If we have understood his psychology, we can readily imagine the intensity of his inner conflict.

The appearance of his family stirs up Coriolanus's self-effacing tendencies. He feels tenderness toward mother, wife, and child and displays the deference toward Volumnia that we had seen in Rome. Sensing his vulnerability, she tries to arouse sympathy for his family's dilemma. They cannot pray to the gods because of divided loyalties and are bound to lose either him or their country. She arouses his protectiveness and guilt by equating an invasion of Rome with an assault on her womb and by threatening suicide if he should attack. She is seconded in this by Virgilia. These appeals do move Coriolanus, though not in the way Volumnia desires. He is alarmed by his weakening resolution and rises to escape:

> Not of a woman's tenderness to be
> Requires nor child nor woman's face to see.
> I have sat too long.
>
>   (5.3)

Volumnia's success in arousing his tenderness is very threatening to Coriolanus, since he has taboos against being womanly and cannot bear to be perceived as weak. If he gave into her, moreover, he would dishonor himself with the Volsces. Since he can move neither toward nor against his mother, he tries to deal with his conflict by moving away.

Volumnia deters him, however, and sensitive to his psychology, assures him that her suit is not "poisonous of [his] honour," for she seeks a peace for which both sides will bless him. Though he will not lose his honor if he makes peace, he will lose it if he destroys Rome:

>   . . . the benefit
> Which thou shalt thereby reap is such a name,
> Whose repetition will be dogg'd with curses,
> Whose chronicle thus writ, "The man was noble
> But with his last attempt he wip'd it out,
> Destroy'd his country, and his name remains
> To th' ensuing age abhorr'd."
>
>   (5.3)

These lines have a powerful impact upon Coriolanus. He has tried to divorce himself from Rome, to persuade himself that he can forge a new name for himself "i' th' fire" of his native city. What Volumnia is saying is that he cannot win glory by conquering Rome; instead, he will lose all the glory he has hitherto won and will make his name abhorred to ensuing ages. Coriolanus has lived for posterity; he has been ready to die in order to gain honor and renown. The only fame that can mean very much to him is that which he can have in Rome; it is the Roman community to which he belongs and by which he wishes to be remembered. Having always imagined himself going down in history as one of his country's greatest heroes, he finds it horrible to face the prospect of being loathed as its destroyer.

In the remainder of her speech, Volumnia alternates between addressing his sense of honor and appealing to his pity and affection. She reminds him that he has "affected the fine strains of honour" and asks if it is "honourable for a noble man / Still to remember wrongs?" (5.3). Revenge is acceptable on behalf of the community, but personal revenge is not a virtue. When this approach does not produce the desired effect, Volumnia points pathetically to his weeping wife and his son and reminds him of his bond to her and of her devotion to him. When this does not work either, she cites the obedience he owes to her as his mother and warns that "the gods will plague" him if he is undutiful. When Coriolanus turns away, she has the ladies go upon their knees to "shame him," says that they will "home to Rome / And die among [their] neighbors," points to the pleading gestures of the boy, and finally gives up: "Come, let us go. / This fellow had a Volscian to his mother; / His wife is in Corioles, and this child / Like him by chance" (5.3). It is at this point that Coriolanus gives in.

What has been going on inside of Coriolanus while his mother has been speaking? As I read his character, his silence is indicative not of refusal, but of inner conflict. He cannot say yes, he cannot say no, and so he says nothing. He has repressed his lifelong dispositions in order to embrace his mission of revenge, but this is bound to be an unstable solution. His mother plays skillfully upon his bond to his family, his sense of duty, and his desire for a glorious place in history. On the other side of the conflict are his reluctance to give up his revenge, his fear of seeming effeminate, and his concern about losing his honor.

His desire for revenge has led Coriolanus to violate his code and to promise his "traitorous services" to the Volsces. Once he does this, he can neither proceed nor withdraw without losing his honor. Despite his mother's efforts to reassure him, he knows that his honor will be poisoned if he does what she wants. When he gives in, Aufidius immediately observes that he has "set [his] mercy and [his] honour / At difference" (5.3). There is no way he can justify making peace with the Romans; the Volsces will not give him "the all-hail." This is their golden opportunity to take revenge for their humiliations, and they are bound to feel that he

has "given up, / For certain drops of salt, [their] city Rome / . . . .
Breaking his oath and resolution like / A twist of rotten silk" (5.6).
When Coriolanus relents, he is aware of the danger:

> O my mother, mother! O!
> You have won a happy victory to Rome;
> But for you son—believe it, O believe it!—
> Most dangerously you have with him prevail'd,
> If not most mortal to him.
>
> (5.3)

I do not think that Coriolanus has hesitated for fear of the personal danger, however, but because of the other considerations I
have been examining.

It is understandable that Coriolanus submits to his mother's
wishes, but it is also understandable that he finds it difficult to do
so. He capitulates when his mother gives up the argument. As
long as she pleads with him, he has no need to make a final
decision, and he can feel the force of the counterarguments.
When there is no more need to resist, her words take effect. Her
statement that he "had a Volscian to his mother" affects him
profoundly. Coriolanus has tried to divorce himself from Rome,
but with the appearance of his family, he realizes that he cannot
do so. Having taught him this lesson, his family now threatens to
divorce itself from him and to deny him a Roman identity. If he
carries out his attack, he will be truly alone in the world, without
the family and the city that have given his life its meaning.

When he agrees to make peace, he is left in a difficult position.
He cannot divorce himself from Rome, but he is too resentful to
return, and he has jeopardized his position with the Volsces by
having relented. He senses his danger but is ready to "let it
come," since he has nothing left to live for. By not destroying
Rome he has preserved his future glory, but there is nothing
meaningful for him to do with the rest of his life.

The manner of his death is still a matter of great importance. He
has devoted himself to showing that he prefers "A noble life before
a long" (3.1), and the confirmation of such a life is a noble conclusion. Coriolanus does die nobly, defending his idealized image
against Aufidius's attack. He was afraid of relenting because it
would expose him to charges of weakness and dishonor, and
these are precisely the charges Aufidius brings against him. He
accuses him of "perfidiously" betraying their business and of
whining "away [their] victory" "at his nurse's tears" (5.6).

Coriolanus has not only been moved by his family's weeping but has wept himself, and Aufidius delivers the final insult by calling him a "boy of tears" (5.6). Coriolanus is so threatened by these charges because they reinforce the self-accusations against which he has been struggling. He must repel them and restore his pride at all costs. He does so by reminding his auditors of the beatings he has given them and of his great triumph when he entered their city alone. He is deliberately insulting to Aufidius and the Volsces as a way of affirming his courage, of showing them that he is not afraid to die. Indeed, he invites them to kill him: "Cut me to pieces, Volsces. Men and lads, / Stain all your edges on me" (5.6). He does this, I think, because he really wants to die. As Menenius had said earlier, "He that hath a will to die by himself fears it not from another" (5.2). With Aufidius against him, Coriolanus has no future with the Volsces, even if he is exonerated. A defiant death in defense of his honor is the best thing that can happen to him. It saves him from an ambiguous situation in which he is subject to self-hate and reproach from others, and it confirms for all time his nobility and courage.

The ending of the play has a wish-fulfillment quality, as Coriolanus is glorified by the Volsces after his death. "Let him be regarded / As the most noble corse that ever herald / Did follow to his urn" (5.6). Even Aufidius is struck with sorrow and testifies to his nobility:

> Though in this city he
> Hath widowed and unchilded many a one,
> Which to this hour bewail the injury,
> Yet he shall have a noble memory.

> (5.6)

The play ends with Coriolanus's feats being remembered and his grandeur acknowledged, even by his enemies. Coriolanus has lived and was always prepared to die in order to leave behind a noble memory, and he has attained that end not only in Rome, but also in Corioles. He could preserve his noble memory in Rome only by relenting and in Corioles only by paying for that act with his life.

Conclusion

My argument has been that the central characters in Shakespeare's history and Roman plays are imagined human beings who can be understood in motivational terms and that we cannot do justice to Shakespeare's genius in mimetic characterization unless we so understand them. I have found the theories of Karen Horney to be remarkably congruent with Shakespeare's portrayal of characters and relationships, and I have tried to recover his psychological intuitions by analyzing his plays with the help of these theories. When we understand Shakespeare's mimetic characters in motivational terms, we find that they are, in E. M. Forster's phrase, "creations inside a creation" who tend to subvert the larger structures of which they are a part.

One way of approaching the subversive action of such characters is to examine the relationship between rhetoric (the devices employed to shape our moral, emotional, and intellectual response to the characters) and mimesis (the concrete portrayal of thoughts, feelings, and actions). Often the rhetoric seeks to induce a set of responses that are not in harmony with the mimetic portrait of the character. When we understand the character as an imagined human being, we find ourselves resisting the rhetoric. Critical controversies are frequently generated by the fact that most critics respond primarily to the rhetoric while some respond primarily to the mimesis. The relatively few critics who respond to both rhetoric and mimesis tend either to find the work confusing or to develop elaborate strategies for reconciling the conflicting messages they are receiving from the text. My approach is to acknowledge that there are conflicting messages and to explain them by recognizing rhetorical inconsistencies, disparities between rhetoric and mimesis, and authorial blind spots and inner conflicts.

Though mimetic characterization usually subverts the structures within which it exists, the problem is not with the mimesis; the fact that a character tends to "kick the book to pieces" is a sign of the character's richness. The problem is that realistic writers are usually much less gifted as interpreters and judges than they are as creators of psychological portraits. This is true even of Shakespeare. In some of his plays there are disparities between what we are shown and how we are asked to respond, while in others the rhetoric is not even consistent with itself. When the rhetoric is inconsistent, some of it may be in harmony with the characterization and some of it may not. It is the confusion or inadequacy of the rhetoric combined with the tendency of mimetic characters to take on a life of their own that makes such characters a subversive force.

All the phenomena I have described occur in *Antony and Cleopatra,* where Shakespeare's characterization of the protagonists is consistent but his rhetorical treatment of them is not.[1] Through the first three acts of the play, the rhetoric calls our attention to the self-destructiveness of Antony's behavior and the manipulativeness of Cleopatra's, but in the last two acts it obscures the responsibility of the protagonists for their own fates and reinforces their self-glorification. If we examine Antony and Cleopatra as mimetic characters, we find that they are bound together in a relationship that cannot work until they are defeated because their inner conflicts lead them to have contradictory needs of each other. The rhetoric is in harmony with the mimesis in the first three acts, where it is critical of the protagonists' behavior, but it clashes with it in the last two, where it romanticizes resignation, morbid dependency, and death.

The critics who see the play as a depiction of folly and self-deception are responding to the rhetoric of the first three acts and to the mimetic portrait of the protagonists throughout, but they tend to ignore or to rationalize away the glorifying rhetoric of the conclusion. Those who see Antony and Cleopatra as triumphant at the end are justified by the rhetoric of the last two acts, but they allow it to blind them to the fact that the lovers are cheering themselves up. A number of recent critics recognize that the play sustains both of these readings, but they disagree about whether it somehow transcends its contradictions or is torn apart by them.

I do not feel that the play is aesthetically coherent, but I think we can make sense of its inconsistencies if we see them as expressions of Shakespeare's ambivalence toward the self-effacing side of himself. Antony has many things in common with the poet of the sonnets. He is a doting lover who is bewitched by a dark lady of dubious reputation and who is given both to compulsive sensuality and to self-disgust. The first three acts of the play are governed by Shakespeare's contempt for the side of himself embodied in Antony, while the last two acts rewrite the story of the sonnets and make the self-effacing bargain work.

The second tetralogy has also generated a great deal of controversy. Like *Antony and Cleopatra*, *Richard II* begins as a tragedy of character in which the flaws of the protagonist are responsible for his destruction. As the play proceeds, however, the rhetoric becomes sympathetic to Richard, who is portrayed as a man more sinned against than sinning. It begins as a political play full of illustrative characters, but after Richard's return from Ireland, it develops into a psychological drama in which the political issues become elusive. Richard's suffering, like Lear's, is so vividly portrayed that it tends to obscure his faults and the thematic issues associated with them. His poetry casts such a powerful spell that many critics are deceived by his self-dramatization and believe that he attains a greater moral stature by the end. These may be blind spots of the author as well, for he allows Richard to achieve a sense of victory in his defeat, as he does with Antony. The brilliance of Richard's characterization is at once the glory of the play and the source of many of its difficulties.

Shakespeare's presentation of Prince Hal in the two parts of *Henry IV* has also sponsored conflicting interpretations. Critics are divided between those who feel Hal to be an ideal prince from the start and those who feel that he undergoes a process of reformation. Those who feel that he is virtuous from the start point to the opening soliloquy in which he announces his intention of throwing off his loose behavior at the appropriate moment; but this soliloquy is itself a subject of controversy, since it makes Hal appear a calculating schemer who heartlessly uses (and later rejects) Falstaff for his own political purposes. This view of Hal does not take into account, moreover, his feelings of guilt, his tormenting behavior toward his father in part 1, and his reversion to such behavior in part 2, after the reconciliation at Shrewsbury. Hal's backsliding in part 2 creates problems for the reformation theory as well, since it seems to negate the pattern of growth that preceded it. Seeing Hal as undergoing reformation is inconsistent with his opening soliloquy, moreover, in which Shakespeare appears to be letting us know that Hal's beauty, like that of the sun, is there all along, even when it is obscured by "base contagious clouds" (1.2). When Hal speaks of his "reformation" in this soliloquy, he is not referring to an inward process of change, but to the way he will appear to others.

Some critics see the plays, then, as having a vindication pattern in which the prince's detractors come to recognize his merit, while others see them as having an education plot in which the immature prince must come to terms with adult restraints and responsibilities. I feel that both readings can be supported, the first by the rhetoric of the plays and the second by the mimesis. The relation between the two parts is confusing when we follow the rhetoric, for part 1 creates expectations that part 2 disappoints; but the plays are unified mimetically, for, when we understand Hal's motives, his personality is consistent throughout. Indeed, motivational analysis binds together all the plays in which Hal appears by enabling us to understand why the playful, multidimensional prince of *1 and 2 Henry IV* becomes the rigid, humorless king of *Henry V.*

In *Henry V,* there is once again a disparity between rhetoric and mimesis. Those who feel that Henry is an exemplary monarch are responding to Shakespeare's glorification of him, largely by means of the Chorus, while those who feel he is not point to many details in the mimetic portrait that undercut his heroic pretensions. Some critics contend that Henry is a cardboard character who has no internal coherence, but I find him to be an imagined human being whose contradictions make psychological sense. He has not only the perfectionistic and self-effacing traits that are glorified by the rhetoric, but also aggressive tendencies that have led some to describe him as a hypocrite or a Machiavel. Henry's conflicts seem to reflect those of the author, for whom the play releases aggressive impulses in a way that does not conflict with his needs for rectitude and humility.

Julius Caesar is usually discussed in terms of its political themes, but I think it is primarily a tragedy of character, the outcome of which is determined by the interaction of Brutus, Cassius, and Caesar. The relationship between Cassius and Brutus is portrayed with great subtlety and is one of the most complex in Shakespeare. Rhetoric is less prominent in this play than in the histories, but there are shifts in the treatment of both Cassius and Brutus that lead to interpretative problems. Cassius is presented as a villain at the beginning, but he becomes a sympathetic figure once Brutus joins the conspiracy, and he achieves victory despite his defeat—not only from his own point of view but from that of the play as well. Though Brutus is presented as self-deceived through most of the play, the rhetoric at the end supports his version of himself as the noblest Roman of them all. I have an explanation for the shift in the treatment of Cassius, but I cannot account for the inconsistent presentation of Brutus. Once again the problem is in the rhetoric rather than in the mimesis, which consistently shows Brutus to be full of illusions about himself.

There is a different kind of tension between rhetoric and mimesis in *Richard III*. Richard is the first of Shakespeare's great mimetic characters, and, like most of the Machiavels, he seems to be well understood both intuitively and at the conscious level. Richard deceives most of the characters, but not the author, whose rhetorical treatment of him is consistent both with itself and with the mimetic portrait. Richard subverts the rhetoric not by being better or worse than it suggests but by arousing responses that are inappropriate to his role as villain. His soliloquies provide so much insight into his pain and the sources of his malicious behavior that they generate a good deal of sympathy. He is not a motiveless villain, but a suffering human being who has been rejected because of his deformity and who is trying to compensate for feeling unloved by pursuing vindictive triumphs. He does this with so much gusto and ingenuity that we take a scandalous delight in his success. We disapprove of his behavior, but it is Richard about whom we care and in whom we are chiefly interested. This confusion of effect is an inevitable result of Shakespeare's techniques of characterization, for, as Wayne Booth (1961) points out, we tend to be seduced by deep, inside views of villains. It may also be the result of an ambivalence on Shakespeare's part toward characters like Richard, through whom he simultaneously expresses and repudiates his own aggressive impulses. He criticizes his Machiavels severely, but he draws them with such force that they are often magnetic figures.

Antony and Cleopatra, Hal, Cassius, Brutus, and the two Richards are all creations inside a creation whose problematic relation to the work as a whole has generated critical controversy. As I have tried to indicate, there are various kinds and degrees of tension between rhetoric and characterization. The rhetoric seems appropriate to the characterization at the beginning of *Richard II*, *Julius Caesar*, and *Antony and Cleopatra* but not at the end. It is in harmony with the characterization of Richard III, even though our deep, inside views of him sometimes subvert its intended effects, and it is inappropriate to the characterization of Hal in all of the plays in which he appears.

Coriolanus is at once the most fully rendered of the characters I have discussed and the least engaged in treason against his role in the play. Despite Shakespeare's apparent sympathy with patrician attitudes, the irrationality with which Coriolanus espouses his positions makes it difficult to see the play as affirming his political philosophy. The rhetoric does not induce much identification with this protagonist, and we never lose sight of the fact that it is his compulsive behavior that brings about his downfall. Like many of Shakespeare's protagonists, Coriolanus undergoes a psychological crisis because of the breakdown of his bargain with fate, and he behaves self-destructively in his effort to restore his pride and to find a new set of defenses. *Richard II, Julius Caesar,* and *Antony and Cleopatra* all begin as tragedies of character, but in each of these plays the pattern is obscured by a shift in the rhetoric. *Coriolanus* is a tragedy of character throughout.

Notes

Chapter 1. "Creations inside a Creation"

1. Nuttall attempts "to show that literature can engage with reality" and directs his argument "against formalism, that is, against the resolution of matter into form, reality into fiction, substance into convention" (1983, vii). He opposes the following theorems of structuralism and poststructuralism: "1. The world consists not of things but of relationships. 2. *Verum factum:* truth is something made. 3. The ultimate goal of the human sciences is not to constitute man but to dissolve him. 4. Language is prior to meaning. 5. Verisimilitude is the mask in which the laws of the text are dressed up" (1983, 8).

2. "Imagined human beings" is W. J. Harvey's term (1965). A. D. Nuttall calls such characters "possible human beings" (1983, 168), Martin Price calls them "fictional persons" (1983, 64), Seymour Chatman calls them "constructed imitations" (1978, 118), and R. S. Crane calls them "concrete semblances of real men and women" (1953, 16). All of these critics are concerned with how mimetic characters "differ from real persons and yet must refer to them and draw their force from what we know their experience to be like" (Price 1983, xiv).

3. There is a good discussion of the differences in characterization between Shakespeare's realistic and unrealistic plays in Adelman (1973, 1–13). See Newman (1985, chap. 9) for a discussion of the similarities.

4. As Chatman observes, "A viable theory of character should preserve openness and treat characters as autonomous beings, not as mere plot functions" (1978, 119). All characters have aesthetic functions, but mimetic characters are more than their functions, and doing justice to their complexity is a legitimate objective of criticism, since, as Martin Price says, "the creation of character is a form of art" (1983, 47). Mimetic characters are both functional and autonomous, and critics tend to focus on one or the other of these aspects.

A. D. Nuttall's distinction between "opaque" and "transparent" criticism is useful here. Opaque criticism is "external, formalist, operating outside the mechanisms of art and taking those mechanisms as its object," whereas transparent criticism is "internal, realist, operating within the 'world' presented in the work." Opaque criticism "throws upon the screen of critical consciousness all the formal devices of a work in such a way that the eye is arrested by them. Formal characters, in order that they should be the more visible, are deliberately made opaque." In the second form of criticism, "formal devices are, like windows, transparent" (1983, 80). In opaque criticism "explanation is generally sought in terms of what happens in other works of art, or elsewhere in the present work," whereas in transparent criticism "no tabu exists against explaining fictitious behaviour by analogy with real-life equivalents" (1983, 81). Both forms of criticism are legitimate, but Nuttall prefers, as do I, the transparent mode. I am also interested, however, in the relation (often the tension) between a character's mimetic and functional aspects, and that requires switching back and forth between the two perspectives.

5. Seymour Chatman notes that "the views of the Formalists and (some) structuralists resemble Aristotle's in a striking way. They too argue that characters are products of plots, that their status is 'functional,' that they are, in short, participants or *actants* rather than *personnages*, that it is erroneous to consider them as real beings. . . . They wish to analyze only what characters do in a story, not what they are—that is, 'are' by some outside psychological or moral measure" (1978, 111). Though Todorov distinguishes between plot-centered and character-centered narratives (1977, 66), Chatman himself is the only structuralist (to my knowledge) who actually makes a case for motivational analysis of realistically drawn characters. Indeed, he provides a powerful response to many of the structuralist objections to the mimetic view of character.

There is a good discussion of the structuralist view in Culler (1975, 230–38). Culler recognizes that the structuralist emphasis on function is an extreme and inadequate position: ". . . for the roles proposed are so reductive and so directly dependent on plot that they leave us with an immense residue, whose organization structural analysis should attempt to explain rather than ignore" (1975, 232). It is this "immense residue" that I attempt to explain through psychological analysis.

6. Brian Vickers documents the fact that "the best critical work of the period was produced in responding to Shakespeare's characters" (1981, 12), but he does not connect this to the rise of the novel.

7. For excellent responses to Knights, see Crane (1953, 14–16) and Nuttall (1965). As V. Y. Kantak argues, when we regard the great characters "only as more or less abstract counters which serve as vehicles for Shakespeare's poetry . . . the result is that character, event, action and the motives behind action, all lose the normal sense we attach to them, leaving us with a continuous dramatic poem—in reality more like a lyric—which only because of certain extraneous features we call drama" (1977, 81). This shows "a fundamental misconception about the category 'drama'. Is it possible to talk about that category without assuming that a simulation of the kind of unity of motive and behaviour that characterize the actions of living human beings is essential to it?" (1977, 77). It is a mistake to separate images from the speeches in which they occur and speeches from the characters who utter them: "The poetry that a character speaks, in an important sense, 'belongs' to and is revelatory of that character. It cannot simply be regarded as though it 'belonged' only to Shakespeare in the way lyric poetry belongs to an author" (1977, 77).

8. E. D. Hirsch argues that valid interpretation involves a "re-cognition of the author's meaning." If we could establish "that Shakespeare did not mean that Hamlet wished to sleep with his mother," then a Freudian interpretation which states that Hamlet did have this wish would be invalid; and it would be "irrelevant" that the play permitted such an interpretation. Since it is highly unlikely that Shakespeare meant us to understand his characters in the way that we do with the use of modern psychological theories, Hirsch's position would seem to exclude the approach I am defending. He goes on to argue, however, that "for some genres of texts . . . the principle of including or excluding implications is not what the author is aware of, but whether or not the implications belong to the *type* of meaning that he wills." If we reject the implication that Hamlet wished to sleep with his mother, it is not because Shakespeare "could not have stated the implication in distinctly Freudian terms," but because "it was not, on our prem-

ise, the kind of trait that belonged to the type of character Shakespeare imagined. . . . the principle for including or excluding implications is to ask whether they are embraced by the author's will to mean 'all traits belonging to this particular type' " (1967, 121–24).

Hirsch's position is not incompatible with mine if we assume, as I do, that in some instances Shakespeare intended to create imagined human beings whose behavior could be understood in the same way that we understand the behavior of real people. Shakespeare could not have been conscious of all of the traits that belong to such a character, but he intended the character to be naturalistically motivated. It is appropriate to try to make sense of such a character, therefore, in psychological terms, even if our mode of discourse is very different from the one Shakespeare would have used had he written a critical analysis.

According to Hirsch, validity in interpretation depends upon a correct identification of the type of meaning willed or of the intrinsic genre of the work. As he himself acknowledges, however, there is no way to establish the correctness of a generic identification. My interpretation of Shakespeare will seem valid only to those who agree with my conception of the nature of his plays.

9. In *Artificial Persons: The Formation of Character in the Tragedies of Shakespeare,* J. Leeds Barroll argues that Shakespeare's contemporaries had sophisticated theories of human behavior, that these theories may well have stimulated Shakespeare's impulse toward realistic characterization, and that they offer a way of understanding the complexity of Shakespeare's greatest characters in Renaissance terms. Impressive as his demonstrations are, and useful as they are for historical understanding, I remain convinced that twentieth-century theories are more adequate to Shakespeare's mimetic portrayal of psychological phenomena. Barroll argues that we do not have to reject historicity in order to do justice to Shakespeare's characterization (1974, 20–21), but I do not believe that understanding them in terms of Renaissance theory makes their behavior intelligible to us.

10. In an essay entitled "Reductionism and Its Discontents," Frederick Crews points out that such developments within the Freudian tradition as ego psychology and object-relations theory "still give the greatest weight to infantile themes" and that, therefore, "the method itself blocks the path of a critic who would avoid reductionism" (1975, 176).

11. Norman Holland's work with identity themes (1975, 1985), which is inspired by the theories of Heinz Lichtenstein, employs a synchronic mode of analysis that is more suitable to character study (although Holland does not use it that way) and that is similar in some respects to the approach I employ.

12. For a fuller account of Third Force psychology and of the relation of Maslow and Horney, see Paris 1986a, chap. 1. This volume contains a bibliography of Third Force psychologists and of literary criticism that employs their theories. See Kelman (1971), Rubins (1978), and Quinn (1987) for useful accounts of the development of Horney's theory; Westkott (1986) for Horney's contribution to feminist thought; and Paris (1989) for a survey of interdisciplinary applications of Horney.

13. See Paris 1991 for discussions of these and other listed characters who are not in the history and Roman plays.

14. Horney speaks of "aggressive" and "compliant" solutions in *Our Inner Conflicts* (1945) and of "expansive" and "self-effacing" solutions in *Neurosis and Human Growth* (1950). I use these terms more or less interchangeably, depending upon which is most appropriate to the character and behavior under discussion.

The division of expansive solutions into narcissistic, perfectionistic, and arrogant-vindictive occurs in *Neurosis and Human Growth*.

Chapter 2. Richard III

1. There are interesting psychological analyses of Richard in the essays by
Neill (1975) and Wheeler (1971–72). For other psychological studies of Richard,
see Adler (1936), Holland (1966, 334–36), and Krieger (1959).

2. I am indebted to Randal Robinson for making me more vividly aware of
the destructive influence of his mother upon Richard. In an unpublished essay,
"The Identity and Temptations of Richard III," he points out that, when she stops
Richard on his way to battle, the Duchess, "like others in the play before her,
calls her son a toad . . . . comical though the word may be in itself, it expresses
the intolerance the Duchess feels toward Richard's physical deformity, and thus
it reveals a prejudice which must have been present since Richard's birth."
Robinson argues that the Duchess "used every possible development to reassure
herself that Richard deserved her scornful treatment—including his long stay in
the womb, the difficulty she had in his delivery, his entrance into the world
deformed, and his disagreeable behavior as an infant. . . . [She] gave Richard
hate instead of love, . . . rejected his demands for support, and . . . made it
impossible for Richard to connect himself with her in a direct, natural fashion."
Adler and Neill also discuss the Duchess's destructive effect upon Richard, Adler
from an Adlerian and Neill from a Laingian point of view.

3. I shall be using the Kittredge-Ribner edition of Shakespeare throughout.
In this chapter, when no title is given, the reference is to *Richard III*.

4. Freud includes Richard among those who feel that they are an exception
because of "some experience of suffering to which they had been subjected in
their earliest childhood, one in respect of which they knew themselves to be
guiltless, and which they could look upon as an unjust disadvantage imposed
upon them." What Richard's opening soliloquy in *Richard III* "thus means is:
'Nature has done me a grievous wrong in denying me the beauty of form which
wins human love. Life owes me reparation for this, and I will see that I get it. I
have a right to be an exception, to disregard the scruples by which others let
themselves be held back. I may do wrong myself, since wrong has been done to
me' " (1958, 86, 88).

5. The strongest case for the psychological realism of the scene between
Richard and Anne has been made by Donald R. Shupe (1978).

Chapter 3. *Richard II*

1. For valuable discussions of this issue, see Rabkin (1967, 80–94), Sanders
(1968, 158–93), and Manheim (1973, 15–17 and 53–75).

2. Critics who stress Richard's responsibility include Stirling (1951), McPeek
(1958), French (1967), Sanders (1968), and Wangh (1968).

3. For interesting analyses of Richard's character, see Sanders (1968), McPeek
(1958), Wangh (1968), Ure (1956), and Humphreys (1967).

4. Martin Wangh's thesis is that the blood of Gloucester = the blood of Gaunt
= the blood of the Black Prince, Richard's father. Richard "felt unconsciously
guilty of usurpation and parricide" and "in order to become free of the pressure

of this unconscious guilt he provoked the law of the talion against himself" (1968, 228).

5. The special pride of the narcissistic person, says Horney, "resides in 'effortless superiority' " (1950, 314). Having to accomplish his objectives through "consistent effort" constitutes a "threat to the illusion of unlimited powers." As a result, "he simply does not know how to work" (1950, 315). Richard's not knowing how to work—i.e., how to use realistic means to get what he wants— contributes greatly to his sense of weakness when his wishes are frustrated.

6. Peter Ure has offered a similar interpretation of Richard's behavior in this scene. According to Ure, Richard's suffering arises from "the paradox of the rightful king who is without power to substantiate his right. . . . There is a kind of denial of his faith which springs from the difficulty of holding it when the startling fact of the *king's* helplessness seems to mock at its truth or efficacy. . . . Richard suffers, too, in performing the acts which his dilemma enforces upon him because they make him conscious of their contradiction of his claims . . . and this leads to the striving to escape from the dilemma, the wish to be no longer the 'god on earth' who is so manifestly at the mercy of his subjects" (1956, 83–84).

Chapter 4. Prince Hal

1. For other examples of this position, see Sjoberg (1969) and Shaaber (1957). Sjoberg argues that "royalty is Hal's by nature; frivolous pleasure, his cloak" (1969, 13). Shaaber claims that "there is no real reformation: the prince always knows what is right and prefers it; only appearances are against him" (1957, 16).

2. I arrived at the conclusion that Hal is rationalizing independently of other critics, but in reviewing the criticism, I find that I have been anticipated, though not in detail, by several others. The ever-astonishing Bradley observes: "You may think he deceives himself here, you may believe that he frequented Sir John's company out of delight in it and not merely with this cold-blooded design; but at any rate he *thought* the design was his one motive" (1963, 254). Aarons observes that "behind this adolescent sophistry is a compulsion to continue his delinquent ways a little longer" (1970, 330). And the Lichtenbergs comment that "in his thoughts to himself, the young Prince rationalizes that his 'knowing' what he is doing really means that he has the ego control over his drives to discontinue it at will. This gives the adolescent a temporary feeling of stability that is belied over and over again by his repetitious returns to similar impulse-ridden actions" (1969, 879).

3. S. P. Zitner comes close to my reading of Hal when he characterizes him as "a Prince who would and would not be king" and observes that "for Hal . . . the prospect of responsibility is not idyllic, but the prospect of shirking it is even worse" (1968, 66, 68).

Chapter 5. *Henry V*

1. For additional accounts of the controversy, see Reese (1961, 317–18), Rabkin (1981, chap. 2), and Smith (1976). The favorable view of Henry can be found in many places. The negative view is most powerfully stated by Hazlitt (1964) and by Goddard (1951, vol. 1, chap. 17).

2. A number of critics have noted the disparity between rhetoric and mimesis, which is more striking here than it was in *1 and 2 Henry IV*. "What we heard from the Chorus," observes William Babula, "does not match what we see on the stage" (1977, 50). Norman Rabkin concludes that there is often "an eloquent discrepancy between the glamor of the play's rhetoric and the reality of its action" (1981, 55).

3. Peter Erickson has observed that Henry's character is "divided and that this division is best seen as a struggle between compassion and aggression. . . . The impression of inauthenticity comes from the fact that the conflict between the two feelings of pity and anger is unresolved and therefore produces a fitful oscillation" (1979–80, 19).

4. William Babula agrees with Tillyard: "Thus in *Henry V* we simply do not have Hal. Shakespeare repeats the theme concerned with the education of a prince, but it is a different prince. Overlooking this fact has led many a critic astray who could not locate the Hal of the earlier plays in this one. He's not there" (1977, 59).

5. Henry's soliloquy on "ceremony" would seem to indicate that his solutions are not working as well as I have suggested. On this one occasion when we see him reflecting on his role rather than playing it, he sounds much like his father envying the "happy low" and complaining about his lack of repose. All that he gets in exchange for the sacrifice of his personal happiness is "ceremony," which he finds to be worthless. It will not cure sickness, produce true homage, or bring peace of mind; and though it creates "awe and fear in other men," he is "less happy, being feared, / Than they in fearing" (4.1). This speech gives us our only intimate view of Henry, and we cannot help wondering if it expresses a sense of the hollowness of regal glory that he always feels. It may; but lest we give it too much importance, we should put it in context and recognize that it is a response to Williams' effort to make him responsible for the fate of his men's souls. The soliloquy is motivated by resentment, by a need to rebel against the excessive burden that Williams would place upon him, and by an impulse toward self-pity and self-glorification. Henry is defending himself in part by seeing himself as a martyr who suffers for the sake of his unappreciative people. It is not they but he who is making the sacrifice. This may reflect feelings that he always has in some degree, given his father's fate and his own anxieties about becoming king, but that he seldom feels so acutely. Despite its narrowing of his personality, most of the time he seems to enjoy being king.

6. Edward Berry sees the tension in the play as being between epic ideals and political realities: "Sidney praises Virgil because he has embodied in Aeneas the virtues of a perfect prince; Bacon praises Machiavelli because he writes of what men do and not what they ought to do. Shakespeare, characteristically, requires that we somehow accommodate both perspectives. The Chorus envisions a golden world true to the imagination, a world that Bacon excludes from his new philosophy; the action of the play, more often than not, presents the brazen truth of history, which Sidney excludes from the epic" (1979, 6).

Chapter 6. *Julius Caesar*

1. My position is thus close to that of John Dove and Peter Gamble, who argue that "the relationship between Brutus and Cassius provides the vital unifying force in the drama, spanning the pre- and post-assassination scenes

and developing to a revelatory denouement" (1979, 543). I differ from them in my emphasis upon the Brutus-Cassius-Caesar triangle and in my interpretation of the Brutus-Cassius relationship.

2. Andrew Wilkinson sees Cassius as the ego and Brutus as the superego, with Cassius needing "that authority for his actions which the superego gives. . . . Under the circumstances it is not surprising that Cassius, whom Caesar describes as impatient of rule, becomes more and more under the power of Brutus. He is overruled repeatedly in a way which would seem quite remarkable were it not for the fact that Brutus exemplifies for him 'Rome' and the patriarchal virtues which he so honours and so denies. It is this conflict which incapacitates him; he becomes, to modify the phrase, but a limb of Brutus" (1979, 75–76).

3. As Henry Ebel observes, "the words of Brutus that drive [Cassius] to the apex of his frenzy—'Away, slight man'—precisely recapture his nightmare vision of Caesar as a Colossus and himself as a petty man. Brutus is now his Caesar" (1975, 123).

Chapter 7. *Antony and Cleopatra*

1. For other discussions of Antony and Cleopatra's pursuit of glory, see Holloway (1961, 99–120) and Alvis (1978).

2. See Kuriyama (1977, 339–40) for a discussion of the regressive character of Antony's Alexandrian revels.

3. As Janet Adelman observes: "To the extent that we are engaged with the protagonist, his judgment will be our judgment; and to that extent it will be dramatic fact. Throughout most of *Antony and Cleopatra*, we are not permitted to become wholly engaged with the protagonists. In fact, most of the structural devices of the play prevent our engagement. But toward the end of the play the dramatic techniques change radically. We tend more often to accept the lovers' evaluations of themselves, to take them at their word, because we are more often permitted to identify ourselves with them. And as we are permitted to become involved with the lovers, their evaluations tend to take on the status of emotional fact even in despite of the literal fact. . . . the dramatic structure now . . . works to give us the feeling of assent in spite of all logic" (1973, 158–59). Although Adelman explains how Shakespeare gets the audience to change its attitude toward Antony and Cleopatra, she does not account for *his* change of attitude.

4. Ernest Schanzer puts the issue another way: ". . . towards its end the play becomes much less concerned with the presentation of the choice between two opposed modes of life and increasingly with the glorification of the choice which Antony has made" (1963, 134). I think that Constance Kuriyama is right in saying that "the primary source of the ironic equipoise which some critics perceive is not in Shakespeare's play, but in the biases and presuppositions" of the critics (1977, 327).

Chapter 8. *Coriolanus*

1. The best of the psychological studies are Browning (1955), Hofling (1957), Barron (1962), Putney (1962), Stockholder (1970), Adelman (1980), and Kahn, (1981, 151–72).

2. According to Besdine, the intense living through the child that characterizes Jocasta mothering, while it "represents a deviation and pathology in terms of the mothering process," also "creates compensations for the character and sexual limitations frequently imposed on geniuses. The character structure is geared to achievement and scaling the heights, which in turn appears to stimulate the capacity for creativity" (1968, 596).

3. As Matthew Proser observes, Coriolanus's "loathing" for the people is "among other things, a method of self-definition, a way of 'proving' his heroic superiority over the 'reechy' people" (1965, 141).

4. See especially Stockholder (1970, 229–33); Putney (1962, 374); and Kahn (1981, 159–60). Kahn employs R. D. Laing's notion of a "false-self system," which is very similar to Horney's conception of the idealized self.

Conclusion

1. The phenomena I have described are by no means confined to the history and Roman plays. For other instances in Shakespeare see Paris 1991.

Works Cited

Aarons, Alexander. 1970. "Normality and Abnormality in Adolescence, with a Digression on Prince Hal: 'The Sowing of Wild Oats.'" *The Psychoanalytic Study of the Child* 25: 309–39.

Adelman, Janet. 1973. *The Common Liar: An Essay on "Antony and Cleopatra."* New Haven: Yale University Press.

———. 1980. "'Anger's My Meat': Feeding, Dependency, and Aggression in *Coriolanus*." In Schwartz and Kahn, *Representing Shakespeare.*

Adler, Charles. 1936. "Richard III—His Significance as a Study in Criminal Life-Style." *International Journal of Individual Psychology* 2: 55–60.

Alter, Robert. 1989. *The Pleasures of Reading in an Ideological Age.* New York: Simon and Schuster.

Alvis, John. 1978. "The Religion of Eros: A Re-interpretation of *Antony and Cleopatra*." *Renascence* 30: 185–98.

Aristotle. 1952. *Poetics.* Translated by S. H. Butcher. In *Criticism: The Major Texts,* edited by Walter Jackson Bate. New York: Harcourt, Brace & World.

Babula, William. 1977. "Whatever Happened to Prince Hal? An Essay on *Henry V*." *Shakespeare Survey* 30: 47–59.

Barber, C. L. 1959. *Shakespeare's Festive Comedy.* Princeton: Princeton University Press.

Barroll, J. Leeds. 1973. *Artificial Persons: The Formation of Character in the Tragedies of Shakespeare.* Columbia: University of South Carolina Press.

———. 1984. *Shakespearean Tragedy: Genre, Tradition, and Change in "Antony and Cleopatra."* Washington: The Folger Shakespeare Library.

Barron, David B. 1962. "*Coriolanus:* Portrait of the Artist as Infant." *American Imago* 19: 171–92.

Bayley, John. 1976. *The Uses of Division.* New York: Viking.

Berry, Edward. 1977. "The Rejection Scene in *2 Henry IV. Studies in English Literature* 17: 201–18.

———. 1979. "'True Things and Mock'ries': Epic and History in *Henry V*." *Journal of English and Germanic Philology* 78: 1–16.

Besdine, Matthew. 1968. "The Jocasta Complex, Mothering and Genius." *Psychoanalytic Review* 55: 259–77, 574–600.

Bogard, Travis. 1955. "Shakespeare's Second Richard." *PMLA* 70: 192–209.

Booth, Wayne C. 1961. *The Rhetoric of Fiction.* Chicago: University of Chicago Press.

Bradley, A. C. [1904] 1964. *Shakespearean Tragedy.* London: Macmillan.

———. [1909] 1963. "The Rejection of Falstaff." In *Oxford Lectures on Poetry.* London: Macmillan & Co.

————. [1929] 1969. "Coriolanus." In A Miscellany. Freeport, N.Y.: Books for Libraries Press.

Bredin, Hugh. 1982. "The Displacement of Character in Narrative Theory." The British Journal of Aesthetics 22: 291–300.

Browning, I. R. 1955. "Coriolanus: Boy of Tears." Essays in Criticism 5: 18–31.

Bullough, Geoffrey, ed. 1964. Narrative and Dramatic Sources of Shakespeare. Vol. 5, The Roman Plays. New York: Columbia University Press.

Charney, Maurice. 1963. Shakespeare's Roman Plays: The Function of Imagery in the Drama. Cambridge: Harvard University Press.

Chatman, Seymour. 1978. Story and Discourse. Ithaca: Cornell University Press.

Coleridge, Samuel Taylor. 1960. Shakespearean Criticism. Edited by T. M. Raysor. London: Dent.

Crane, R. S. 1953. The Languages of Criticism and the Structure of Poetry. Toronto: University of Toronto Press.

Crews, Frederick. 1975. Out of My System: Psychoanalysis, Ideology, and Critical Method. New York: Oxford University Press.

Culler, Jonathan. 1975. Structuralist Poetics. Ithaca: Cornell University Press.

Docherty, Thomas. 1984. Reading (Absent) Character: Towards a Theory of Characterization in Fiction. Oxford: Oxford University Press.

Dove, John and Peter Gamble. 1979. " 'Lovers in Peace,' Brutus and Cassius: A Re-examination." English Studies 60: 543–54.

Ebel, Henry. 1975. "Caesar's Wounds: A Study of William Shakespeare." Psychoanalytic Review 62: 107–30.

Erickson, Peter B. 1979–80. " 'The Fault / My Father Made': The Anxious Pursuit of Heroic Fame in Shakespeare's Henry V." Modern Language Studies 10: 10–25.

————. 1985. Patriarchal Structures in Shakespeare's Drama. Berkeley and Los Angeles: University of California Press.

Faber, M. D. 1970a. "Falstaff Behind the Arras." American Imago 27: 197–225.

————, ed. 1970b. The Design Within: Psychoanalytic Approaches to Shakespeare. New York: Science House.

Feldman, Harold. 1952. "Unconscious Envy in Brutus." American Imago 9: 307–35.

Fish, Stanley. 1976. "How to Do Things with Austen and Searle: Speech Act Theory and Literary Criticism." Modern Language Notes 91: 983–1025.

Foakes, R. A. [1954] 1963. "An Approach to Julius Caesar." In the Signet Classic edition of Julius Caesar, edited by William and Barbara Rosen. New York: New American Library.

Forster, E. M. [1927] 1949. Aspects of the Novel. London: Edward Arnold.

————. [1951] 1969. In "Julius Caesar": A Casebook, edited by Peter Ure. London: Macmillan & Co.

Frattaroli, Elio. 1987. "On the Validity of Treating Shakespeare's Characters As If They Were Real People." Psychoanalysis and Contemporary Thought 10: 407–34.

French, A. L. 1967. "Who Deposed Richard the Second?" Essays in Criticism 17: 411–33.

Freud, Sigmund. 1958. "Some Character-Types Met with in Psycho-Analytic Work." In On Creativity and the Unconscious, edited by Benjamin Nelson. New York: Harper and Row.

Frye, Northrop. 1965. *A Natural Perspective: The Development of Shakespearean Comedy and Romance*. New York: Columbia University Press.

Galsworthy, John. 1931. *The Creation of Character in Literature*. Oxford: The Clarendon Press.

Gerenday, Lynn de. 1974. "Play, Ritualization, and Ambivalence in *Julius Caesar.*" *Literature and Psychology* 24: 24–33.

Givan, Christopher. 1979. "Shakespeare's *Coriolanus*: The Premature Epitaph and the Butterfly." *Shakespeare Studies* 12: 143–58.

Goddard, Harold. 1951. *The Meaning of Shakespeare*. 2 vols. Chicago: University of Chicago Press.

Harding, D. W. 1969. "Women's Fantasy of Manhood: A Shakespearean Theme." *Shakespeare Quarterly* 20: 245–53.

Harvey, W. J. 1965. *Character and the Novel*. Ithaca: Cornell University Press.

Hazlitt, William. [1818] 1965. In Signet Classic edition of *Henry V*, edited by John Russell Brown. New York: New American Library.

Hirsch, E. D. 1967. *Validity in Interpretation*. New Haven: Yale University Press.

Hochman, Baruch. 1985. *Character in Literature*. Ithaca: Cornell University Press.

Hofling, Charles K. 1957. "An Interpretation of Shakespeare's *Coriolanus.*" *American Imago* 14: 407–35.

Holland, Norman. 1966. *Psychoanalysis and Shakespeare*. New York: McGraw-Hill.

———. 1970. "Romeo's Dream and the Paradox of Literary Realism." In *The Design Within: Psychoanalytic Approaches to Shakespeare*, edited by M. D. Faber. New York: Science House.

———. 1975. *5 Readers Reading*. New Haven: Yale University Press.

———. 1985. *The I*. New Haven: Yale University Press.

———, Sidney Homan, and Bernard J. Paris, eds. 1989. *Shakespeare's Personality*. Berkeley and Los Angeles: University of California Press.

Holloway, John. 1961. *The Story of the Night: Studies in Shakespeare's Major Tragedies*. London: Routledge & Kegan Paul.

Horney, Karen. 1945. *Our Inner Conflicts*. New York: Norton.

———. 1950. *Neurosis and Human Growth: The Struggle Toward Self-Realization*. New York: Norton.

Humphreys, A. R. 1967. *Shakespeare: Richard II*. London: Edward Arnold.

Jenkins, Harold. [1956] 1965. "The Structural Problem in Shakespeare's *Henry the Fourth.*" In *Henry IV, Part Two*, edited by Norman Holland. New York: The New American Library.

Kahn, Coppélia. 1981. *Man's Estate: Masculine Identity in Shakespeare*. Berkeley and Los Angeles: University of California Press.

Kantak, V. Y. 1977. "An Approach to Shakespearean Tragedy: The 'Actor' Image in *Macbeth.*" In *Aspects of "Macbeth,"* edited by Kenneth Muir and Philip Edwards. Cambridge: Cambridge University Press.

Kelman, Harold. 1971. *Helping People: Karen Horney's Psychoanalytic Approach*. New York: Science House.

Kirschbaum, Leo. [1949] 1968. "Shakespeare's Stage Blood and Its Critical Significance." In *Twentieth Century Interpretations of "Julius Caesar,"* edited by Leonard Dean. Englewood Cliffs, N.J.: Prentice-Hall.

Kittredge, George Lyman and Irving Ribner, eds. 1966. *The Tragedy of Julius Caesar.* New York: John Wiley & Sons.

Knight, G. Wilson. 1963. *The Imperial Theme.* New York: Barnes & Noble.

———. 1965. *Wheel of Fire.* New York: Barnes and Noble.

Knights, L. C. 1933. *How Many Children Had Lady Macbeth?* Cambridge: The Minority Press.

———. 1965. *Further Explorations.* Stanford: Stanford University Press.

Krieger, Murray. 1959. "The Dark Generations of *Richard III.*" *Criticism* 1: 32–48.

———. 1964. *A Window to Criticism: Shakespeare's Sonnets and Modern Poetics.* Princeton: Princeton University Press.

Kris, Ernst. 1957. *Psychoanalytic Explorations in Art.* London: Allen & Unwin.

Kuriyama, Constance Brown. 1977. "The Mother of the World: A Psychoanalytic Interpretation of Shakespeare's *Antony and Cleopatra.*" *English Literary Renaissance* 7: 324–51.

Levine, George. 1981. *The Realistic Imagination.* Chicago: University of Chicago Press.

Lichtenberg, J. D. and C. 1969. "Prince Hal's Conflict: Adolescent Idealism and Buffoonery." *Journal of the American Psychoanalytic Association* 17: 873–87.

MacCallum, M. W. [1910] 1967. *Shakespeare's Roman Plays and Their Background.* New York: Russell & Russell.

McPeek, James A. S. 1958. "Richard and His Shadow World." *American Imago* 15: 195–212.

Mack, Maynard. 1965. Introduction to Signet Classic edition of *Henry IV, Part One.* New York and Toronto: New American Library.

Manheim, Michael. 1973. *The Weak King Dilemma in the Shakespearean History Plays.* Syracuse: Syracuse University Press.

Maslow, Abraham. 1970. *Motivation and Personality.* 2d ed. New York: Harper & Row.

Mill, J. S. 1961. *The Philosophy of John Stuart Mill.* Edited by Marshall Cohen. New York: Random House.

Mudrick, Marvin. 1960. "Character and Event in Fiction." *The Yale Review* 50: 202–18.

Neill, Michael. 1975. "Shakespeare's Halle of Mirrors: Play, Politics, and Psychology in *Richard III.*" *Shakespeare Studies* 8: 99–129.

Newman, Karen. 1985. *Shakespeare's Rhetoric of Comic Character.* New York and London: Methuen.

Nuttall, A. D. 1965. "The Argument about Shakespeare's Characters." *Critical Quarterly* 7: 107–20.

———. 1983. *A New Mimesis: Shakespeare and the Representation of Reality.* London: Methuen.

Palmer, John. 1948. *Political Characters of Shakespeare.* London: Macmillan.

Paris, Bernard J. 1974. *A Psychological Approach to Fiction: Studies in Thackeray, Stendhal, George Eliot, Dostoevsky, and Conrad.* Bloomington: Indiana University Press.

———. 1978. *Character and Conflict in Jane Austen's Novels: A Psychological Approach.* Detroit: Wayne State University Press.

————. 1983. "Richard III: Shakespeare's First Great Mimetic Character." *Aligarh Journal of English Studies* 8: 40–67.

————, ed. 1986a. *Third Force Psychology and the Study of Literature*. Rutherford, N.J.: Fairleigh Dickinson University Press.

————. 1986b. "The Disparity between Rhetoric and Mimesis in Shakespeare's Presentation of Prince Hal." In *Essays on Shakespeare in Honour of A. A. Ansari*, edited by T. R. Sharma. Meerut, India: Shalabh Book House.

————. 1987. "Brutus, Cassius, and Caesar: An Interdestructive Triangle." In *Psychoanalytic Approaches to Literature and Film*, edited by Maurice Charney and Joseph Reppen. Rutherford, N.J.: Fairleigh Dickinson University Press.

————. 1989. "Interdisciplinary Applications of Horney." *The American Journal of Psychoanalysis* 49: 181–88.

————. 1991. *Bargains with Fate: Psychological Crises and Conflicts in Shakespeare and His Plays*. New York: Insight Books.

Peterson, Douglas. 1973. *Time, Tide, and Tempest: A Study of Shakespeare's Romances*. San Marino: The Huntington Library.

Plutarch. 1964. "Life of Marcus Antonius." Translated by Sir Thomas North. In *Narrative and Dramatic Sources of Shakespeare*, vol. 5, *The Roman Plays*, edited by Geoffrey Bullough. New York: Columbia University Press.

Price, Martin. 1983. *Forms of Life: Character and Moral Imagination in the Novel*. New Haven: Yale University Press.

Proser, Matthew. 1965. *The Heroic Image in Five Shakespearean Tragedies*. Princeton, Princeton University Press.

Putney, Rufus. 1962. "Coriolanus and His Mother." *Psychoanalytic Quarterly* 31: 364–81.

Quinn, Susan. 1987. *A Mind of Her Own: The Life of Karen Horney*. New York: Summit Books.

Rabkin, Norman. 1967. *Shakespeare and the Common Understanding*. New York: Free Press.

————. 1981. *Shakespeare and the Problem of Meaning*. Chicago: University of Chicago Press.

Reese, M. M. 1961. *The Cease of Majesty*. New York: St. Martin's Press.

Ribner, Irving. 1971. "The Political Problem in Shakespeare's Lancastrian Tetralogy." In *Twentieth Century Interpretations of "Richard II,"* edited by Paul M. Cubeta. Englewood Cliffs, N.J.: Prentice-Hall.

Rossiter, A. P. 1961. *Angel with Horns and Other Shakespeare Lectures*. Edited by Graham Storey. New York: Theatre Arts Books.

Rubins, Jack L. 1978. *Karen Horney: Gentle Rebel of Psychoanalysis*. New York: The Dial Press.

Sanders, Wilbur. 1968. *The Dramatist and the Received Idea: Studies in the Plays of Marlowe and Shakespeare*. Cambridge: Cambridge University Press.

Schanzer, Ernest. 1963. *The Problem Plays of Shakespeare*. New York: Schocken Books.

Scholes, Robert and Robert Kellogg. 1966. *The Nature of Narrative*. New York: Oxford University Press.

Schwartz, Murray M. and Coppélia Kahn, ed. 1980. *Representing Shakespeare*. Baltimore: The Johns Hopkins University Press.

Sewall, Arthur. *Character and Society in Shakespeare.* Oxford: The Clarendon Press.

Shaaber, M. A. 1957. Introduction to *The First Part of King Henry the Fourth.* Baltimore: Penguin Books.

Shaw, Bernard. 1934. *Prefaces by Bernard Shaw.* London: Constable & Company.

Shupe, Donald R. 1978. "The Wooing of Lady Anne: A Psychological Inquiry." *Shakespeare Quarterly* 29: 28–36.

Sidney, Sir Philip. 1952. *An Apology for Poetry.* In *Criticism: The Major Texts,* edited by Walter Jackson Bate. New York: Harcourt, Brace & World.

Sjoberg, Elsa. 1969. "From Madcap Prince to King: The Evolution of Prince Hal." *Shakespeare Quarterly* 20: 11–16.

Skura, Meredith Ann. 1981. *The Literary Use of the Psychoanalytic Process.* New Haven: Yale University Press.

Smith, Gordon Ross. 1959. "Brutus, Virtue, and Will. *Shakespeare Quarterly* 10: 367–79.

———. 1976. "Shakespeare's *Henry V:* Another Part of the Critical Forest." *Journal of the History of Ideas* 37: 3–26.

Stirling, Brents. 1951. "Bolingbroke's 'Decision.' " *Shakespeare Quarterly* 2: 27–34.

Stewart, J. I. M. 1949. *Character and Motive in Shakespeare.* London: Longmans, Green & Co.

Stockholder, Katherine. 1970. "The Other Coriolanus." *PMLA 85: 228–36.*

Tillyard, E. M. W. 1944. *Shakespeare's History Plays.* London: Chatto & Windus.

Todorov, Tzvetan. 1977. *The Poetics of Prose.* Translated by Richard Howard. Ithaca: Cornell University Press.

Toole, William B., III. 1974. "The Motif of Psychic Division in *Richard III." Shakespeare Survey* 27: 21–32.

———. 1978. "Psychological Action and Structure in *Richard II." Journal of General Education* 30: 165–84.

Traversi, Derek. 1963. *Shakespeare: The Roman Plays.* Stanford: Stanford University Press.

Ure, Peter. 1956. Introduction to the Arden Shakepeare edition of *Richard II.* London: Methuen.

Vickers, Brian. 1981. "The Emergence of Character Criticism, 1774–1800." *Shakespeare Survey* 34: 11–21.

Wangh, Martin. 1968. "A Psychoanalytic Commentary on Shakespeare's *The Tragedie of King Richard the Second." Psychoanalytic Quarterly* 37: 212–38.

Wentersdorf, Karl. 1976. "The Conspiracy of Silence in *Henry V." Shakespeare Quarterly* 27: 264–87.

Westkott, Marcia. 1986. *The Feminist Legacy of Karen Horney.* New Haven: Yale University Press.

Wheeler, Richard. 1971–72. "History, Character, and Conscience in *Richard III." Comparative Drama* 5: 301–21.

Wilkinson, Andrew. [1966] 1970. "A Psychological Approach to *Julius Caesar."* In *The Design Within,* edited by M. D. Faber. New York: Science House.

Zitner, S. P. 1968. " 'Anon' or, a Mirror for a Magistrate." *Shakespeare Quarterly* 19: 63–70.

Zuk, Gerald. 1957. "A Note on Richard's Anxiety Dream." *American Imago* 14: 37–39.

Index